RETHINKING CORRUPTION

Why have anti-corruption efforts often failed? Current thinking on corruption has largely overlooked the profound implications of its contested nature, which paradoxically makes it an effective yet highly dysfunctional "tool of government." As a tool of government, it helps execute policies and guarantees a degree of political order. Moreover, anti-corruption measures are wielded as political instruments, strategically embraced by governments and oppositions to further their respective agendas. Based on an analysis of Russia, Brazil, and the United States, *Rethinking Corruption* takes a fresh look at corruption and critiques the prevailing view of anti-corruption policies. Embarking on a captivating journey through these countries, this book encompasses the notion of legal corruption and invites a comprehensive reconsideration of corruption, with a focal point on questions of economic and political equality.

Lucio Picci is Professor of Economics at the University of Bologna. He has written three books and published articles in the *American Journal of Political Science*, the *Review of Economics and Statistics*, *Research Policy*, and the *World Bank Economic Review*.

Rethinking Corruption

Reasons Behind the Failure of Anti-Corruption Efforts

LUCIO PICCI
University of Bologna

Shaftesbury Road, Cambridge CB2 8EA, United Kingdom

One Liberty Plaza, 20th Floor, New York, NY 10006, USA

477 Williamstown Road, Port Melbourne, VIC 3207, Australia

314–321, 3rd Floor, Plot 3, Splendor Forum, Jasola District Centre, New Delhi – 110025, India

103 Penang Road, #05–06/07, Visioncrest Commercial, Singapore 238467

Cambridge University Press is part of Cambridge University Press & Assessment, a department of the University of Cambridge.

We share the University's mission to contribute to society through the pursuit of education, learning and research at the highest international levels of excellence.

www.cambridge.org
Information on this title: www.cambridge.org/9781009468800

DOI: 10.1017/9781009468824

First published 2024

A catalogue record for this publication is available from the British Library

A Cataloging-in-Publication data record for this book is available from the Library of Congress

ISBN 978-1-009-46880-0 Hardback

To the memory of Sergio Picci, who tried to teach me how to build things

Contents

Figures

Preface

The idea for this book has been with me for quite some time. It gradually emerged as I observed cracks in the prevailing paradigm about the timeless question of corruption and how to fight it. This paradigm established itself approximately in the mid-1970s, when researchers trained in economics applied their rational choice tool kit to the study of corruption and displaced previous theories of a sociological nature. Over time, I became convinced that certain themes that are often seen as almost incidental characteristics of corruption within the current debate, such as the difficulty in defining it and the politicization of its fight, deserve much more centrality. In fact, I believe that to truly understand corruption, we must move these themes from the edges to the center of the debate.

At the beginning of this project, I realized that to make progress in this direction, I needed to take a broad perspective and to adopt a multidisciplinary approach. This consideration made my research more complex, also because it is based on detailed studies of three different countries: Brazil, Russia, and the United States. For these reasons too, the assistance I received from colleagues and friends was invaluable.

Some of the ideas that I present in Chapter 3 result from joint work with Laarni Escresa. Other ideas of this book started to develop as Alberto Vannucci and I wrote a book in Italian humorously titled *Zen and the Art of Fighting Corruption*. I am grateful to Marco Albertini, Michele Alecevich, Rachel Brewster, Nicola Bruno, Tito Cordella, Giulia Gortani, Ian Jacobs, Michael Johnston, Elisabetta Lalumera, Mark Philp, Shitong Qiao, Mauro Sylos Labini, Federico Varese, and Maurizio Viroli for reading part of the manuscript, and to Octavio Amorim Neto, Osvaldo Croci, Luciano da Ros, Brandon Garrett, Fernanda Odilla, Benedetto Ponti, Matthew Taylor, Daniel Treisman, and Alberto Vannucci for finding the time to read it in its entirety. Also, two anonymous reviewers of the manuscript provided valuable feedback. Without the comments and criticisms of these persons, I would not have completed this project.

I had the fortune of discussing particular questions of interest with Larry Bartels, Elizabeth David-Barrett, Marco Bertamini, Luigi Curini, Mario del Pero, Esther Dweck, John French, Giampiero Gallo, Diego Gambetta, Miriam Golden, Tatiana Guarnizo Useche, Sergiei Guriev, Rodrigo Janot, Nia Johnson, Daniel Kaufmann, Judith Kelley, Paul Lagunes, Alena Ledeneva, Ben Noble, Lucio Renno, Richard Sakwa, Luca Savorelli, Dmitriy Skougarevsk, James Snyder, and Jennifer Wolak. I thank all of them. In the last few years, I also presented my developing ideas at various workshops: at the European University at Saint Petersburg, Jindal University, the University of Perugia, Tbilisi State University, Duke University Law School, the University of St. Andrews, and the Federal University of Santa Catarina. I am grateful to these institutions for hosting me and to the audiences of those meetings for their comments and criticisms.

I completed this book while on sabbatical leave. I thank my *alma mater*, the University of Bologna, for the support. I also acknowledge funding from the Italian Ministry of University and Research under project PRIN 2022 "Scalpo" (State Capture and Legal Political Corruption). At Cambridge University Press, I am indebted to Robert Dreesen, for his help in making this book a reality, to Sable Gravesandy and Narmadha Nedounsejiane, for their work on the production of the volume.

This book that emerged from such efforts, and collaborations, has a contrarian slant, but it does not contradict a basic element of the prevailing paradigm, according to which corruption is worse than bad. In this regard, my long journey has not taken me far from the point of departure. At a certain point in my work, a literal lack of movement was imposed by the coronavirus pandemic. As a result, I wrote a significant part of this book not far from where a gifted political scientist who also was interested in corruption, Niccolò Machiavelli, famously taught us to forget about "*cose*," things, as they are imagined, to consider how they are in reality. This book is my attempt to do so.

PART I

LAYING THE GROUNDWORK

1

Introduction

How was Brasilia born? The answer is simple. Like all great initiatives, it arose from almost nothing.

Juscelino Kubitschek[1]

Brasília was built at the end of the 1950s in the remote and previously almost uninhabited highlands of Brazil. It is shaped like a bird or an airplane, with two gently curved wings intersecting a long fuselage. The plan of the city was the vision of a handful of modernist architects, and to its different parts were assigned distinct functions. The main subdivision is between the residential wings and a long central body, where the political and administrative buildings are located.

I was in Brasília while researching this book on October 28, 2018, the day of the second round of the presidential elections that were to be won by Jair Bolsonaro. My hotel was located in the aptly named "hotel sector," near the crossing of the residential wing with the governmental section. Brasília is a city envisioned for motor vehicles; there were not many pedestrians around me when, as the sun was setting on a clear day, I headed toward the tip of the fuselage, where the most important political institutions are located. I walked across the vast esplanade from which the cathedral emerges as a flower, and I soaked into the vision of that and other modernist buildings by Oscar Niemeyer, who designed much of Brasília's iconic architecture. I saw a sad-looking girl, draped with a red flag, walking away alone, I thought, from some last-ditch political event. On the flag, written in block letters, I could read the name of Haddad, the candidate of the *Partido dos Trabalhadores* (Workers' Party, or PT) and the loser of the day.

[1] Kubitschek 2000 [1976], 5. In this book, all translations into English are mine, when not stated otherwise.

I walked past a string of ministries, most of them built alike, and finally reached the political heart of the city and the National Congress. Slowly, Bolsonaro's fans started to assemble for what unanimous opinion polls had announced would be a historic victory. There were vendors selling Brazilian flags and assorted Bolsonaro merchandise, a few food trucks, and a truck with loudspeakers blasting out pro-Bolsonaro songs. One person, wearing a black robe with a hood and holding a long sickle in his hands, was available for anyone who wanted to take a selfie with Death. More opportunities for selfies became available once a large cardboard cutout of a smiling Bolsonaro started making the rounds in front of the esplanade facing the parliament building. A honking motorcade started soon after the results of the elections were made public, only hours after the polls closed, thanks to Brazil's modern voting infrastructure.

The election of Jair Bolsonaro as president of Brazil followed a series of major corruption scandals, collectively known as "*Lava Jato*," or "Car Wash," which engulfed the PT and other political parties. *Lava Jato* uprooted Brazil's political life and resulted in the impeachment of its serving president, Dilma Rousseff, and the imprisonment of her predecessor, Luiz Inácio Lula da Silva. The widespread popular mobilization of Brazilians opposing corruption ultimately enabled the election of an unlikely candidate: Jair Bolsonaro, a far-right, long-term member of parliament known for his sexist and homophobic remarks, who defended Brazil's dictatorship, which ended in 1985, torture, and killings by a police force known for its abuses.

Brazil is a great and fascinating country that four decades ago managed a peaceful and largely successful transition from dictatorship to democracy, though certainly while displaying contradictions. The presence of pervasive corruption has been one of them, but democratic Brazil also carried out a long string of anti-corruption reforms. Ironically, they contributed to *Lava Jato* itself and placed at center stage a judiciary that would also be embroiled in controversy. Following a major leak of private conversations by *The Intercept Brazil*, an online news organizations, it became apparent that the heroes of the anti-corruption drive, Sérgio Moro (then a federal judge) and Deltan Dallagnol (then a federal public minister), had been involved in collusive practices that at a bare minimum were very inappropriate. Moro's decision to accept the offer from newly elected President Jair Bolsonaro to become minister of justice further convinced many that justice had been weaponized to serve partisan interests. The raucous public debate that followed the *Lava Jato* case also makes Brazil a paradigmatic example.

Brazil's anti-corruption reforms were not perfect, but to the extent that public policy is, of necessity, "muddling-through,"[2] they were more ambitious than many other corruption-ridden countries could realistically hope for. They also aligned with the principles of the prevalent anti-corruption playbook. Civic society involvement, in particular, was nothing short of spectacular in the Brazilian case, if we are to judge from the massive popular mobilization in support of *Lava Jato*. When considering Brazil's failure, as with all medicines that are not efficacious in a particular case, it might be argued that the doctor was inept or the patient recalcitrant. However, the lack of successful anti-corruption policies globally suggests that the problem may not lie with their implementation, but rather indicate the presence of more fundamental weaknesses. In fact, only a few countries are considered to have significantly reduced corruption levels in recent decades. The list of achievers varies depending on the observer, but it tends to include Hong Kong, Singapore, and a few other small countries.[3] The United States, during the late nineteenth and early twentieth centuries, is also an example of a country that transitioned from high to low levels of corruption. However, these changes occurred over long periods of time and were part of broader societal transformations, rather than solely anti-corruption reforms.

The lack of success in anti-corruption efforts and accusations of political motives behind them, as seen in the case of Brazil, should give us pause. The recurrent accusations that anti-corruption efforts pursue political projects that have little to do with their stated objectives, again as it happened in Brazil, where many saw the motivations behind *Lava Jato* to be less than honest, also suggest that it is time for reckoning, and that we should rethink corruption. More to the point, we should rethink what, at a risk of simplification, I call the prevailing paradigm about corruption. In the decades that followed World War II, sociological functionalism affirmed that corruption may have positive "latent" functions. For example, in certain historical situations, it may have enabled forms of social inclusion when alternatives were absent. A different view gradually took hold toward the end of the 1970s. This developed in the United States using the economists' methods of analysis and focused on individual

2 Lindblom 1959.

3 Mungiu-Pippidi 2015, 85, and Mungiu-Pippidi and Johnston 2017. Da Ros and Taylor 2022, 4–6 and 199–200 provide a summary of what we know about successful attempts to reduce corruption. More precisely, I should say, *what we think we know*, since (as Chapter 3 argues) we are at a loss when trying to measure changes of corruption over time.

behaviors, often observed through the lens of a principal–agent model. Later, theoretical considerations were supplemented by empirical analyses that appeared to confirm that corruption had negative implications and no redeeming qualities, while also shedding light on its presumed determinants and effects. Theoretical considerations and empirical evidence combined to indicate policy solutions to fight corruption. An emerging tool kit of anti-corruption measures gradually became institutionalized, with contributions from a diverse group of actors. There was active involvement from international organizations, such as the World Bank and the United Nations. An influential anti-corruption international nongovernmental organization, Transparency International, was founded in Berlin in 1993. National governments also became involved, and in 1977, the passage in the United States of the Foreign Corrupt Practices Act had important implications and reverberations worldwide. Researchers at universities and other institutions, in the United States and elsewhere, became increasingly interested in corruption, and an industry of specialists on anti-corruption (and, more broadly, on governance issues) developed.

This, using a very broad brush, is what I mean by the current thinking on corruption. How should we correct it? I anticipate the main ideas of this book, together with a brief description of the methodology that I adopt.

RETHINKING CORRUPTION AS A CONTESTED CONCEPT: CORRUPTION AS A SOCIAL CONSTRUCT

I derive most of my conclusions from a detailed analysis, using both primary and secondary sources, of three countries: Brazil, Russia, and the United States. These countries have varied levels of corruption as we measure it, which would rule out the problem of "selection on the dependent variable."[4] However, the choice of these cases has not been random. As a precondition, I selected countries whose national language I understood at least well enough to be able to read primary sources. These countries were also chosen because I found them instructive in different ways, to the point that observing them over many years has partly shaped my theses. I could then be accused of a selection of cases, if not on the dependent variables, on the covariates, to the extent that, in leading me to the conclusions that I like, they would make me a victim of confirmation bias.

4 Which would occur when the dependent variable displays little variation. King et al. 1994, 128–129.

While such accusations could be leveled at all "small 'n'" studies, it is possible that the three countries that I have chosen represent unique quirks in a world that otherwise manifests regularities of a different type.[5] I aim to convince the reader of the generality of my conclusions in two ways: first, by providing good reasons to believe that they have a degree of generality, in that their motives are plausibly of wide application; and second, by summoning further evidence that supports my theses. I adopt an interpretative framework that is influenced by historical institutionalism and highlights the importance of contextual information. Additionally, my analysis of the country cases is not solely comparative, as I also consider each one of them individually for what they may teach us. Last, while occasionally I will refer to the most recent events or data, I conclude my analysis before the beginning of the COVID-19 pandemic, because of its exceptional nature.

I propose a methodological approach to thinking about corruption that distinguishes between two focuses of analyses. One I call "corruption-as-phenomenon," and it is familiar as it pertains to investigations that are conditional on a given definition of corruption. Within analyses of corruption-as-phenomenon, we ask questions such as how much corruption there is (e.g., in the form of bribes to public officials) and what its causes and effects are. Most current research on corruption falls under this category.

However, I am mostly interested in a distinct focus of analysis that emerges when we observe the debate on corruption from a distance. There has always been much disagreement about what and who deserves the label of corrupt. This is also evident from the cases that I consider. In Brazil, the anti-corruption protagonists of *Lava Jato* were eventually seen by many to be corrupt. In Russia, the state used its power to frame the leader of an anti-corruption movement, Alexei Navalny, as a criminal, while it sponsored a friendly anti-corruption movement. In the United States, there has been a concomitant, long-run increase in economic and social inequality. To account for these changes, I consider the concept of "legal corruption," which goes beyond the currently prevailing narrow definition of corruption. As different as they are, all these cases, which the chapters ahead consider in detail, indicate the contested nature of the concept of corruption.

We should, however, do more than recognize that corruption is an elusive and contested concept, as if such characteristics were ancillary or

[5] Referring to themes considered in Chapter 4, they could express small "dapples" (Cartwright 1999) in an otherwise un-dappled world.

incidental, and perhaps reflective of a not-yet-achieved perfection in providing a satisfactory definition of what corruption really is. To the contrary, the impossibility of proposing an agreed-upon definition is perhaps what characterizes corruption the best, together with the struggle to influence such an understanding and, at least occasionally, to ensure that its infamous label falls on our enemies and not on ourselves.[6] In this light, corruption emerges as a concept that is always contested and that, as such, cannot be defined univocally. This contested and elusive character of corruption is at the center of my analysis, together with an invitation to go beyond a common understanding of corruption as a set of behaviors, to be appropriately defined, studied, and hopefully eradicated with the right treatment.

Corruption emerges from these considerations as a socially constructed concept, one that may be articulated in different problematic areas. One of them I simply mention without considering it further. It is the *problematization* of corruption, a term that I use in a loose Foucaldian sense. How and when did it happen that humans started to think about corruption? When did they elaborate such a concept, and when did they start arguing about competing definitions of it? When, in different words, did corruption begin to be considered a problem? I can only speculate that it happened together with the appearance of the first proto-states, which possibly also marked the emergence of forms of codified punishment that could be meted out to persons guilty of such "corruption." These are just suppositions, as a "deep history" of the concept of corruption has never been written and probably cannot be written due to lack of documentary evidence.

A second element regards the *politicization* of corruption, that is, the possible instrumentality of accusations of corruption in the political arena (as a "tool of politics," as I will propose later). The politicization of corruption is part of the broader activity of social construction of the concept, which doesn't only include intentional uses of corruption as a tool of politics. In fact, many attempts to influence the debate on corruption do not have an explicit political objective. However, and regardless of conscious intentions, they all contribute to our understanding of corruption and have a political effect (this book being no exception). Therefore, as a focus of analysis, the social construction of corruption is general enough to include all the relevant elements (problematization, politicization, and

[6] As Giorgio Blundo puts it, "It is possible to avoid the dead end of definition by concentrating on the processes of qualification of behaviors termed deviant or transgressive from an emic point of view: in a Beckerian optic, corruption would then be 'an act to which this label was successfully applied'" (Blundo 2007, 29, citing Lascoumes 1999, 49).

participation in the debate on corruption) that characterize the contested nature of the concept.[7]

The thesis that corruption is a socially constructed phenomenon, and that we will never conclusively agree upon what and who is corrupt, may be criticized for being dangerously relativistic. If we deny the possibility of agreeing on a definition of our object of inquiry, perhaps we are left in a vacuum where no interesting statement about corruption might be heard or uttered. I am convinced that this is not the case and that in fact an adequate recognition of the contested nature of corruption is a prerequisite to progress in its study. While much of this book attempts to demonstrate and to give substance to this thesis, here I would like to preliminarily justify it while referring to an important antecedent to the idea that a concept might be subject to endless contestation.

Walter Bryce Gallie proposed that some concepts "are not resolvable by arguments of any kind" and inevitably involve "endless disputes." An example of such "essentially contested concepts," as he called them, would be art.[8] Recognizing that art is an essentially contested concept does not stop us from going to museums and, more generally, from participating in the endless discussion about whether what we see there is, or isn't, an expression of art. We are perfectly able to engage the debate on art at two distinct levels: from a distance, while recognizing that it will never be resolved conclusively; and also from within, where we weigh in with our opinions. If we successfully do so, while distinguishing these two focuses of analysis, our participation in the debate on art may become more mature and nuanced.

Gallie claims in fact that "one very desirable consequence of the required recognition in any proper instance of essential contestedness might therefore be expected to be a marked raising of the level of quality of arguments in the disputes of the contestant parties."[9] Such conclusion provides the main justification that has been proposed for the introduction of the category of essentially contested concepts, which is perhaps understandable

[7] My choice of terms echoes that in Granovetter 2007, but similar arguments may also be found elsewhere in the literature.

[8] Gallie 1956. On accusation of relativism, Collier et al. 2006 note that "Both Gallie himself, and subsequent commentaries on his contribution, have expressed concern that the approach can encourage a conceptual relativism that is undesirable and destructive." They also conclude that this is not the case.

[9] Gallie 1956. Several concepts, besides art, have been considered to be essentially contested, for example, democracy and the rule of law (Collier et al. 2006). Surprisingly, to the best of my knowledge, no one has suggested that corruption also is an essentially contested concept.

if we consider that philosophers, such as Gallie, are naturally preoccupied with questions that pertain to the quality of intellectual disputes. This line of reasoning certainly would also apply to the debate on corruption. However, I am convinced that, at least in the case of corruption, at stake there is more than the quality of the debate. Corruption is not just *any* concept. It is, and perhaps has always been in history, the most negative value in politics – on par, in some places and epochs, with crimes of heresy, or of high treason in times of war. Influencing a societal understanding of what and who is corrupt is a very high-stakes game, and we should consider it as such.

To do so, we should keep the two levels of analysis that I propose – that of corruption as a phenomenon, and that of corruption as a social construct – distinct. And since, as I will argue, any definition of corruption as a phenomenon hinges on values and on a normative view of society (or at least, on a standard of action), doing so requires that we as researchers are forthcoming about our values, to the extent that they shape our own understanding of what and who deserves the label of corrupt.[10] I advocate for transparency in this regard, recognizing that whenever we discuss corruption-as-phenomenon, we participate in the very high-stakes game of the social construction of corruption. My value judgments, normative views, and perhaps my idea of justice, as they pertain to a discussion of corruption, may be briefly summarized as follows: Democracy is desirable, and a working democracy cannot exist in the presence of pronounced inequalities. The reader will observe these convictions of mine emerge in the pages ahead.

CORRUPTION IS A TOOL OF GOVERNMENT, AND ANTI-CORRUPTION IS A TOOL OF POLITICS

A focus on the social construction of corruption leads to the two main conclusions of this book.

First, corruption is a powerful *tool of government*, in part because it offers reasons for elites to remain cohesive. These incentives may be in the form of both benefits and punishments. To the first type belong the enticements of corruption, and they are reinforced whenever the ruler has the possibility to assign at will the label "corrupt" and the ensuing punishments. This helps rulers solve an existential *problem of control*. I use this term in the Madisonian sense that "you must first enable the government to control

[10] Collier et al. 2006 express a similar consideration in the context of the wider debate on essentially contested concepts, in vouching for a "a frank recognition that research in the social sciences routinely has a normative component."

the governed,"[11] or, seen from a different angle, that it is necessary for a government to have a degree of control in the choice and in the execution of policies. Control in government is a prerequisite for political order and a vital necessity of any political system. However, corruption as a tool of government has fundamental flaws,[12] and a polity should strive to develop better ways of governance. This is easier said than done, and occasionally there may be no concrete alternative solution to the problem of control in government but the use of corruption, as is the case in Russia and Brazil.

My second broad conclusion is that anti-corruption is a *tool of politics*, because it can be used to pursue a political agenda. Rulers may politicize corruption in a self-serving way, as we observe in the imprisonment for alleged corruption of Aung San Suu Kyi in Myanmar.[13] Additionally, corruption is a tool of politics that is available more widely, because it is a powerful "valence issue," that is, one of those issues on which most people agree, either negatively (as in the case of corruption) or positively (as it would be for, e.g., "competence"). As such, it is a compelling political rallying cry, as populist movements around the world know well. However, as a tool of politics, anti-corruption has many shortcomings. The case of Brazil suggests that it is rather unpredictable in its outcomes; in Russia, anti-corruption efforts have led to state repression, instead of positive reforms. Perhaps, then, anti-corruption should be avoided as a political platform, but in concrete situations, this might be difficult to do for lack of feasible alternatives.

The two main conclusions of the book – that corruption is a tool of government and anti-corruption is a tool of politics – derive from the distinction between the two levels of analysis discussed earlier. This distinction reveals an interesting symmetry between corruption and anti-corruption, as both are tools, one of government and one of politics. Both have serious shortcomings, but in certain situations, they may be almost inevitable. By acknowledging such symmetries between corruption and anti-corruption, one appears as the obverse of the other.

THE CHAPTERS AHEAD

This book is divided into three parts. In Part I, I provide a critique of the current prevailing view on corruption and propose a methodological

11 Hamilton et al. 2008 [1788], 256–261 (Federalist paper n. 51).

12 For a summary of the effects of corruption, see Fisman and Golden 2017, 84–112. Chapter 4 of this book, however, casts doubt on the possibility of a causal discourse on corruption.

13 Ratcliffe 2022.

framework to move beyond it. In Part II, I consider the cases of Russia, Brazil, and the United States. In Part III, I take stock of these cases and I discuss and elaborate upon the conclusions of my research.

While arguing that we should think differently of corruption, I have said little until now of the shortcoming of the view that prevails today. Chapter 2 describes its main traits in more details. In particular, the current consensus view on corruption is all but monolithic, and at its "soft edges" we find themes that in fact deserve center stage, such as the elusive and contested nature of the concept.

One aspect of the currently prevailing view is the emphasis on quantifications of corruption, which have been used to research its causes and effects and to gauge the progress of anti-corruption reforms around the world. Chapter 3 is dedicated to these measures. Corruption country scores are an example of so-called Global Performance Indicators (GPIs), which have become popular since the 1990s; they assume that by taking the right initiatives, countries can improve their ranking in a given GPI. However, the available measures of corruption are not well suited to assessing changes of corruption over time. A more general conclusion also emerges from this chapter. In studying social phenomena using quantitative techniques of analysis, it is considered important to draw a sharp line between the definition of a concept, which should come first, and attempts at measuring it, which should be conditional on the definition chosen. However, when measures of social phenomena are successful, they take on a life of their own and contribute to an ossification of the concept they refer to. Consideration of the extent to which the prevailing concept of corruption and its most popular measures have shaped each other also provides a good angle from which to discuss corruption more generally.

Chapter 4 discusses attempts to estimate the effects and causes of corruption. Results obtained using the linear regression models have suggested a list of the determinants, and of the effects, of corruption. They also have implicitly promoted a view according to which we read the observed associations between corruption and other factors in causal terms. I propose a critical assessment of whether the counterfactual of a significantly different level of corruption from the one observed may be legitimate. Corruption emerges from this discussion as a part of a dense historical matrix, one where it is difficult to contemplate changes in individual factors while leaving others unmodified.

Chapter 5 concludes Part I. I first focus on corruption-as-phenomenon and summarize the concept of corruption, contrasting two perspectives that have coexisted. From one perspective, corruption is seen as a degradation of the social body, often within an organic view of society, while in the other, it is defined in terms of public office, for example, as the abuse of entrusted power (or more specifically of public office) for private gain, which is the definition prevailing today.[14] Following these considerations, I clarify that all definitions of corruption (as phenomenon) have common ingredients; in particular, they depend on a normative view of the polity. These characteristics may be expressed using a geographic metaphor; later in the book I propose new such "geographies." I also consider the social construction of corruption and its different actors.

With these premises, Chapter 5 discusses a simple analytical framework that permits us to consider corruption as closely linked to other phenomena and as highly dependent on context. I surmise that historical processes do not proceed linearly but are characterized by historical junctures, which are moments of fast-paced historical change. I distinguish between two types of historical change. One takes place in a "lower sub-system," which is concerned with day-to-day history. These changes occur without modifications in the ways in which the problem of control of government is solved and political order is guaranteed. The other, which occurs in a "higher sub-system," implies modifications in that respect. For example, in Brazil, there was much change following *Lava Jato*, but likely no reduction in corruption. In my interpretation, this is because the need for corruption as a tool of government remained largely unmodified. *Lava Jato* affected, and even shocked, the lower subsystem, but not the subsystem higher up.

This methodological compass guides me in the second part of the book, dedicated to the description of the cases of Russia, Brazil, and the United States (Chapters 6–8). When considering the first two of these cases, the two important conclusions of the book emerge: Corruption is a tool of government, and anti-corruption is a tool of politics. When considering the United States, I expand beyond a narrow view of corruption and discuss its legal forms.

In Part III, I consider the implications of the case studies. As I stressed, definitions of corruption depend on a normative view of the polity, and such dependence should be recognized when debating corruption. In Chapter 9, I do so, in the context of a discussion of corruption in the United States, arguing for the relevance of new "geographies of corruption," and, in particular, of legal forms of corruption. My interpretation of legal corruption

14 As used e.g. by Transparency International ("entrusted power") or the World Bank ("public office") in several of their official documents.

in the United States is framed within a dynamic relationship between economic and political inequality, which may be mutually reinforcing.

Chapter 10 presents the conclusion that corruption is a tool of government. The cases of Brazil and Russia indicate how corruption can function as a tool of government by providing powerful incentives, both positive and negative, that help maintain elite cohesion and implement policies. These cases demonstrate how corruption can become a trap, as it may be the only viable solution for maintaining control in government, despite its deficiency as a tool. The differences between Russia and Brazil, and other cases that I consider, emphasize the importance of context-dependent information and of case studies.

Chapter 11 argues that anti-corruption is a tool of politics. This is true as soon as we recognize that it is also a tool of government, because assuring the viability of government is an essential political problem. I examine this issue from a wider perspective, viewing corruption as a "valence issue." Parties, politicians, and civil society organizations may take advantage of the widespread popular opposition to corruption, and campaign on an anti-corruption platform, especially if it is difficult for them to differentiate themselves in other ways. The decreased relevance of ideological differences in recent decades, particularly following the collapse of the Soviet Union, has contributed to the increased interest in corruption that has accompanied the establishment of the current consensus view. Also, for this reason, adopting an anti-corruption political platform has occasionally been an inevitable choice for reform-minded political actors.

I also explore further why anti-corruption reforms have largely failed. Besides Brazil and Russia, I briefly consider other cases, such as Italy, which in the early 1990s witnessed a spectacular anti-corruption campaign, *Mani Pulite* ("Clean Hands"). These examples highlight the risk of unforeseen consequences of anti-corruption efforts, even when they may be apparently successful. I interpret these difficulties in light of the model of historical change of Chapter 5, which argues that long-term changes require the development of tools of government other than corruption. I also analyze the reforms that took place in the United States over several decades, beginning in the late nineteenth century, which were accompanied by a decrease in corruption.

***

In this book, by emphasizing the elusive and contested character of corruption, I adopt a perspective that aims to be sufficiently detached from its object of study. Anti-corruption efforts struggle against the perverse aptness of corruption in satisfying that prerequisite of government, which is control. Anti-corruption efforts also fall victim to the function it serves as a tool of politics. From this perspective, I derive a pessimistic view on the prospects of anti-corruption efforts that are narrowly defined, on which I present some concluding considerations in Chapter 12. They vouch for a broader approach to the question of corruption, and they touch upon the idea of modernity and one of its key ingredients: the possibility of human agency.

2

The Consensus on Corruption

Although corrupt behavior can arise in a number of different contexts, its essential aspect is an illegal or unauthorized transfer of money or an in-kind substitute
Susan Rose-Ackerman[1]

On June 15, 1978, Giovanni Leone resigned as the president of the Italian Republic, following a smear campaign that accused him of direct involvement in corruption. He was alleged to be the main figure in a scandal that had rocked Italian politics, mesmerized the public, and acquired an aura of mythical mystery that seemed to be reflected even in its vocabulary. "Hercules" was the name of the airplanes that the US Lockheed Corporation had bribed Italian officials into purchasing, and the public had long wondered about the identity of the main recipient of bribes, whose foreign code name, *Antelope Cobbler*, seemed straight out of a noir novel. An explosive book by Camilla Cederna, an investigative journalist, alleged that this "cobbler" was, in fact, the only animal capable of having the upper hand on the antelope: the lion, Leone, the president.[2]

Regarding Leone's responsibilities, I ask the reader to be patient and apply a presumption of innocence. I will return to this particular case in Chapter 11, considering it as an example of the politicization of anti-corruption efforts. Here, I am interested in the broader picture provided by the Lockheed scandal, which was quite extensive as it involved several

[1] Rose-Ackerman 1975.

[2] Cederna 1978. In Italian, the jargon expression "*fare le scarpe*" (literally, "to make shoes" for someone) approximately means "to have the upper hand" (on someone). I base my account on Caprara 2001 and Vecchio 2018.

countries besides the United States and Italy. Its origins can be found in the break-in of the Democratic National Committee, in the Watergate Office Building in Washington, DC, in June of 1972. The long series of events that followed that burglary eventually led to the passage of an important US Federal Statute, the Foreign Corrupt Practices Act (FCPA) of 1977, which marked a significant shift in how corruption is perceived and addressed.

These political developments occurred at the same time as new ideas on corruption were taking hold in academia. Until the 1970s, an influential perspective had considered corruption through the lens of then popular sociological functionalism. This resulted in opinions about corruption that had a counterintuitive streak, as it was noted that corruption occasionally performed useful functions. However, from the 1970s, and following the impetus of researchers trained in economics, a new consensus emerged that underlined the negative aspects of corruption and tended to identify it with the corresponding crime, as in the quotation of Susan Rose-Ackerman opening this chapter. Quantifications of corruption became prominent during the 1990s. They were to play an important role in benchmarking levels of corruption at the country level with the aim of reform, a question that I will consider in detail in Chapter 3. Also, these measures have been used widely to study the causes and effects of corruption, often using econometric methods that I will discuss in Chapter 4, and that contributed to framing in causal terms the way we think about corruption and how to fight it. This chapter considers several of these developments.

John Maynard Keynes famously asserted that the ideas of economists, whether right or wrong, are "more powerful than is commonly understood," to the point that "the world is ruled by little else."[3] The fortunes of ideas, be them of economists or of different thinkers, depend on contingent conditions that influence whether they thrive or not outside of their centers of production. The ideas of economists have certainly been consequential within the debate on corruption. Brewing in academic circles during the 1970s, they were successful because a set of largely fortuitous reasons contributed to a fertile ground. They took advantage of domestic factors, as represented by the political events following the Watergate scandal in the United States. They were helped by geopolitical considerations such as the presence first, and demise afterward, of the Soviet Union. And certainly, they also profited from factors that belong more directly to the realm of ideas, as we will see for instance when considering the uses of quantifications of corruption. The interaction of different reasons eventually encouraged the activation of

[3] Keynes 1936, 383–384.

powerful processes of institutionalization, which was a key element in the establishment of the current consensus on corruption.

These features, both of a political and intellectual nature, led to the emergence of a broadly consensual view of corruption that shares many common traits, that this chapter considers. This view is far from monolithic, and here, we also begin exploring its less coherent and occasionally contradictory elements. They represent the soft edges of the current debate, and they are central to the ideas of corruption that we will develop in Parts I and II of this book.

A SHIFTING THEORY OF CORRUPTION

A sociological, functionalist view of corruption was highly influential in the decades following World War II. In 1949, Robert Merton pointed out that city "political machines", that in the United States came to epitomize corruption, were also functioning as providers of public services to disadvantaged people while the state was relatively absent. These machines offered opportunities for integration into society and social mobility.[4] Two decades later, James Scott applied similar reasoning, when he noted that corruption in developing countries represented opportunities for disenfranchised populations to at least influence policy execution through bribery, given that they could not legally influence policy choices.[5]

A diverse group of scholars proposed functionalist interpretations of corruption. Researchers broadly belonging to the field of postcolonial studies noted that corruption could be functional to processes of modernization of developing countries, several of which had only recently acquired independence. For them, a functionalist reading of corruption, being at least partly exculpatory, allied with a desire to escape a moralizing ethnocentrism. At the opposite end of the intellectual spectrum, Samuel Huntington, whose ideas of social stability were considered to be those of a political hawk, also wrote influential considerations on corruption using a functionalist approach, noting, for example, that "corruption may be the means of assimilating new groups into the political system by irregular means."[6]

4 Merton 1968 [1949], 124.

5 Scott 1969.

6 Huntington 1968a, 61. See also Huntington 1968b. On Huntington's views, see Gawthorpe 2018. A variation of these functionalist readings, more couched into economic analysis, surmised that corruption under certain circumstances could be "efficient" – for example, in bypassing ill-conceived government regulations. See Leff 1964 and a summary of arguments in Fisman and Golden 2017, 84–86.

Interpretations of corruption along these lines waned in the early 1970s for various reasons. The functionalist perspective, which saw social structures as conduits for social order, was seen as out of step with reality as the world increasingly appeared to be dominated by social strife. A younger generation of scholars, particularly in the United States, rejected functionalism in favor of conflict theory, which was more in line with the spirit of the times.[7] Additionally, a string of failures by developing countries to modernize and democratize, as seen in coups in Brazil (1964), Chile (1973), and Argentina (1976), led to much soul searching among developmental economists[8] and seemed to contradict any reasoning within the modernization discourse. As functionalism lost popularity, other approaches to sociology did not focus on the question of corruption, leaving an empty space to be filled.

In the 1970s, as part of a broader encroaching into other disciplines, economists began to offer a new individualistic view on corruption that ignored sociological considerations. The conceptual framework for this perspective was provided by a principal–agent conceptual framework, as in Susan Rose-Ackerman's trailblazing 1978 book "Corruption: A Study in Political Economy."[9] This book and the broader perspective it represents signaled an effort by economists to study corruption using their own tools of analysis and the assumption of instrumental rationality. Corruption was seen as a failure in the principal–agent relationship, where a public administrator (the agent) may abuse his power for self-serving motives, rather than acting in the best interests of the citizenry (the principal).

Studies of corruption began to take a quantitative approach as measures of corruption became available, initially as by-products of preexisting country risk assessments, and later through dedicated efforts. However, as discussed in Chapter 3, these measures have been problematic. Despite this, they have been in high demand in an intellectual context dominated by economists who believed scientificity was partly reliant on the use of quantitative methods, particularly classical hypothesis testing. The

7 Osrecki 2017.

8 An example being provided by Albert O. Hirschman. Michele Alacevich, considering his intellectual trajectory, mentions how the whole subdiscipline of development economics was eventually reincorporated into economics *tout court*, as the idea took hold that the discipline, following its pretenses of scientificity, of necessity had to be unitarian (Alacevich 2021: 312–313). Such was the *esprit du temps* when the economist's toolbox came to be widely applied to the analysis of corruption, as we are about to consider.

9 Rose-Ackerman 1978. It was preceded by a journal article published three years earlier and significantly titled "The economics of corruption" (Rose-Ackerman 1975).

quantification of corruption spurred a research industry that used econometric methods to research the causes and consequences of corruption, and that was initiated by a seminal article by Paolo Mauro.[10] These studies indicated that corruption is highly pernicious in all respects, contradicting the more nuanced conclusions of the functionalist tradition. In Chapter 4, I will argue that the use of widely available econometric methodologies had an important framing effect on contemporary corruption studies whose effects persist to this day. Representative studies of the older functionalist tradition continued to be cited in the academic literature, and they are to this day, but mostly as a reminder of an exotic past age and of an almost romantic idea of corruption.[11]

The focus on quantification in studies of corruption also reflects a narrowing of its conceptual scope. The functionalist readings had often opted for broad definitions of corruption. For example, James Scott considered forms of "legal" corruption, and how similar behaviors could be a crime of corruption in one country (or historical period), but not in a different one.[12] The new paradigm on corruption has embraced a narrower view that, coherently with an individualistic analytical approach, centers on a concept of public service. Such conceptual narrowing is also reflected in developments in the sphere of politics, starting with the already cited FCPA of 1977.

THE FOREIGN CORRUPT PRACTICES ACT AND THE OECD ANTI-BRIBERY CONVENTION

The passage of the FCPA of 1977 made the United States the first country to criminalize foreign bribery and represented an early milestone in the field of modern anti-corruption. As part of the revelations of the Watergate scandal, it was disclosed that several American companies had unabashedly bribed abroad to secure contracts. The case of the largest US military contractor Lockheed Corporation (now, Lockheed Martin), which had recently been saved from bankruptcy thanks to a federal grant, was particularly significant because of the size of the bribes and of their widespread

10 Mauro 1995.

11 Most frequently cited, it appears, together with Huntington 1968a and 1968b is Nye 1967, and, less frequently, Scott 1969. This intellectual tradition has been kept alive in anthropological studies that present a radical critique to the dominating paradigm. However, they occupy a small niche in the academic debate and have had no appreciable impact within policy circles. See, for example, Anders and Nuijten 2007 and Torsello and Venard 2016.

12 Scott 1969.

political repercussions. As we saw, bribes had been disbursed in Italy with momentous consequences. Lockheed had also bribed the Japanese Prime Minister Tanaka, Prince Bernhard of The Netherlands, and politicians in Germany. The scandal, which represented a huge embarrassment for the United States, contributed to the election as president of an outsider, Jimmy Carter, in 1976.[13]

Geopolitical considerations influenced the political climate of the post-Watergate years, leading to the groundbreaking FCPA of 1977. The Cold War also entailed a competition for the moral high ground, and as Rachel Brewster notes, "the alternative narrative offered by the Soviet Union was one that vilified corporations as capitalist institutions that undermined economic justice, co-opted local elites, and biased public policies."[14] Moreover, it was feared that foreign bribes by US corporations would create hidden allegiances with foreign leaders and result in a security threat. Senator Frank Church, Chairman of the US Senate Select Committee that played an essential role in discovering Lockheed's corruption, embraced both arguments when noting that "the Communist bloc chortles with glee at the sight of corrupt capitalism," and that "U.S.-based corporations should not be supporting political factions antithetical to those supported by the U.S. Government."[15]

These debates trace the genesis of the most visible provision of the FCPA, namely, the outlawing of foreign bribery. However, preoccupations of a different type led to further consequential provisions regarding accounting practices. The legislative drafters were well aware that the mere possibility of paying illegal bribes rested on the availability of slush funds. The Securities and Exchange Commission (SEC), in particular, realized that the presence of slush funds impinged on its mandate to guarantee rigorous accounting standards. Responding to these preoccupations, the new statute imposed stringent record-keeping requirements on issuers.[16]

[13] Abbott and Snidal 2002, who note that he was elected "on a foreign policy platform premised heavily on moral considerations."

[14] Brewster 2017 (also on the security threat of foreign bribes, *infra*). On the restraining effects that Cold War competition had on US economic and political elites, see Gerstle 2022, 10–12. For a detailed story of the FCPA, see Koehler 2012, who thus summarizes its motivations: "foreign policy was the primary policy concern from the discovered foreign corporate payments which motivated Congress to act. However, foreign policy was not the sole reason motivating Congress. The legislative record also evidences that congressional motivation was sparked by a post-Watergate morality, economic perceptions, and global leadership."

[15] Cited in Koehler 2012.

[16] See the discussion in Brewster 2017 and references therein.

These provisions eventually made the FCPA an important "practice area for American lawyers in white-collar crime, mergers and acquisitions, and corporate compliance law,"[17] and more generally a promoter of a model of "governance by compliance."

The concept of compliance is a crucial part of current anti-corruption policies and deserves further discussion. Before I turn to this question, I note that the FCPA was the origin of subsequent developments that resulted in a reinforcement of its principles and their propagation globally. The political climate that led to the approval of the FCPA evaporated rather quickly, as domestic concerns about the competitiveness of US companies abroad made its enforcement unpalatable. During the Reagan years, unwillingness to make good on the promises of the FCPA resulted in its very modest enforcement, and business interests occasionally suggested that it be repealed. However, such option was politically unfeasible. In the crucial final decade of the Cold War, the United States was still fighting for the world's heart and soul, and a repeal would have amounted to an admission of guilt against the worst accusations toward its capitalism.

The United States chose instead to lobby internationally to convince other countries to also outlaw foreign bribery, eventually succeeding after a protracted effort. In December of 1997, the members of the Organization for Economic Cooperation and Development (OECD) signed the Convention on Combating Bribery of Foreign Public Officials in International Business Transactions (in short, OECD Anti-Bribery Convention), which came into force in 1999. It is an international treaty that requires signatory countries (currently, 44, including some non-OECD members, with Brazil and Russia among them) to legislate measures intended to combat foreign bribery in their own jurisdictions. The entry into force of the OECD Anti-Bribery Convention finally created the conditions for a significant increase in the enforcement of the FCPA. Importantly, the United States adopted a broad interpretation of the extent of its jurisdiction, which covers companies registered with its SEC and, generally, entities carrying out part of their businesses in the United States. Some very high-profile cases involving foreign companies contributed to pressure other countries to also increase enforcement, or else. In the words of Rachel Brewster, after an "enforcement silence" lasting two decades, there followed an "enforcement explosion."[18]

[17] Brewster 2017, also for the following summary of events leading to the OECD Anti-Bribery Convention.

[18] Brewster 2017. On the effects of US extraterritorial enforcement of the FCPA, see Kaczmarek and Newman 2011.

The FCPA and the OECD Anti-Bribery Convention, which drew inspiration from it, presupposed a particular view of corruption. By addressing a problem of bribing, they were broadly in accord with the concomitant conceptual narrowing occurring within the academic debate. The affirmation of a narrower definition of corruption had a framing effect, and in particular, concentrating on corruption as a crime also diverted attention away from its broader contextual conditions, which had been more prominent in the previous sociological reading of corruption. The 1960s and early 1970s had been marked by a protagonism of the Global South, which included elements of a critique of the corrupting role of multinational corporation. For example, then President of Chile Salvador Allende had condemned "the increasingly obvious conflict between the public interests of the wealthy nations (those which are of real benefit to their peoples) and the private interests of their great international corporations."[19] Equating corruption with the crime of corruption, to the extent that it attracts attention on the criminal acts of individuals or firms, also deviates attention away from broader considerations. In particular, it implicitly denies the possibility that corruption may in fact be an intrinsic component of a given economic or political arrangement. In Chapter 9, we will observe a similar framing effect when considering the debate on corruption in the United States during the last decades, particularly with reference to ideas on "state capture."

Both the FCPA and the OECD Anti-Bribery Convention were coherent with new ideas on anti-corruption policies and contributed to their institutionalization. The OECD Anti-Bribery Convention, in particular, also requires that the signatories adopt appropriate accounting and auditing standards to avoid off-the-book transactions, and that penalties are in place in case of omissions or falsification.[20] I consider these developments next.

AN EMERGING CONSENSUS ON ANTI-CORRUPTION POLICIES

Functionalist interpretations did not focus on elaborating a theory for combating corruption, which after all was viewed as occasionally useful. However, within the new consensus, emphasis on personal incentives and the assumption of instrumental rationality had direct implications for anti-corruption policies, which came to be seen as an exercise in aligning

[19] UNCTAD 1973, cited in Katzarova 2019, 77, who considers this debate in detail. Garavini 2012 offers a reconstruction of the broader historical picture regarding the rise of the "Global South" during the 1960s and 1970s.

[20] See Article 8 in OECD 1997.

incentives between the public and those in power. Empirical evidence from quantitative studies which I critically consider in Chapter 4 implicitly framed the problem as one amenable to "policy fixes", and provided both support to a set of prescriptions and a bridge between theoretical considerations and observed behaviors.

The emerging anti-corruption prescriptions were consistent with a broader view of the relationship between individual incentives and institutional outcomes, as exemplified in James Madison's consideration that "ambition must be made counteract ambition"[21]: The ambition of the fearless journalist, for example, can be harnessed to confront the ambition of a corrupt politician that she investigates. When these proposed solutions emerged in the late 1970s they were expressed in terms of modern economic theory, but the broad ideas underlying them were already in the air at the times of Madison, when it was posited that "passions and interests" could be used for the common good. As Albert Hirschman notes, the "idea of engineering social progress by cleverly setting up one passion to fight another became a fairly common intellectual pastime in the course of the eighteenth century".[22]

These concepts, with their old pedigree, have contributed to modern cures for corruption. Within a principal–agent view of the problem of corruption, blueprints for institutional reform were designed to realign incentives, as interest in corruption increased both as a topic of research and within societal discourse. The concrete contents of recommended anti-corruption policies vary, as does emphasis on the relative importance of their ingredients within policy packages, but they tend to include the following elements.[23] The assumption of instrumental rationality implies the relevance of deterrence, which is provided by adequate enforcement of anti-corruption laws. Reforms of the judiciary and the police force aimed at increasing enforcement are a mainstay of anti-corruption policy packages. Transparency is also considered important because it permits both horizontal and vertical accountability. The emergence of the current consensus on anti-corruption policies has coincided with the affirmation of the Internet as a major communication infrastructure. Debates on ways to fight corruption have been

[21] Hamilton et al. 2008 [1788], 257 (Federalist No. 51).

[22] Hirschman 1977, 26.

[23] See the considerations in Kroeze et al. 2017, 3, who summarize this intellectual tradition, which they criticize, by affirming that "anticorruption and good government tended to be equated with the historical development of democracy, accountability, transparency in public affairs, Weberian-style bureaucracy and the rule of law, all emblematic aspects of countries that are consistently ranked among the least corrupt in the world."

influenced by the emergence of the Internet, and by considerations on how it may enable improvements of governance more generally, permitting more transparency, accountability, and citizens' participation. Concrete uses of the Internet have been recommended, for example, in the field of public procurement, where many countries now manage and monitor vast repositories of open data on individual public purchases.[24]

It is also recognized that while corruption has a high social cost, individuals may have weak incentives to oppose it, which can result in high-corruption equilibria. To avert them, emphasis has been placed on public education, aimed at elucidating the public on the high costs of corruption and the importance to fight it, also at the individual level (e.g., though whistleblowing) and through involvement in civil society. Particularly in recent years, as the failure of anti-corruption efforts has become more evident, policy fixes emphasizing the need for collective action have acquired more prominence.[25] By focusing on collective behaviors, these proposals also introduce an element of contradiction with respect to the prevailing individualistic outlook on corruption.

Anti-corruption policies crystallized also following powerful processes of institutionalization. Transparency International, an international NGO based in Berlin, was founded in 1993 with the explicit goal of fighting corruption worldwide by a former regional director for the World Bank, Peter Eigen, and became very influential. Starting in 1995 and under the presidency of Jim Wolfensohn, the World Bank shifted from a hands-off approach to a decidedly anti-corruption stance.[26] Attention to corruption was part of a greater emphasis on questions of governance that took place in those years. While references to a so-called Washington Consensus should be considered with prudence, if we consider the acquired vagueness of the term, the shift that took place during the late 1990s at the World Bank may identify the affirmation of a broader version of such a "consensus," that came to include corruption (and more generally sound governance) as a preoccupation.[27] A visible product of this shift was the introduction of

[24] See Fazekas and Kocsis 2020, and, also on more general uses of the Internet, Adam and Fazekas 2021.

[25] Rothstein 2021, suggesting a "social contract" to fight corruption, is an example of this tendency.

[26] For an account of these developments, written by a protagonist, see Kaufmann 2005.

[27] John Williamson, who in 1989 was the originator of the expression "Washington Consensus," considers that in the late 1990s some "deviations" with respect to its original version emerged, also with respect to "institutional issues, especially regarding governance and corruption, in the case of the [World] Bank [...]" (Williamson 2009).

a wide set of "governance indicators,"[28] part of the increasing presence and visibility since the 1990s of various global performance indicators that I will discuss further in Chapter 3.

In 2003, a vast majority of United Nations Member States signed the United Nations Convention against Corruption, which aimed at a stronger and internationally coordinated effort to fight corruption.[29] The United Nations Office on Drugs and Crime has been tasked with promoting anti-corruption policies and in assisting countries in carrying them out.[30] Regional international organizations have taken initiatives along similar lines. Anti-corruption policies have progressively been codified and institutionalized through the establishment in many countries of anti-corruption agencies and other types of dedicated administrative units.

At the level of individual organizations, views on governance were influenced by parallel developments in organizational culture. In the public sector, anti-corruption policies were approximately coeval with the development of a "New Public Management" movement, which emphasized the importance of personal incentives among public officials and reflected a wider application of economic methods. One general recommendation of New Public Management was the adoption of organizational principles used in the business sector, such as performance-based pay.[31]

The term "compliance," which can be applied to both organizations and countries, has become an important catchword in the debate on anti-corruption and governance. It is presumed that compliance with suitable organizational models and codified business practices can encourage efficient, effective, and honest behavior. The FCPA and the OECD Anti-Bribery Convention have played a significant role in promoting this approach for both companies and countries. The FCPA encouraged companies to implement compliance programs, either to prevent serious damage in case of indictment or by requiring them as part of deferred or non-prosecution agreements. This effect extended internationally with the implementation of the OECD Anti-Bribery Convention, which led the United States to robustly enforce the FCPA also with respect to foreign corporations. Enforcement of the Convention was also demanded to individual countries, both by OECD as the custodian of the

[28] Kaufmann et al. 1999a and 1999b.

[29] United Nations 2004.

[30] Under direction of the Conference of the States Parties, "the main policymaking body of the United Nations Convention against Corruption" (UNODC n.d.).

[31] See Engels 2017, 168.

Anti-Bribery Convention and by other bodies and organizations, such as Transparency International.

The case of Italy is instructive in this respect. Following its adherence to the OECD Convention, Italy modified its penal code to include the crime of foreign bribery on September 29, 2000. The Convention established a monitoring mechanism to ensure its implementation, carried out by the OECD Working Group on Bribery, in the form of periodic "Country reports." The report on Italy dated 2004 noted favorably that Italy had "enacted Legislative Decree 231 on 8 June 2001 which imposes administrative liability against legal persons for the offense of foreign bribery," while adding that it represented "a milestone in Italy's legal history, as legal persons were not previously liable for any criminal offenses."[32] This innovation in fact put Italy on the same footing as the United States, where corporate (criminal) liability had been established at the beginning of the twentieth century.[33] In Italy, liability of legal persons was accompanied by the introduction of so-called organizational and managerial models in companies. In fact "article 6(1)(a) [of Legislative Decree 231] provides that legal entities shall not be held liable if 'before the fact was committed, (management) offices had adopted and effectively implemented organisational and management models so as to prevent offences of the kind which occurred'." The anti-corruption drive contributed to a trend of convergence of the Italian civil law system to principles that are more familiar in the Anglo-Saxon, and more particularly, US common law tradition. As in the United States, these developments in Italy also promoted a compliance industry of lawyers and consultants of different stripes.

A decade later, Italy passed an important piece of anti-corruption legislation, Law 190 of November 6, 2012. The law extended to public administrations the same broad principles introduced to private business by Legislative Decree 231 of 2001. It established an independent National Anti-Corruption Authority (*Autorità Nazionale Anticorruzione*, or ANAC) responsible for overseeing anti-corruption policies and ensuring that all public administrations appoint an official "responsible for corruption prevention and transparency." Italian public administrations must also comply with an "anti-corruption plan" that they themselves must draft under ANAC's guidance. This also represents an organizational model of sorts, but this time as applied to public administrations.[34]

[32] OECD 2004, also for the citations that follow in the paragraph.
[33] Garrett 2014, 4.
[34] Picci and Vannucci 2018, 139–149.

In conclusion, in Italy we witness the same "logic of compliance" applied first to firms (Legislative Decree 231 of 2001) and later to public administrations (Anti-Corruption Law 190 of 2012). We also observe compliance with respect to an international consensus on anti-corruption policies, as Italy was spurred in that direction by both domestic and international actors. We will see state compliance at work also in Brazil, where forms of corporate liability were established in 2013. To a limited extent, and with important caveats, similar considerations will apply even to the case of Russia. In fact, anti-corruption established itself as a "global regime," as defined by Stephen Krasner: "a set of 'implicit or explicit principles, norms, rules, and decision-making procedures around which actors' expectations converge in a given area of international relations."[35]

The anti-corruption recipes that define it are rooted in institutional practices that are considered to be appropriate and legitimate. To the extent that these practices have become routine within formal organizations, they have moreover acquired a veneer of "myth and ceremony," as in John Meyer and Brian Rowan Brian's classic analysis.[36] They observed that ritualization is an element of organizational "decoupling," which is a relative disconnect between the formal structure of the organization and its day-to-day operations that serves to maintain legitimacy. Also, under this light, compliance with the dictates of anti-corruption plans has become an important element of organizational routines, at constant risk of turning into a box-ticking ritual. As the Italian Anti-Corruption Authority noted disconsolately, when judging that the compulsory anti-corruption plans drawn by Italian public administrations showed a "widespread attitude of mere compliance."[37]

THE SOFT EDGES OF THE CONSENSUS ON CORRUPTION

The consensus view on corruption has not been monolithic. As is often the case with systems of ideas that become hegemonic, it has been characterized

[35] Krasner 1982.

[36] Meyer and Rowan 1977. See also, in the contest of the anti-corruption international regime on which I will return in a later chapter, Zaloznaya and Reisinger 2020. Alina Mungiu-Pippidi argues that anti-corruption is an element of soft power within the European Union activity of "norms promotion" (Mungiu-Pippidi 2020).

[37] Autorità Nazionale Anticorruzione 2016, 82. My treatment of the theme of compliance has not been exhaustive. I have ignored for simplicity important developments, such as the regulatory reforms that followed the financial crisis of 2007–2009, and how they may have influenced anti-corruption policies, and ideas and practices of compliance more generally.

by both internal contradictions and contamination with external ideas. One significant internal contradiction derives from its reliance on highly disputable measures of corruption, discussed in Chapter 3. Additionally, although a narrow concept of corruption has predominated, it is acknowledged that the concept is elusive and its nature contested.

Another theme at the edge of the current debate concerns the relationship between corruption and other social phenomena. While much effort has been dedicated to understanding the causes and effects of corruption, it is often recognized that the concept of corruption, being elusive, is also multifaceted and cannot be considered in isolation. To the extent that corruption has come to be seen as part of a broader idea of governance, it is agreed that it is one of its characteristics and that it can be understood only in the context of governance more generally. A more extreme version of this point of view is reflected by occasional references to so-called systemic corruption, a concept that has come to identify cases where corruption is pervasive and very entrenched in the way that the business of government is carried out.

Recognizing that corruption is an elusive concept contradicts the numerous attempts to assess its causes and consequences, since these attempts assume that corruption can be clearly defined and distinguished from other phenomena that it may cause or result from it. The perceived necessity of adopting precise definitions of the social phenomena under study has led to intense efforts to make the concept of corruption less elusive through qualifications or classifications aimed at pinning it down, and perhaps also reflect a researcher's *horror vacui* that pin it down we cannot. These recurring themes hint at an unresolved tension between the core tenets of the consensus view on corruption and different ideas and methods of analysis. For example, the reference to the concept of systemic corruption resuscitates a functionalist view, as something that is systemic must have functions within the system. Additionally, when observing systemic failures, implicit reference is made to social mechanisms that are not the result of a straightforward aggregation of individual behaviors, as in the rational choice, individualistic approach. In other words, a more sociological reading of corruption naturally reemerges as counterpoint to the prevailing view on corruption.

Last, although much emphasis has been attributed to anti-corruption policies with the presumption that human agency can reduce corruption, the difficulties involved are widely recognized. As I mentioned earlier, corruption is often portrayed as a stubborn societal equilibrium, as Ray Fisman and Miriam Golden argue that "conceiving of corruption as an equilibrium offers a powerful way to both frame the problem and to think about what to do about it," while noting that "sometimes – not often, but sometimes – corruption does unravel."[38] Part of the problem is seen to derive from a degree of instrumentality that anti-corruption efforts may have. Anti-corruption is "very often deployed as a rhetorical weapon in political conflicts over power, the rules by which it was exercised and the distribution of resources," as note Ronald Kroeze, André Vitória and Andre Geltner, who further anticipate ideas that I will expand upon: "Much like accusations of crime in the social sphere and magic in the religion sphere, charges of corruption in the political sphere were frequently used as a cudgel by rival individuals and factions wishing to undermine the moral standing of their opponents and their claims to legitimate authority." They add that the political use of accusations of corruption "should be understood in a broad way: corruption played (and plays) a role in legitimizing and in undermining the political legitimacy of those holding public authority."[39]

These themes represent the soft edges of the current thinking on corruption and are related with the main propositions of this book. As we proceed, I aim to move them from the edge to the center of the debate.

CONCLUSION: A COMPLEX SET OF MOTIVES LED TO THE CONSENSUS VIEW

The ideas of economists, as Keynes proposed, can go a long way, as we see also in the case of modern thinking on corruption. Their success was the result of a fortuitous interplay of different motifs. In the 1970s, when the new thinking on corruption emerged, it was part of a broader encroachment by economists into neighboring disciplines. While the ideas of economists were new, they were also consonant with an older tradition that we traced back to the seventeenth-eighteenth century. The fact that these were, to some extent, old ideas in new clothes may have helped their reception in the United States, where they resonated particularly well.

The individualistic approach proposed by economists to study corruption, along with the implications drawn in devising anti-corruption policies, found a receptive audience due in part to the contemporaneous debate on what was then called "New Public Management." Fortuitous historical events, such as the Watergate scandal, set the political stage for the FCPA of 1977, while subsequent developments led to the OECD Anti-Bribery

[38] Fisman and Golden 2017, 14–15.
[39] Kroeze et al. 2017, 3.

Convention. It is interesting to consider the unwitting role of the Soviet Union in these developments. First, its presence helped convince US legislators, who sought moral high ground and were concerned with national security, to approve the FCPA. Later, it was the absence of the Soviet Union that became relevant. As ideological differences diminished and free-market ideology became dominant, corruption became a more enticing issue in the domestic political arena.[40] I will explore these issues in greater depth in Chapter 11, which is dedicated to the study of corruption as a political tool.

As the demand for anti-corruption policies grew, so did their supply, leading to the creation of an anti-corruption industry comprising specialists, organizations, and various organizational functions. This, in turn, generated vested interests in perpetuating the prevailing view of corruption upon which the industry was founded.[41]

Multiple factors contributed to the conceptual narrowing of corruption, which is a hallmark of the current consensus view. This narrowing was consonant with the individualistic approach of economists, who are naturally interested in the actions of individual actors. The emphasis on quantification and this narrowing played into each other's hands, contributing to a crystallization of ideas. I explore this issue in Chapter 3, while Chapter 4 considers how quantifications of corruption were used to study its determinants and effects. Here too, a fortuitous factor emerged: the availability of econometric methods that implied a causal interpretation of results, reinforcing the presumption of human agency in curing corruption. These two chapters conclude my critique of the prevailing view on corruption. Throughout the previous pages, I also have highlighted themes that we find at the periphery of that view, and that will be central to Parts II and III of the book.

[40] On the zenith of the neoliberal order, see Gerstle 2022, and in particular its chapter 6, significantly titled "Hubris."

[41] For a critical view, see Sampson 2013 and Krastev 2004.

3

The Mutual Shaping of Measures and Concepts

The Bribe Payers Index (BPI) is a measure of how willing a nation's multinational corporations appear to engage in corrupt business practices.

Wikipedia, accessed on May 6, 2023

On October 27, 2017, the Italian Ministry of Foreign Affairs organized a "High-level Workshop on Corruption Measurement" within the framework of the Italian G7 Presidency. The invitation to the meeting stated that ongoing discussions on anti-corruption strategies showed the necessity of adopting "more objective indicators" because country rankings that use perception-based measures "are often flawed." Transparency International's corruption perception index was singled out and blamed.[1] This initiative arose from Italy's relatively poor showing in such perception-based rankings, in the face of those protracted efforts of compliance to the global anti-corruption regime that I have summarized in Chapter 2. Coordinated by an official of ambassadorial rank, Italy's move hints at the importance that measures of corruption have acquired, and to which this chapter is dedicated.

I consider two main questions. One is only apparently of a technical nature and regards the difference between assessing levels of corruption versus its changes over time. The available indices are particularly poor at measuring the latter, which is a fatal flaw when we task them to

[1] I was among the recipients of the invitation. At the international level, the Italian effort eventually contributed to a Resolution (n. 8/10), of the Conference of the States Parties to the United Nations Convention against Corruption (Abu Dhabi, December 16–20, 2019), also affirming "the importance of developing an international statistical framework for measuring corruption, grounded in objective methodologies and reliable data sources." See UNODC 2019.

assess the outcome of anti-corruption policies. I will discuss this question within the broader debate on global performance indicators (GPIs) that have become very popular during the last decades and that instead presuppose an ability to measure a country's progress. I moreover consider the contrast between amounts of corruption and propensity to corruption. It is an important distinction that we ignore at our own risk, as I will show when considering the "Bribe Payers Index" (hence, TI-BPI), a Transparency International's ill-fated and now defunct measure. The fact that these important distinctions have mostly been ignored reflects a degree of analytical confusion within the prevailing view, and it also suggests that the available measures of corruption are even more problematic than it is usually recognized.

The analysis of measures of corruption also serves as an introduction to Chapter 4, where their uses will be critically evaluated, and it helps to clarify our understanding of corruption itself. The relationship between corruption and how we measure it reminds me of M. C. Escher's "Drawing Hands" lithograph, which depicts two hands drawing each other.[2] Metaphorically, one hand represents corruption and the other its quantification. The process of measuring corruption requires a conceptualization of the underlying phenomenon, but it also prompts its questioning: The conceptualization and the measurement of corruption are mutually shaping.

MEASURES OF CORRUPTION BASED ON PERCEPTIONS AND ON EXPERIENCE

Transparency International first published its "Corruption perception index" (hence, TI-CPI) in 1995. According to the organization's founder and then President, Peter Eigen, the index resulted from "an assessment [...] in which existing polls of international business interests and financial journalists have been analyzed and collated," and provided "a picture of how international business sees the levels of corruption in the 41 countries ranked in the survey."[3] Since then, the index has been published yearly, with a country coverage that increased over time.

The TI-CPI is "a composite index, a combination of 13 surveys and assessments of corruption, collected by a variety of reputable institutions,"[4]

2 On this "strange loop," see Hofstadter 1979, 689, and following.

3 Transparency International 1995.

4 Transparency International 2020. Baumann 2020 notes that "the vast majority [of data sources used by Transparency International] were either produced for sale to corporate

so that its precise definition of corruption is unclear and should be seen as a combination of definitions of the included surveys. Some of the sources on which the TI-CPI is based had already been employed as measures of corruption. For example, in a very influential article published in 1995 on which I will return in Chapter 4, Paolo Mauro used a country risk assessment of corruption in order to estimate the effects of corruption on economic growth.[5] While similar assessments of corruption had been used by professionals in the field, the TI-CPI was the first to bring perception-based measures of corruption to the attention of a broad audience.

The world map of corruption according to TI-CPI indicates that it is a serious problem in most countries.[6] Canada and the United States have relatively low levels of perceived corruption compared to the rest of the Americas, where levels of perceived corruption are high, with the partial exception also of Costa Rica, Uruguay, and Chile. In Africa, corruption is perceived to be very high in all countries, with the partial exception of Namibia, Botswana, and South Africa at the southern tip of the continent. Countries in Asia and the Middle East are perceived as highly corrupt with the exception of Singapore. In the Far East and Pacific, Japan and, even more so, Australia and New Zealand are perceived to be virtuous. Europe overall has a level of corruption below the world average, but with variations across countries, with Southern and particularly Eastern European countries faring worse. A pattern of corruption perceived to be less severe in richer countries has remained consistent since the introduction of the TI-CPI in 1995. It also emerges from consideration of other perception-based measures, such as the "Control of Corruption Indicator" (WB-CCI), one of those governance indicators that, as we have seen in Chapter 2, the World Bank introduced in the 1990s.[7]

One of the few available alternatives to perception-based measures is surveys on personal experiences of the phenomenon. The best known

clients or were based on surveys of business elites," and affirms that people at Transparency International "are Gramscian intellectuals who put forward an interpretation of corruption that is non-threatening to corporate capital."

5 He used a total of nine indicators, "[...] proxying for corruption and various other institutional variables" from the same source, "Business International (BI), now incorporated into The Economist Intelligence Unit" (Mauro 1995).

6 For example, Transparency International titles its press release for the 2017 edition of their index: "Corruption Perception Index 2017 shows high corruption burden in more than two-thirds of countries" (Transparency International 2018).

7 Kauffmann et al. 2011. The WB-CCI was first published in 1996, then in 1998, in 2000, 2002, and yearly afterward. It is based largely on the same sources of the TI-CPI, with which it is very highly correlated.

of them is Transparency International's "Global Corruption Barometer" (hence: TI-GCB), which was first presented in 2003 and has been published yearly until 2007, and every two or three years ever since.[8] The TI-GCB and the TI-CPI convey approximately similar messages.[9] The observed overall coherence between these two distinct measures brings credence to their overall validity and to the prevailing narrative on levels of corruption worldwide to which they contribute. However, such conclusion would be premature, as we will discuss shortly.

Transparency International proposed a further perception-based indicator, the "Bribe Payers Index" (hence, TI-BPI), published intermittently between 1999 and 2011. It was not meant to measure levels of corruption in a given country (as in the case of the TI-CPI and the TI-GCB), but its "supply side," defined as "the likelihood of firms from the world's industrialized countries to bribe abroad."[10] The introduction of the TI-BPI provided a degree of balance to Transparency International's assessment of corruption worldwide. Whereas the TI-CPI was accused of partiality against poorer countries, the TI-BPI focused on richer countries and on the proclivity of their companies to buy their way into foreign markets, thus "exporting" corruption, to the Global South in particular. However, the TI-BPI was characterized by fatal conceptual flaws, which soon we will discuss.

Before proceeding further, I present a simple measure of the visibility within the academic debate of the four indicators of corruption mentioned (TI-CPI, WB-CCI, TI-GCB, and TI-BPI), using the search engine scholar .google.com, which is dedicated to scientific publications. A search using appropriate keywords permits to compute the number of documents that mention one or more of those four measures of corruption (Figure 3.1). The TI-CPI has been divided by 10 to make it comparable with the other measures considered and is by far the most popular one. The visibility of the World Bank Control of Corruption Indicator (WB-CCI) and the Transparency International Global Corruption Indicator (TI-GCI) is much lower and similar. More visible was the TI-BPI that however has lost ground in the more recent years, a fact that I will interpret shortly.

[8] It lists eight different types of public services and asks whether the respondent "has paid a bribe to any of [them] in the past 12 months" (Transparency International 2013, 11).

[9] Their correlation in 2013 equaled −0.67 and −0.74 for rank correlation. The negative sign is expected, since the TI-CPI, unlike the TI-GCB, is inversely related to levels of corruption. Measures such as the TI-GCB address different questions and have different shortcomings, with respect to perception-based measures. See Escresa and Picci 2017 and references therein.

[10] Transparency International n.d.c. After 1999, it was published also in 2002, 2006, 2008, and 2011. On its being ceased after 2011, see also Fisman and Golden 2017, 73.

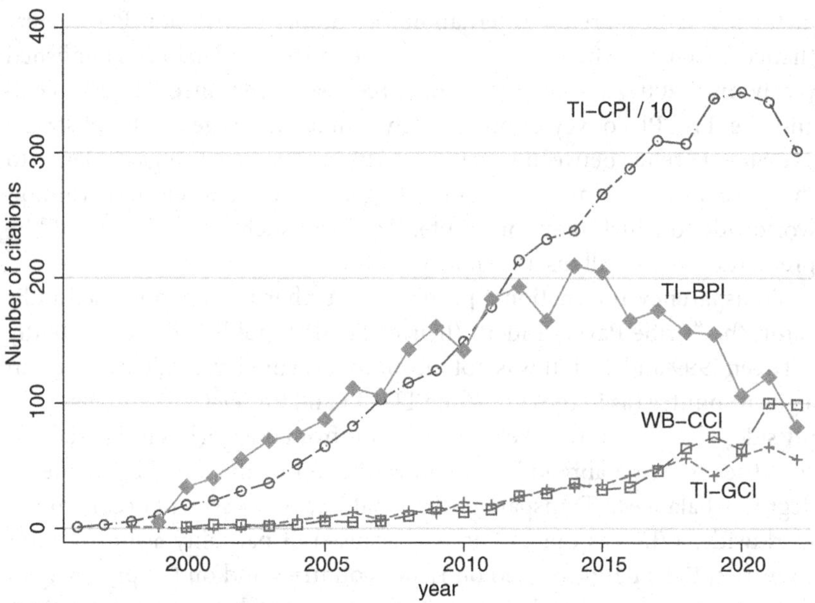

Figure 3.1 TI-CPI, WB-CCI, TI-GCB, and TI-BPI: Google Scholar Citations
Citations of TI-CPI are divided by 10. Hits correspond to a search of: "Corruption Perception Index" and/or "Corruption Perception Indicator" (TI-CPI); "Control of Corruption Indicator" and/or "Control of Corruption Index (WB-CCI)"; "Global Corruption Index" (WB-GCI); "Bribe Payers Index" (TI-BPI).

CROSS-BORDER BRIBES AND THE PUBLIC ADMINISTRATION CORRUPTION INDEX

To assess the validity of the TI-CPI, we compare it with a measure obtained using a completely different methodology and data. The data refer to recorded occurrences of bribes that firms headquartered in a given country allegedly paid to public officials or politicians abroad. Use of these data in fact gives rise to two measures: the "Public Administration Corruption Index" (hence, PACI), to be compared with the TI-CPI, and the "Bribe Payers Corruption Index" (BPCI), aimed at capturing the "supply side" of corruption, as was the TI-BPI, to which it will be compared later.[11]

I mentioned in Chapter 2 that the OECD Anti-Bribery Convention led to the introduction of the crime of foreign bribery in many countries. The enforcement of these provisions permitted the collection of a database of

[11] The PACI is presented in Escresa and Picci 2017, and the BPCI in Picci 2018.

1,216 cases that have occurred between the years 2000 and 2014.[12] The resulting measures do not derive from a simplistic count of cases, which would be meaningless as it would depend on a country's judicial activism and on other factors that are unrelated to what we desire to measure. Instead, they are based on a more sophisticated consideration of the geographic distribution of cases, as observed from a distant "observation point."

In fact, the geographic distribution of cross-border interactions of various types might be informative of phenomena that are the result of secretive activities more generally. For example, Annette Alstadsæter, Niels Johannesen, and Gabriel Zucman research the distribution of wealth held in tax havens. As a way to test for the robustness of their results, they use data from the Panama Papers leak[13] and consider the geographic distribution "of unique owners of shell companies created by Mossack Fonseca in each of the world's countries (normalized by 2007 GDP)." They argue that it is "informative to analyze who the owners of the shell corporations created by this firm are." In their analysis, Panama serves as a distant observation point with respect to which the geographic distribution of cases might be usefully observed. Using more leaks of the Panama Papers type, each one from a different offshore tax haven, would supply more such observation points from where to consider the geographic distribution of cases *elsewhere.* These different geographic distributions could be combined to provide a single measure of the overall distribution of, in that case, ownership of shell companies. As big datasets of cross-border interactions of various types might become more abundant, be they the consequence of leaks, or other, we would expect more indicators to be developed along these lines. Here, however, we are uniquely interested in the translation of such general intuition to the problem of measuring corruption, which is what the PACI and the BPCI do.

To further clarify how this is accomplished, let us call the country of the firm that allegedly bribed abroad the "headquarters country," while the "foreign country" is where the allegedly corrupt public official resides. We first consider the PACI, a measure of corruption of public officials in the "foreign" country (foreign with respect to the country where the bribing firm is headquartered). As an example of the intuition underlying

[12] I use an updated version (dated December 13, 2022) of the database, with respect to the one presented in Escresa and Picci 2017.

[13] Alstadsæter et al. 2018. The Panama Papers are the publication by the International Consortium of Investigative Journalists, in the Spring of 2016, of the names and addresses of the owners of all the shell companies created by the Panamian firm Mossack Fonseca.

Table 3.1 *Cases of cross-border bribery, 2000–2014*

	Total cases	Positive cases	Ongoing cases
Of which, first enforced in:	1216	761	355
Headquarters country	518	334	124
Foreign country	222	94	120
Third-country jurisdiction: United States	236	169	49
Third-country jurisdiction, other than the United States	240	164	62

Source of the data: updated version (December 13, 2022) of the dataset described in Escresa and Picci 2017. The "headquarters country" is where the firm which allegedly bribed public officials abroad is headquartered. The "foreign country" is where the act of alleged corruption took place. "Third-country jurisdiction" refers to cases that were first enforced neither in the headquarters, nor in the foreign country. *Positive cases* refer to cases that were concluded with a judgment in favor of the prosecution or a settlement. *Ongoing cases* are those that are still pending or for which no further information is available.

this index, assume that half of all the cases concerning US firms involve Chinese public officials. That would be a signal that public sector corruption in China is relatively high. Obviously, such a conclusion should take into account the bilateral transactions that could be vulnerable to corruption (the United States interacts more often with China than, say, Denmark). As a suitable proxy for the intensity of bilateral cross-country interactions, export figures from the headquarters to the foreign country are used. Also, both the PACI and the BPCI consider and combine cases arising not only from a single jurisdiction, but from all for which there are suitable data.

A summary of the data is provided in Table 3.1, where cases are distinguished according to the jurisdiction that "first enforced" them, that is, where a given case emerged for the first time. Most cases (518 out of 1216, or 43%) were first enforced in the headquarters country. A total of 222 cases, or 18% of the total, emerged instead in the foreign country. The remaining cases were first enforced in so-called third-country jurisdictions. In this category, the United States stands out with 236 cases, because of the expansive interpretation of its jurisdiction which I mentioned in Chapter 2. Other 240 cases emerged in different countries that also represent third-country jurisdictions.

I mentioned that a jurisdiction where cases were first enforced constitutes an "observation point" with respect to which the geographic distribution of those cases *elsewhere* might be considered. In particular, cases that emerged in the headquarters country might be used to assess corruption in the foreign country, leading to the computation of the PACI ("Public Administration Corruption Index"), which expresses the propensity to corruption of public officials in a given country. The less numerous cases first enforced in the foreign country are useful for computing the BPCI ("Bribe Payers Corruption Index"), which assesses the propensity of firms in a given country to corrupt abroad.[14] Cases first enforced in third-country jurisdictions, on the other hand, are useful for the computation of both indices, since those jurisdictions are distant from both from the foreign and the headquarters country. Considering Table 3.1, this implies that a total of 994 cases are informative for the task of computing the PACI (the sum of 518, 236, and 240), while 698 are used to compute the BPCI (the sum of 222, 236, and 240). Let me stress once more that the PACI, which I now discuss, is an index of corruption that is based on observed occurrences of corruption: not on perceptions of the phenomenon, as is the case of the TI-CPI or the WB-CCI, and not on the voluntary "confessions" of persons who experience corruption, as is the case of the TI-GCB and of similar indices. Another important novelty is that the PACI's definition of corruption is precise and circumscribed (cross-border bribing), while the TI-CPI is vague in what it measures.[15]

The paucity of the data available does not permit the computation of the PACI on a yearly basis. For this reason, I present the index for a rather long period, 15 years (from 2000 to 2014), implicitly assuming that levels of corruption are rather constant over time, and I compare it with the TI-CPI of 2007. With all these caveats in mind, it is perhaps surprising that a comparison of the logarithm of the PACI with the TI-CPI shows a remarkable degree of coherence, with a correlation coefficient equal to −0.80 (Figure 3.2).[16] These two measures of corruption, so very dissimilar in nature, produce similar evidence on the levels of corruption worldwide.

[14] The conditions that have to be met in order for the proposed measures to be valid, and all technicalities that are relevant for the construction of the two indices, are described in Escresa and Picci 2017 and Picci 2018.

[15] Regarding the PACI's "external validity," and in particular on whether cross-border bribes are informative of their purely domestic variant, see the discussion in Escresa and Picci 2017, 2020.

[16] The PACI attributes higher scores to higher levels of corruption, while the TI-CPI does the opposite, hence the negative sign of their correlation coefficient. On the reasons and implications behind the use of the logarithm transformation for the PACI, see the considerations in Escresa and Picci 2017.

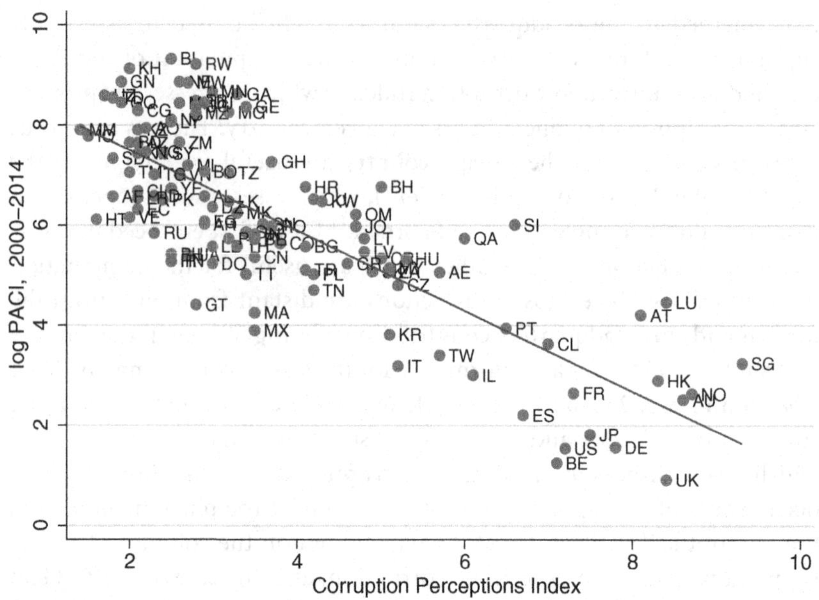

Figure 3.2 The PACI versus the TI-CPI
Labels are ISO two-letter country codes. Log of the Public Administration Corruption Index (PACI, 2000–2014), and Transparency International's Corruption Perception Index (TI-CPI) (year 2007), with ordinary least squares regression line. See Escresa and Picci 2017 for details.

Michaela Saisana and Andrea Saltelli show that the constituent measures of the TI-CPI are highly coherent,[17] and we have just observed that a further measure of corruption, the PACI, obtained using completely different data and methods, also provides rather similar results. Perhaps it might be concluded that how corruption is defined does not really matter and perceptions tend to be on target. Additionally, it might be thought that if perception-based measures are approximately correct to assess variations of corruption across countries, they must also be useful to measure the changes of corruption over time within countries. However, such conclusions would be premature.

A comparison of the variations in time of the TI-CPI and the PACI is complicated by the fact that the PACI cannot be computed on a yearly basis because of the paucity of the available data. For these reasons, with Laarni Escresa, I focused on 19 "world regions" – geographic aggregates that are

[17] Saisana and Saltelli 2012.

wider than the country – and computed the PACI for three five-year periods. Changes over time of these measures are not correlated with suitable ones obtained using the TI-CPI – in fact, their correlation, if anything, tends to indicate opposing messages regarding changes of corruption in time.[18]

To summarize, both the TI-CPI and the PACI offer similar information on the level of corruption, but they disagree with each other when used to assess changes in corruption over time. This apparent contradiction should not surprise. If a phenomenon, such as corruption, exhibits significant variation across countries, but only minimal changes over time, then an imprecise measure might be acceptable in one case but not in the other. Later in this chapter, I will discuss the reasons behind the shortcomings of perception-based measures to assess changes of corruption in time. First, I consider a distinction whose importance is underappreciated: that between the quantity of corruption and the propensity to engage in corruption.

PROPENSITIES VERSUS QUANTITIES OF CORRUPTION AND CHANGES OF CORRUPTION OVER TIME

Different human activities may be more or less vulnerable to corruption. Let us consider, in country *i*, *N* different types of transactions, indexed *j*, that involve public administrations. They could include, for example, public purchases, granting building permits, and administering traffic tickets. Each type of transaction *j*, in country *i* (Transactions_{ji}), has an associated probability of being corrupt, $Pr\left(\text{corruption}_{ji}\right)$. These probabilities often vary significantly. For example, it could be that in a given country the police force is honest and cannot be bribed in order to avoid a speeding ticket, while at the same time public tenders are often corrupt.

A reasonable measure of corruption in country *i* is provided by the ratio between the number of corrupt transactions (which we equal to its expected number) and the total number of transactions:

$$\text{Corruption}_i = \frac{\sum_{j=1}^{N} Pr\left(\text{corruption}_{ji}\right)\cdot \text{Transactions}_{ji}}{\sum_{j=1}^{N} \text{Transactions}_{ji}} \tag{3.1}$$

It is bounded between 0 (absence of corruption) and 1 (all transactions are corrupt). The numerator of Eq. (3.1) states that the overall level of

[18] Escresa and Picci 2016.

corruption depends both on the probability of each type of transaction to be corrupt, and on how many transactions there are of each type.[19] To fix ideas, a decrease in corruption could happen either because the probability of corruption for one or more types of corruption decreases, or because the composition of types of transactions shifts in favor of those that are characterized by lower probabilities of corruption.

I apply this simple intuition to consider corruption in Spain, with a focus on the years before and after the financial crisis of 2007–2009. Daily interactions of Spanish citizens with public administrations tend to be honest: According to the 2013 edition of TI-GCB, only 2% of the population surveyed declared that, in the previous 12 months, they had paid a bribe.[20] Perception-based measures such as the TI-CPI, however, tell a partially different story and rank Spain as a relatively virtuous country at the world level, but not when compared to other countries in the European Union. Besides what the TI-CPI indicates, media coverage of corruption scandals suggests that Spain has had a rather serious problem of grand corruption.

We would like to consider how the perceptions of corruption in Spain have changed over time according to the TI-CPI. Transparency International has been rather inconsistent in its consideration of its time variations. A list of "Frequently Asked Questions" states that "the score of a country in the 2018 [TI-]CPI [can] be compared with the previous year," but that "because of the update in the methodology" [...] "scores before 2012 are not comparable over time."[21] Previously, Transparency International had been much more prudent on the possibility of comparing the scores in time. The question "How can the 1996 Ranking be compared to the 1995 Ranking?" was answered in a nuanced way, and the reader was reminded that "a changing performance *may* be due to actual regime shifts and a trend towards increasing or decreasing corruption over time" (emphasis mine).[22] At the same time, in its reports accompanying the publication of new releases of the TI-CPI, Transparency International has regularly commented changes in time (or lack thereof) of its indicator as if they mattered.

[19] The formula could admit weights reflecting a greater importance attributed to grand corruption (such as corruption in public tenders) than to petty corruption (such as bribes to cancel a speeding ticket). The formulation proposed is the simplest possible for my purposes.

[20] Transparency International 2013.

[21] Transparency International 2019.

[22] Transparency International n.d.a. On changes in the methodology of the TI-CPI over time, see also Baumann 2020.

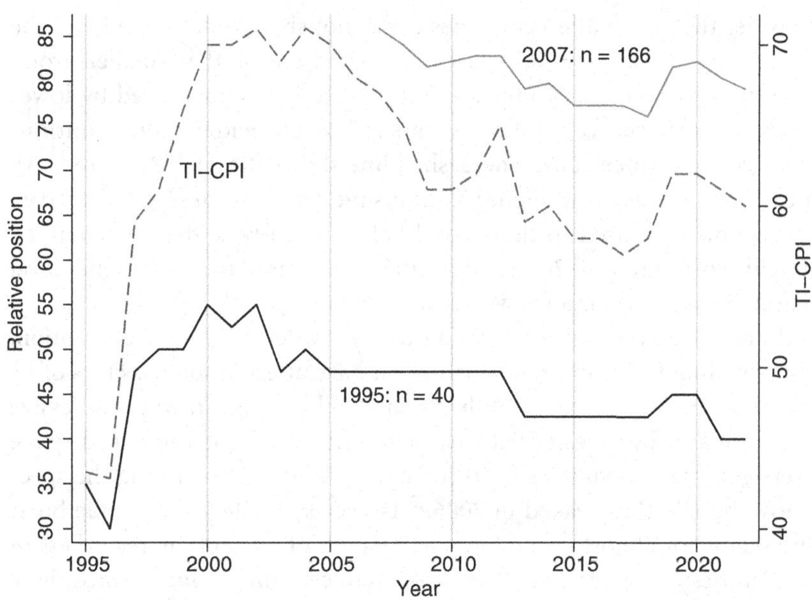

Figure 3.3 TI-CPI and its relative position (Spain)
Dashed line: TI-CPI (right axis; values before 2012 are multiplied by 10). Relative positions (left axis): Percentiles, relative to group of countries (of size *n*) continuously present from a given date. Higher relative positions (and values of the TI-CPI) correspond to less perceived corruption. See Escresa and Picci 2016 for details.

Considering these somehow contradictory messages, I also evaluate the evolution in time of the country rankings. The number of countries covered by the TI-CPI has varied considerably, and it has increased in time, so that I compute rankings within groups of countries that have been continuously covered since a given year.[23] In particular, I consider two groups of countries that have been covered continuously: since 1995 and since 2007. For example, the 1995 edition of the TI-CPI covered 41 countries. Of these, 40 have been continuously covered ever since (Spain is one of them). I chose 2007 as the starting point for the second comparison because it marked a significant increase in country coverage.

Relative rankings in Figure 3.3 indicate the percentage of countries faring worse than Spain. For example, if we consider the group of countries continuously covered by the TI-CPI since 2007 (166 of them), Spain fares rather well, placed as it is in the top 20% of the list, or better. If we

[23] This simple methodology is further illustrated in Escresa and Picci 2016.

consider the group of 40 countries continuously covered since 1995 (the lowest line in Figure 3.3), it fares less well because that smaller group includes several richer countries that tend to be characterized by lower levels of perceived corruption, compared to the wider group continuously covered since 2007. The dashed line shows the TI-CPI score.[24] All measures considered in Figure 3.3 transmit a similar message: Perceived corruption decreased in the second half of the 1990s, then it remained roughly constant until 2012, and in 2013, it increased to a new higher level that it maintained for a few years.

As noted, Spain is characterized by very low levels of petty corruption, but troubling forms of grand corruption have affected some sectors of its economy. Poor governance of the private building sector, where excessive discretionary power rested with local authorities in the absence of adequate oversight, made it vulnerable to corruption, particularly during the speculative bubble that peaked in 2006.[25] However, in 2009 the bubble burst and the sector almost ground to a halt. *Levels* of corruption, regardless of *propensities to engage in corrupt acts*, were certainly reduced since there were not nearly as many high-risk transactions as before, contrary to what is indicated in Figure 3.3. Public investments, which also are at risk of corruption, also decreased in number following the financial crisis.[26] Levels of corruption in Spain certainly decreased after such significant negative economic shock. The increase of perceived corruption after 2013 (Figure 3.3) likely derives from a series of high-level corruption scandals.[27]

The case of Spain highlights an important and overlooked shortcoming of perception-based measures of corruption, such as the TI-CPI; these perceptions are not retrospective. When scandals become highly visible, individuals revise their perceptions of corruption upward not only for the present but also for the past. This is so not only because those scandals often refer to events that may have happened years earlier, but perhaps

24 Values of the TI-CPI before 2012 have been multiplied by ten, to reflect a change of scale that took place in that year.

25 See Barroso Vargas 2012, Jiménez Sánchez 2008, Garcia Quesada et al. 2013, Villoria 2015, and Villoria and Jiménez- Sánchez 2012.

26 In Picci 2018, I present supporting data both on housing permits and on public investments. The reorientation of public resources toward social expenditure might have resulted in an increase of corruption in those sectors. However, such effect was likely modest, since most transfers were the result of the application of objective rules. Cases such as that of the *Expedientes de regulación de empleo* (regulated layoffs of workers by firms in dire straits) in Andalusia, giving rise to abuses (Barroso Vargas 2012), were likely exceptions to the rule.

27 Villoria 2015.

more importantly because they may change perceptions of the long-term, structural characteristics of a country. However, when surveyed, respondents are asked to provide perceptions only for the most recent year, and the published past measures of corruption such as the TI-CPI cannot be modified retrospectively. This limits the ability of these indicators to assess changes in corruption over time. The case of Spain also indicates the importance of distinguishing between levels and propensities of corruption in assessing changes over time. Referring to Equation (3.1), the conclusion that corruption declined in Spain after the financial crisis derives from considering the sectoral composition of transactions that are vulnerable to corruption. I conclude that after the financial crisis the *quantity* of corruption decreased because there were significantly fewer high-risk transactions.

As for the other channel of change in Equation (3.1), which is variations in the probabilities that a given type of transaction is corrupt, these are difficult to ascertain in the aftermath of a crisis. Two contrasting effects may be at play. Occasionally, we observe "corruption bubbles," times when the number of high-risk transactions is very high. An "anything goes" mentality may prevail, and, at least in some sectors of activity, pervasive bribing becomes a sort of new normal. These corruption bubbles may be encouraged by extraordinary circumstances, as was the case in Spain during the heady years leading to the financial crisis of 2007–2009. Popular culture and everyday language may provide hints of the ongoing excesses, as was the case for the Spanish expression "*hipotecas Cayenne*" (Cayenne mortgages), that in those years came to indicate those mortgages supposedly allowing the purchase not only of a house, but also of the eponymous Porsche SUV. A feeling of impunity may establish itself, resembling the experience of a crowd sacking public properties during a riot, where each one feels protected by the numerous others. Where, moreover, a shared understanding that there will come a day of reckoning paradoxically encourages a get-it-while-you-can voracity.[28] Also suggesting that the end of a bubble may bring lower corruption is the fact that the decrease in the number of transactions vulnerable to corruption may lead to more effective monitoring, resulting in restrain. However, and with an opposite effect, facing diminished opportunities, corrupt networks may fight more fiercely to maintain a minimum of illegal resources which may be essential for their cohesion and survival.

[28] In the years leading the *Mani Pulite* scandals of the early 1990s, Italy also arguably went through a similar experience. See della Porta and Vannucci 2012, chapter 9, describing a "snowball effects" and path dependency. Also consider Hirschman 1982.

It is an open question as to which of these effects might have prevailed in Spain after 2008, but the question is likely of second-order importance, in comparison with the observed very significant decrease in the number of high-risk transactions.

THE PROPENSITY TO BRIBE ABROAD: A TALE OF NATIONAL CULPABILITY

Countries with high levels of perceived corruption according to the TI-CPI are seen as lacking in some way, as they are unable to implement an adequate model of public governance. The goal of the TI-CPI, as it happens for global perfomance indicators (GPIs) more generally, is to encourage these countries to mend their ways. Countries that fail may adopt two broad strategies that are not mutually exclusive. The first is to question the validity of the ranking, as Italy has done in the case of perception-based measures of corruption such as the TI-CPI. The second, which is only available to countries in the Global South, is to deflect blame by claiming that corruption is imported. This thesis is at least plausible, as the Global North is home not only to most corporations that have been involved in foreign corruption, but also to financial institutions that have been instrumental in the payment of bribes and in their laundering.

Within a debate influenced by such considerations, in 1999 Transparency International launched its "Bribe Payers Index" (TI-BPI) to "evaluate the supply side of corruption – the likelihood of firms from the world's industrialized countries to bribe abroad."[29] Transparency International condemned such practices without mincing words, stating that "the scale of bribe-paying by international corporations in the developing countries of the world is massive," while "actions by the majority of governments of the leading industrial countries to curb international corruption are modest," to the point that "some of the world's richest countries turn a blind eye to corruption. When their companies use bribes to win business abroad and are allowed to get away with it, governments are effectively complicit in exporting corruption."[30] The TI-BPI was a perception-based measure computed only for a small group of countries mostly from the Global North. Its fatal shortcomings may be seen as a consequence of having ignored the distinction between levels of corruption and propensity to corrupt, so that consideration of this index presents us with the opportunity to discuss

[29] Transparency International n.d.c.
[30] Transparency International n.d.b and n.d.c.

this important question from a distinct angle. The TI-BPI also offers an interesting example of the mutual shaping between measures of corruption and the concept of corruption, which is one of the defining aspects of the current consensus view, that so much attention has dedicated to measurement issues.

The TI-BPI is highly correlated with the TI-CPI (with a correlation equal to 0.83 in 2011), suggesting that countries with modest levels of perceived corruption also are home to firms that have a lower "likelihood to bribe abroad" – this is the expression used by Transparency International, and it is important to take note. This suggests that there are country factors that are relevant both for domestic corruption and for its exporting abroad. The implied narrative is one where the term "corruption" is cast as in its original etymological meaning, the Latin "*com*" and "*rumpere*," to break. Corruption, both domestically and in its exported variety, would derive from a broken national order, possibly reflecting the presence of a national collective culpability.[31] We are observing once again one of the soft edges of the current prevailing view on corruption where distinct perspectives are interlaced. The logic of GPIs, here applied to a narrow and public-office-centered definition of corruption, interacts with an altogether different view of which I will say more in a Chapter 5, where the label of corruption is applied to a whole "body politic."

The TI-BPI is marred by fatal methodological flaws because it confuses levels of corruption and propensities to corrupt. More precisely, the "likelihood of firms to bribe abroad," the concept of interest of this index, is a hopelessly ambiguous expression since it does not specify if it refers to a generic firm, or to a firm having a concrete possibility to bribe abroad. To clarify, consider a fictitious example. Assume that firms headquartered in Argentina that contest markets abroad offer bribes with a probability that is twice that of Swiss companies facing the same predicament. However, the fraction of Argentinian firms with a concrete chance of contesting markets abroad is much smaller than in Switzerland, a country that notoriously headquarters many important multinational companies. So, the "likelihood of firms" "to bribe abroad" would be twice as big in Argentina, if the assessment is conditional on a firm having a concrete chance to do so (a conditional probability, expressing a propensity to corrupt). However, it would likely be much smaller if we look at all firms in each country (a marginal probability, expressing the probability that a generic Argentinian firm "exports" corruption).

[31] Picci 2018.

The TI-BPI asked firms' representatives to identify countries where they have business relationships (such as suppliers, clients, partners, or competitors) and to rate, on a scale of 1 to 5, "*how often* [...] firms headquartered in those countries engage in bribery" within that country (emphasis is mine).[32] The question left respondents uncertain as to whether they were asked to assess the probability that a transaction is corrupt, given that a cross-border transaction occurs, or the probability that a generic firm engages in foreign bribery, regardless of whether it has the opportunity to do so. Faced with an ambiguous question and in most cases without the benefit of first-hand information, the answers likely reflected an "availability heuristics," which is a tendency to form a judgment on some question on the basis of what is readily brought to mind, where the information is retrieved based on "associative distance."[33] Levels of perceived corruption, such as those of the very popular TI-CPI, provided the necessary cues, resulting in the strong correlation observed between the two measures.[34]

As I anticipated, the data on cross-border bribes that can be used to compute the Public Administration Corruption Index (PACI) may also be used to calculate the Bribe Payers Corruption Index (BPCI), which measures the propensity to corrupt abroad. As is for the case of the PACI, the BPCI is coherent with the definition of measures of corruption provided in Equation (3.1), and a country score represents a percentage relative to a world average level of the propensity to corrupt abroad, which is set equal to 100.[35] Results both for the BPCI and also for the TI-BPI are shown in Figure 3.4, which should be interpreted while considering that the TI-BPI assigns lower values to more corruption while the BPCI does the opposite. The positive correlation between the two measures implies that, in fact, they deliver contrasting messages. The BPCI singles out Switzerland as the country with the greatest propensity to "export corruption," followed by the United Kingdom and The Netherlands. More than anything else, what matters in delivering these results is the opportunity to bribe abroad, so it is those countries that have more multinational corporations that tend to top the list.

To conclude, the narrative of corruption as a national sin, where the most corrupt among the rich countries also are more guilty of exporting

[32] See Appendix A in Picci 2018 for details.
[33] See Schwartz 1998, and Tversky and Kahneman 1973, who introduced the concept.
[34] Picci 2018 shows that the list of shortcomings of the TI-BPI is not limited to this aspect.
[35] See Picci 2018 for a detailed description of the BPCI and of the conditions for its validity.

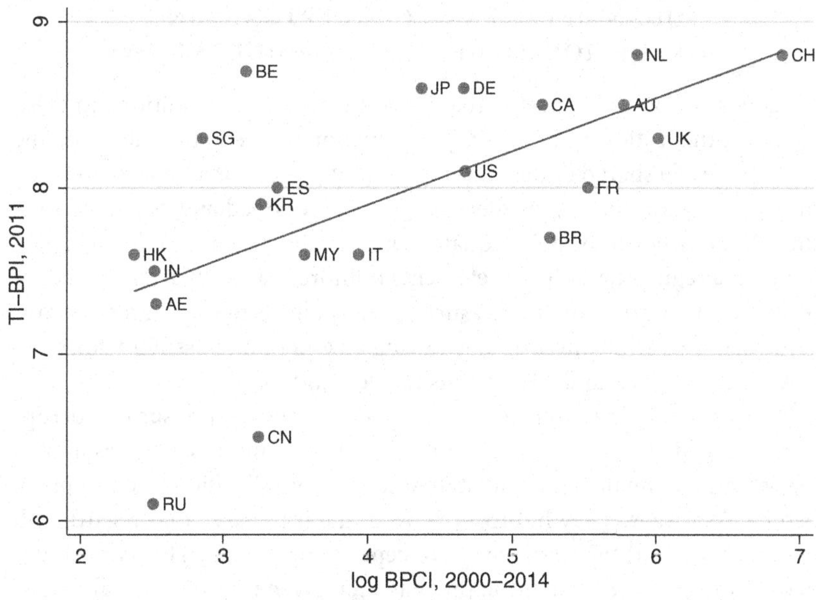

Figure 3.4 The TI-BPI versus the BPCI
Labels are ISO two-letter country codes. Transparency International's Bribe Payers Index (TI-BPI, year 2011) and logarithm of the Bribe Payers Corruption Index (BPCI, years 2000–2014), with ordinary least squares regression line. The BPCI increases in levels of corruption, while the opposite holds for the TI-BPI. See Picci 2018 for details.

it abroad, is the result of misguided empirical research by Transparency International. A faulty measure influences a particular conceptualization of corruption which not only replicates the colors of Transparency International's world map of levels of corruption according to its Corruption Perception Index, but reinforces them by affirming their validity in a new domain.

The TI-BPI was last published in 2011 and around May 2020, according to achive.org, all material related to this index disappeared from its website: Transparency International quietly phased out the TI-BPI without formally retracting it. A Wikipedia entry for the TI-BPI still declares that "The Bribe Payers Index (BPI) is a measure of how willing a nation's multinational corporations appear to engage in corrupt business practices." The TI-BPI has also been used in empirical research on corruption (Figure 3.1). The number of yearly publications citing it has been significantly higher than for the WB-CCI, or TI-GCI, or roughly one-tenth of the TI-CPI. Only after 2014, the number of citations that it received started to decrease.

QUANTIFYING AND CONCEPTUALIZING CORRUPTION: SOME FINAL CONSIDERATIONS

Measures of societal concepts require some broad preconditions to exist. A conceptualization of a certain phenomenon is needed to allow for the emergence of a shared understanding of what it is that is amenable to being measured. Additionally, for measures to be developed and sustained over time, there needs to be an adequate demand and the conditions to supply them on a regular basis. These elements reinforce each other: The presence of an embryonic demand to measure a concept leads to its progressive conceptualization, which in turn, in showing an emerging possibility for measurement, supports and strengthens the demand for it.[36]

Measures of corruption were developed as a new consensus on corruption emerged. Thanks to their popularity, they came to be seen as appropriate and legitimate, and contributed to the crystallization of concepts in two distinct ways. They hid from view all the intricacies that regard both the measures and the underlying concept of corruption. This contributes in explaining the little attention that has been given to two important questions that we have considered in this chapter: the distinction between propensity and quantity of corruption, and the distinction between measuring corruption at a given time and over time. The measures not only contributed to a crystallization of the concept of corruption in selecting what to measure but also in what they left out, which is much, if we consider the narrowness of today's prevailing definition. In particular, they promoted a relative lack of interest for forms of corruption that may not correspond to crimes and for many other borderline phenomena that, for example, we may be unsure as to whether to classify as forms of conflict of interest, or of corruption. To return to the metaphor provided by M. C. Escher's "Drawing Hands," one hand, corruption, drew the other, its measures, which in turn partly shaped our understanding of corruption.

These conclusions would also apply more generally to the score of GPIs that have become popular since the 1990s. In the words of Judith Kelley and Beth Simmons, they have represented "governance by other means" and provided International Organizations ways to "'govern' without explicit legal or regulatory directives."[37] However, measures of

[36] On these relationships, see also Desrosières 1998, in the context of the emergence and affirmation of statistics.

[37] In a situation where their contested role spurred searches for creative and "hybrid" forms of governance. Kelley and Simmons 2021.

corruption such as the TI-CPI (and the very similar WB-CCI) also distinguish themselves from GPIs in general. A desired characteristic of a GPI is that it should be actionable, in the sense that it may place pressure on governments to enact policy responses aimed at improving a country's ranking.[38] The case of the currently available corruption indicators is different: Because of their shortcomings in measuring changes over time in corruption (or worse, as in the case of TI-BPI), they are not actionable, and this is so regardless of what we may think of the concept of corruption that they adopt (and promote).[39] For this reason, whatever positive may be said about the current role of GPIs in global governance, it does not apply to the case of corruption. Perception-based measures of corruption in a certain sense have been free-riding on the success and legitimacy of other GPIs. It is also under this light that we should interpret the frustration that transpires from the invitation of the Italian government, of which I said at the beginning of this chapter, to adopt "more objective indicators." Last, I note that not knowing how to measure changes in corruption in time amounts to not being able to distinguish between compliance to anti-corruption policies that is effective in combating corruption, from that which is not, and such ignorance may favor the ritualization of compliance that I discussed in Chapter 2.

Investigations into the causes and the consequences of corruption have often used the measures of corruption that we have discussed. Such uses involve a series of methodological questions that I consider in Chapter 4. My intention is to continue a critical appraisal of the current consensus on corruption. Once this appraisal will be completed, all the pieces will be in place to provide, in Chapter 5, a series of methodological directives to guide us further ahead.

38 See Kelley and Simmons 2019, particularly their Figure 2 showing "pathways, policy response and reassessment" describing the possible mutual relationship between GPIs and policy changes. Consider Doshi et al. 2019 on such mechanism at play for the World Bank's (eventually retracted) "ease of doing business" index, with particular reference to India.

39 See also Kelley and Simmons 2019: "GPIs are more likely to be influential when they are actionable. It is considerably easier for all countries to change a fee, for example, than it is to quickly improve child mortality or perceptions about corruption."

4

Of Causality and Historical Junctures

I suppose it is tempting, if the only tool you have is a hammer, to treat everything as if it were a nail.

Abraham Maslow[1]

There was a time when many Italians, if asked about the yearly cost of corruption to the country, would have concurred in indicating that it amounted to 60 billion Euros. It was a belief promoted by several authoritative news outlets which included *Corriere della Sera* and *la Repubblica*, respectively, first and second newspapers by circulation in Italy, and *Il Sole 24 Ore*, the most important business daily.[2] The hefty amount of money had been mentioned in televised talk shows and parliamentary debates, most often to support calls for urgent and comprehensive action against corruption.[3]

It took approximately two years for the Italian media system to gradually realize that the 60 billion Euro estimate of the cost of corruption was an invention, resulting from misunderstandings and journalistic errors.[4] This curious case, besides serving as an example of a use of (pseudo) quantitative information in a purely rhetorical fashion, where

1 Maslow 1966, 15.

2 The time was approximately 2012. See Corriere della Sera 2012, La Repubblica 2012, Turno 2012.

3 For example, Honorable Laura Boldrini (then President of the Chamber of Deputy): "Corruption poisons our country and takes away from its honest citizens 60 billion every year" (Boldrini 2013). Bill introduced in the Chamber of Deputy, March 15, 2013: "According to the Annual Report of the Italian Supreme Audit Institution, in 2009, the yearly cost of corruption on the State budget is about 50 or 60 billion Euros" (Camera dei Deputati 2013). In fact, that institution had never expressed such a view.

4 De Luca 2014.

"60 billion" was simply meant to indicate "a lot,"[5] is worth further analysis for the insights it can provide. First, nobody objected to the question itself on the cost of corruption, indicating acquiescence with the view that corruption has a cost that may be expressed (even if perhaps not exclusively) in monetary terms. Also, the question did not define corruption, perhaps because it was thought that there is agreement on the concept. The answer provided implicitly stated that the necessary data and a suitable methodology of analysis were believed to be available. Last, the causal reasoning, where the occurrence of "corruption" is seen as a cause of its "costs," implied a thought experiment where the counterfactual of no corruption is considered legitimate as an alternative to the observed reality. In conclusion, the question on the yearly cost of corruption in Italy was in fact ideological, in the sense that it presupposed acceptance of a set of mutually related ideas.

Estimating the cost of corruption entails the solution of two distinct problems. First, an estimate of the quantity of corruption is needed, a question discussed in Chapter 3. Second, a methodology to translate that quantity into a cost should also be available. Under no circumstance, in fact, the quantity of corruption would correspond to its cost. For example, when corruption is identified with bribery, the total amount of bribes paid in a year (assuming that we knew) would not equate to the cost of corruption. On the one hand, the money of bribes is put to further use, with some of it returning to the state via taxation. On the other hand, bribes distort the allocation of resources, so that they have both direct and indirect costs, and we have good reasons to believe that the latter may trump the former.

Going from a measure of corruption such as the ones discussed in Chapter 3, to an estimate of its costs, requires an appropriate methodology of analysis. The one that has prevailed, and that led to results strongly influencing the current consensus view on corruption, involves the use of the multivariate regression model. I discuss these uses in the pages ahead, to argue that the adoption of the regression model represents an interesting case of "model substitution." This occurs when repeated use of a certain model leads to espouse a theory of reality which is coherent with it: As Abraham Maslow once put it, if all you have is a hammer, then everything looks like a nail.

In this case, "the hammer" conduced to automatically interpret in causal terms the empirical relationship between corruption and other relevant factors. Such causal interpretation implied the belief that counterfactuals

[5] On "rhetorical numbers," see Wolfe 2010.

regarding corruption and other relevant characteristics of governance may be meaningfully contemplated. This belief, in turn, promoted a cognitive framework where the possibility of agency to reduce corruption is assumed. "The hammer" was repeatedly used because it was readily available and visible to all, in the form of popular econometric methods that imply a causal reading of their results. As such, it was considered to be a very legitimate hammer. The ready and convenient availability of those methods represents yet another fortuitous factor that contributed to the affirmation of the current prevailing view on corruption. And while the use of these methods in the said way eventually waned, their previous intense use contributed to crystallize a series of beliefs in the years when the current consensus on corruption was establishing itself, with lasting consequences.

This chapter discusses these themes and lays the foundations for Chapter 5, where an alternative conceptual framework to interpret corruption is proposed.

GROWTH REGRESSIONS AND CORRUPTION

Occasionally, some research article attracts much continued attention and becomes a focal point for future authors. One such article, titled "Corruption and growth" and that to date has been cited more than 14,000 times according to Google Scholar, was published in 1995 in the prestigious *The Quarterly Journal of Economics*. The author was Paolo Mauro, then a researcher at the International Monetary Fund. Drawn from a chapter of his doctoral dissertation at Harvard University, it estimated the effects of corruption on the prospects for economic development and concluded that these were statistically significant and of considerable negative magnitude. On October 1, 1996, the World Bank's President, Jim Wolfensohn, who knew of Mauro's article and had been influenced by it, delivered an important speech that formally marked the Bank's change of stance with respect to corruption.[6]

Mauro's article was part of a lively research agenda that attempted to use "growth regressions," analyzing data from many countries, to shed light on the determinants of economic growth. The year of publication, 1995, coincided with the birth of Transparency International's Corruption Perception Index, which rode on the rising popularity of Global Performance Indicators. Those quantitative measures allowed to compare

[6] See Daniel Kaufmann's account (Kaufmann 2005, and in particular, note 14).

and rank countries along different dimensions and were also used widely in growth regressions either as variables of interest (as was the case for corruption in Paolo Mauro's study) or as control variables. Their use in turn stimulated their supply, in a context where quantitative "large N" studies were believed to be conducive to credible empirical conclusions.

The seminal article in the growth regression literature had been published by Robert Barro four years earlier, also in *The Quarterly Journal of Economics*.[7] According to Steven Durlauf, it "arguably launched the industry of identifying variables that explain cross-country growth differences,"[8] where the use of the linear regression model was justified by referring to the Solow's growth model, so that it might be claimed that the empirical models were "theory-driven."[9] In macroeconomics, much emphasis was placed in those years on its so-called microfoundations, of which the very streamlined representative agent model of dynamic optimization introduced in 1928 by Frank P. Ramsey represented the noble grandfather.[10] Such "growth regressions" were expanded in many different directions.[11] Paolo Mauro introduced corruption as a possible explanatory factor, finding that it led to "lower investments, thereby lowering economic growth."

Eventually, after the "rise" of growth regression, there followed "controversy" and eventually their "fall," and as Steven Durlauf summarized, these empirical exercises "[began] to evolve into a tool for pattern recognition and construction of stylized facts."[12] Seeing those estimates as a tool for pattern recognition, or as representations of multivariate correlations, corresponds to a more cautious interpretation of the estimated coefficients as causal relationships. I will argue soon that this caution also represents a slippery slope. Of more immediate concern to us, I note that

[7] Barro 1991.

[8] Durlauf 2009.

[9] And, consequently, also theory-dependent, in the sense that the validity of the theory, or of some other theory delivering linearity, should be considered as a maintained hypothesis of the empirical model. A maintained hypothesis indicates "all facts, assertions, or assumptions about the probability model of a probability sample that are in common to *H* and *H'*, and that are maintained as true regardless of the outcome of a statistical test of *H* versus *H'*" (Mittelhammer 2013, 543), where *H* and *H'* are, respectively, the null and the alternative hypothesis.

[10] Ramsey 1928. The Solow's model – or more appropriately, the Solow–Swan model – is not micro-founded in the said sense.

[11] Durlauf 2009 reports that "growth regressions have been used to assess over forty distinct growth theories, with over 140 different variable choices to explore these theories," with reference to Appendix 2 of Durlauf et al. 2005.

[12] Durlauf 2009.

not so prudent causal interpretations contributed significantly to the shift in the understanding of corruption that took place in both academia and policy circles.[13]

In its introduction, Mauro referred to previous studies where "[…] some authors have suggested that corruption might raise economic growth, through two types of mechanisms. First, corrupt practices such as 'speed money' would enable individuals to avoid bureaucratic delay. Second, government employees who are allowed to levy bribes would work harder, especially in the case where bribes act as a piece rate." Mauro cited two works[14] that were part of the literature, influenced by sociological functionalism, that in the 1960s and 1970s had offered a nuanced view on corruption. I mentioned that those opinions had already been subject to criticism, for example, by Susan Rose-Ackerman[15] who, in the words of Mauro, "warns of the difficulty of limiting corruption to areas in which it might be economically desirable." Mauro also mentions that empirical evidence pointing to an overall damaging effect of corruption had already started to appear, citing Kevin Murphy, Andrei Shleifer, and Robert Vishny,[16] who "provide evidence that countries where talented people are allocated to rent-seeking activities tend to grow more slowly."

Mauro's work spurred a research program where the linear multivariate regression model was used to uncover the role of corruption, to research both its effects, as Mauro had done, and also its determinants, that is, using a measure of corruption as the dependent variable. While the former case could be rationalized by referring to the Solow model, which delivers linearity, no such theoretical underpinning was available for the regressions that were aimed at studying the determinants of corruption, and the choice of linearity arose out of convenience.[17] The overall conclusions of that large literature, that ebbed and flowed with some delay with respect to the tide of growth regressions in general, were that corruption has an important economic cost and that it is caused by a series of factors on which there was at least partial agreement. Freedom of the press and

[13] A coarse measure of the persistent impact of Paolo Mauro's paper is provided by Google Scholar: Its number of yearly citations peaked only in 2016 at a little more than 800, and in 2021, it received 730 citations, more than it reached in 2014 and in any of the years before.

[14] Leff 1964 and Huntington 1968a.

[15] Rose-Ackerman 1978.

[16] Murphy et al. 1991.

[17] The literature that emerged was eventually summarized in several review papers, such as Ades and Di Tella 1996; Azfar et al. 2001; Lambsdorff 2006; Treisman 2007; and Pellegrini 2011.

transparency were unambiguously indicated as leading to less corruption, while the effects were more nuanced or outright uncertain regarding other characteristics of governance such as levels of democracy, characteristics of political competition, political and fiscal decentralization, and different cultural factors.[18] These conclusions seemed to provide damning evidence against any exculpatory view on corruption. From the mid-1990s onward, the use of inferential statistical analysis supplied an aura of scientificity to such emerging consensus, which new theorizing reinforced. Uses of linear regressions coincided with a view of the world deeply rooted in the history of econometric thought where the possibility of human agency is built into the model. To discuss these themes in the simplest of settings, in the next section I assume away the numerous problems of measurement that we considered in Chapter 3.[19]

ESTIMATING CAUSAL EFFECTS USING THE REGRESSION MODEL

In Chapter 3, I noted that statistics work as "black boxes" that simplify but also obscure. Piercing into them, as we have done, may be tedious, but observing their otherwise hidden assumptions (and occasionally, as we have seen, mistakes) is often instructive. Something similar may be said about statistical methods. They also simplify reality, for example, because their use may be legitimized in the eyes of the reader simply by referring, almost boilerplate-style, to the appropriate and socially accepted academic literature. We are about to pierce into one such black box, as is represented by the linear regression model, to derive important insights into how today's discourse on corruption is framed by causal readings of results.

An estimated coefficient of a multiple regression allows for a causal interpretation of the effect of an independent variable, or regressor, on the dependent variable under a series of conditions. I report them, as they are summarized in a well-known intermediate-level textbook in econometrics.[20] Readers who are already familiar with them are invited to be patient, knowing that what follows is only a summary treatment. Those who are

18 These studies have most often used perception-based measures of corruption and also occasionally the result of surveys assessing the experience of corruption, or both, as in Treisman 2007. Escresa and Picci 2020 assess the determinants of corruption using the data on cross-border occurrences of corruption that I illustrated in Chapter 3.

19 Stock and Watson 2015, 370, offer a textbook introduction to measurement errors in the context of regression analysis.

20 Stock and Watson 2015.

not familiar with the regression model in general should not worry about technicalities, as I will provide intuitive explanations of what matters to us.

The Least Squares Assumptions in the Multiple Regression Model

$$y_i = \beta_0 + \beta_1 \cdot X_{1i} + \beta_2 \cdot X_{2i} + \ldots + \beta_k \cdot X_{ki} + u_i, \cdots\cdots i = 1, \ldots, n.$$

1. u_i has conditional mean zero given $X_{1i}, X_{2i}, \ldots, X_{ki}$, that is, $E\left(u_i \vee X_{1i},_{2i}, \ldots, X_{ki}\right) = 0$

2. $(X_{1i},_{2i}, \ldots, X_{ki}, Y_i), i = 1, \ldots, n$, are independently and identically distributed (i.i.d.) draws from their joint distribution.

3. Large outliers are unlikely: $X_{1i}, X_{2i}, \ldots, X_{ki}$ and Y_i have nonzero finite fourth moments.

4. There is no perfect multicollinearity.

If these assumptions hold, then in large samples the OLS estimators $\widehat{\beta_0}, \widehat{\beta_1}, \ldots, \widehat{\beta_k}$ are jointly normally distributed and each $\widehat{\beta_j}$ is distributed $N\left(\beta_j, \sigma^2_{\beta_j}\right), j = 0, \ldots, k.$

Assumption 1 is very important, and it may be violated in the presence of an "omitted variable bias," which occurs if a variable that is not included in the list of regressors is a determinant of Y_i and also is correlated with at least one of the included regressors. Additionally, Assumption 1 is violated when one or more regressors are "endogenous," meaning that there is mutual causation between a regressor and the dependent variable. The problem of endogeneity is particularly relevant when the goal is to estimate the causes and effects of corruption, as corruption is likely caused by many variables that it also affects. In this case, a different estimator such as one with "instrumental variables" should be used. These "instruments" should have two characteristics in order for the resulting estimates to be unbiased: They should be "relevant" (correlated with the endogenous regressor) and "exogenous" (uncorrelated with the error term). However, the exogeneity condition is notoriously difficult to meet.[21]

The genesis of the use of the terms "exogenous" and "endogenous" in the context of regression analysis helps explain misuses of these models. These terms were first used in the late 1930s as the newborn discipline of econometrics attempted to estimate the simple multi-equation model of

[21] And to verify, see Stock and Watson 2015, chapter 12, for a textbook treatment of these themes. For example, Mauro 1995 uses as an instrument for his measure of institutional efficiency an index of ethnolinguistic fractionalization, and as additional instruments "dummies on whether the country ever was a colony […] and on whether the country was still a colony in 1945."

the neoclassical synthesis of Keynes' General Theory, introduced in John Hicks' 1937 landmark article.[22] The stylized "IS-LM" model, as it was to be called, has two main variables that are determined externally to the model and are therefore "exogenous": the amount of public expenditure, and the money supply, both representing policy choices. These choices then influence the values of the other variables, determined by solving the estimated model (a system of equations), and are therefore "endogenous." These "structural models" allow for the analysis of the impact of different monetary and fiscal policies on the endogenous variables of interest, such as gross domestic product and the unemployment rate.

Hicks' 1937 article was published in *Econometrica*, the journal of the Econometric Society that was founded four years earlier. The effort to estimate and analyze structural models went hand in hand with the development of national accounts and represented a central focus of the new discipline of econometrics during its first decades of existence.[23] These efforts produced numerous macroeconometric models, sometimes of great dimensions in terms of number of equations,[24] that became prominent during the 1960s and the 1970s as econometric methods were perfected and computers became more powerful and accessible. These models were widely used to inform policy choices, during what were the years of "high econometrics," a version of high modernism.[25]

Generations of economists were trained according to these methods until approximately the late 1980s, when a shift in teaching occurred, with

[22] Keynes 1936 and Hicks 1937. "Soon after Keynes published The General Theory, a generation of macroeconomists worked to [turn] his grand vision into a simpler, more concrete model" (Mankiw 2006, providing a summary of these developments).

[23] I touched upon the "reciprocal relation between the availability of data and the methods that make use of them" also in Picci 2011, 104–105. The first Nobel Prize in economics was awarded in 1969 to two early protagonists of such research agenda, Ragnar Frisch and Jan Tinbergen, reflecting the relevance of these developments within the history of economic thought. Other researchers who contributed to this intellectual tradition were awarded the same prize in the following years, such as John Hicks in 1972 and Robert Klein in 1980. What is commonly named the "Nobel Prize in economics" is, in fact, the "The Sveriges Riksbank Prize in Economic Sciences in Memory of Alfred Nobel."

[24] Most significantly, in "Link Project," whose "new developments" are the subject of Klein 1985. It is worth of note that this article was published in the highly respected *American Economic Review*. Those were the last years when articles documenting a research project that was increasingly being seen as outdated could hope to be published in a "top journal." An authoritative comprehensive treatise on the econometric methods that were used to estimate "Keynesian" macro-models is Fair 1984.

[25] Louçã 2007. In the words of Fernández-Villaverde 2008, "there is no purer example of the high modernism impulse in economics than the vision behind the design and estimation of macroeconometric models." On high modernism, see Scott 1998.

a lag with respect to the developments that were taking place in research. Also for this reason, the idea that exogenous factors can be maneuvered to modify the equilibrium value of highly relevant macroeconomic variables is deeply ingrained in the profession. This view of necessity implies a causal reading of the effects of those exogenous variables and goes hand in hand with the idea of macroeconomists as "engineers," or as Gregory Mankiw puts it, as "problem solvers" who occasionally "take a significant job in public policy"[26] in Washington (as Mankiw himself did). It is important to keep these antecedents in mind, as this worldview has also been applied to an altogether different question, that of corruption. In this case, too, economists have proposed themselves as "engineers," following the progressive institutionalization of an anti-corruption discourse and increased demand for policy solutions and specialists.

Let us briefly consider the other assumptions of the multivariate regression model. The second one, affirming that the variables are identically, independently distributed, needs not bother us here. It might in fact be relaxed so as to admit a degree of dependence among the observations, as is typical for time series data. Assumption 3, which rules out the presence of "large outliers," is often brushed away as a technicality. This assumption in fact has an interesting implication in terms of the vision of the world that it assumes, which is one where the relevant variables might be seen as the outcomes of sums of many factors, none of which is preponderant. A simple paradigmatic case would be a world where each relevant variable is the result of the sum of a great number of independent factors of equal importance that can either be switched on (taking value "1") or off (with value "0") with a given (constant) probability. The random variable that they determine would follow the binomial distribution, which may be approximated by the normal distribution, with its rare outliers.[27] Also, the distribution of the error term of the regression should not have big shocks unless they are infrequent, since they would be found in the dependent variable, again contrary to Assumption 3. For these reasons, when we use the linear regression model, we implicitly adopt a view of the world that we

26 Mankiw 2006.

27 Data-generating processes that are different from this particular paradigmatic case could satisfy assumption 3. However, they all imply a view of the world where the regressors are some functions of many events, none of which dominates the others, and where in turn the dependent variable of the regression (a weighted average of the regressors, plus an error term) also has this characteristic. On the emergence of a "normal" view of the world, as an approximation of the binomial distribution, see Desrosières 1998, in particular chapter 2.

might call "additive, multi-factor, none too big." This view is at odds with a different one where events do not evolve in such a well-ordered manner and the observed outcomes at least occasionally are the result of "critical junctures." When studying corruption, such critical junctures should be contemplated, and in Chapter 5 we will do so.

Assumption 4, ruling out perfect multicollinearity, reminds us that within a linear model any linear transformation of the data does not add any usable information. Regressors might certainly be mutually correlated, as long as their correlation is not perfect. The degree of mutual correlation among the regressors is in fact an important question to which I will return.

Unbiasedness of the estimators, which occurs if the previously mentioned four conditions are satisfied, is a precondition for a causal interpretation of the estimated coefficients. A causal interpretation hinges on *ceteris paribus* reasoning: An estimated coefficient of the model, $\widehat{\beta}_j$, represents the (estimated) causal effect of a unit change in X_j on Y_j *while holding all other* $X_i \left(i = 1, \ldots, k; i \neq j\right)$ *constant*. The importance of such line of reasoning and its occasionally neglected implications cannot be exaggerated, as a causal reading using the *ceteris paribus* condition permeates the empirical literature on the study of the effects and causes of corruption. Paolo Mauro himself used a typical expository device to inform the reader of the *magnitude* of the estimated *causal effect* that he found to be statistically significant, proposing a counterfactual: "For example, if Bangladesh were to improve the integrity and efficiency of its bureaucracy to the level of that of Uruguay (this corresponds to a one-standard-deviation increase in the bureaucratic efficiency index [...]), its investment rate would rise by almost five percentage points, and its yearly GDP growth rate would rise by over half a percentage point."[28] Such counterfactual is coherent with the adoption of the linear regression model, and it is not as innocuous as it may appear, as I am about to argue.

COUNTERFACTUALS AND THEIR PLAUSIBILITY

Ceteris paribus reasoning involves considering counterfactuals, which are alternate scenarios distinct from reality. In the words of Philip Tetlock and Aaron Belkin, counterfactuals can be avoided "only if we eschew all causal inference and limit ourselves to strictly noncausal narratives of what actually happened (no smuggling in causal terms under the guise of

[28] Mauro 1995.

verbs such as "influenced," "responded," "triggered," "precipitated," and the like)."[29] Counterfactuals are thought experiments, where one aspect is changed while everything else remains mostly similar, and they can vary in their plausibility. For example, consider what would have happened if Gavrilo Princip had not killed Archduke Franz Ferdinand of Austria in Sarajevo on June 28, 1914. It is possible that for some reason Gavrilo Princip failed to carry out the assassination, thus determining, on that fateful day, the branching off of an alternative world that at the beginning would be exactly as reality but for the fact that Archduke Franz Ferdinand remained alive. To fully consider this thought experiment, we would have to examine all the possible worlds that would have resulted from the counterfactual event.

Let us consider a more problematic counterfactual: "If the partisans of Vilna [during the Second World War] had had a nuclear device at their disposal, they would have prevailed."[30] Martin Bunzl argues, and I concur, that "changing the past to make the antecedent plausible quickly deprives us of our sense of certainty. After all, [the partisans of Vilna] surely would not have had such a device available to them unless others did too, and we are off to the races. In this sense, a counterfactual inference is only as good as the assumptions that one makes about the background conditions (what philosophers call 'co-tenability')."[31] In different words, the counterfactual regarding Gavrilo Princip requires a "minimal-rewrite of history"[32] (such as, him getting drunk the night before and not waking up to his appointment with history), while that on the partisans in Vilna would require a significantly more substantial one.

Philip Tetlock and Aaron Belkin elaborate further on such difficulties when they note that "we cannot manipulate the 'independent' variable in interconnected systems without creating ripple effects that alter the values taken on by other potential causes in the historical matrix, thereby creating 'confounding' variables that render interpretation of the original thought experiment problematic." They also indicate that my choice of the

29 Tetlock and Belkin 1996, 4. The overall question of counterfactuals is all but settled: As Hitchcock 2021 puts, "no analysis of actual causation is widely believed to perfectly capture all of our pre-theoretic intuitions about hypothetical cases," and "there is still very little agreement on the most central question concerning causation: what is it." Fearon 1991 provides a social scientist's reading, as does Elster 1978. The Oxford Handbook of Causation (Beebee et al. 2009) provides an extensive summary of the debate and of the different approaches to the analysis of the problem of causation.

30 Bunzl 2004, citing Tetlock and Belkin 1996.

31 Bunzl 2004.

32 Tetlock and Belkin 1996, 7.

Archduke's murder as an illustrative counterfactual represents a cliché, in noting that "perhaps one reason why assassinations attract so much counterfactual attention is that it is so easy imagining 'getting away with' changing only a few causal antecedents and producing a consequential result."[33] When considering the use of a counterfactual to solve a concrete problem of causation, then, the relevant question is how dense and interconnected the historical matrix is for the problem considered.

Contemplating counterfactuals that involve different degrees of corruption is problematic because the relevant relations of causal interconnectedness are quite dense, as consideration of the regression model will demonstrate. James Fearon contrasts counterfactuals in "case strategy" (qualitative case studies) and "actual case strategy" (such as multivariate linear regression analyses).[34] He argues that in the former, "support for a causal hypothesis [...] comes from arguments about what would have happened. These arguments are made credible (1) by invoking general principles, theories, laws, or regularities distinct from the hypothesis being tested; and (2) by drawing on knowledge of historical facts relevant to a counterfactual scenario." The sketchy discussion of counterfactuals done previously belongs to this category.

Fearon notes that in a regression analysis (an "actual case strategy") "support for a hypothesized causal connection comes principally in the form of a *frequency or magnitude of association across actual cases*" (the emphasis is mine). The observed *covariation* of the regressors is what makes the "virtual worlds" that substantiate the *ceteris paribus* condition of the causal reading of the estimated coefficients plausible. The extent to which the observed variability of the data might automatically provide meaningful counterfactuals deserves clarification. To provide it, I again refer to Mauro's reasoning: "if Bangladesh were to improve the integrity and efficiency of its bureaucracy to the level of that of Uruguay (this corresponds to a one-standard-deviation increase in the bureaucratic efficiency index [...], its investment rate would rise by almost five percentage points, and its yearly GDP growth rate would rise by over half a percentage point."

In considering Mauro's counterfactual, let us first assume that his results are internally valid (the four conditions of the regression model are met), so that his estimated coefficients admit a causal interpretation.

[33] Tetlock and Belkin 1996, 19–20.

[34] Fearon 1991. King et al. 1994 note that "the differences between quantitative and qualitative traditions are only stylistic and are methodologically and substantively unimportant."

If we focus on one variable at a time, Mauro's conclusion seems to hold also in terms of external validity, as he proposes a change in the regressor of interest (a measure of perceived corruption) that is well inside the observed range of variation of the data (from Bangladesh to Uruguay, both of which exist in reality). However, this alone is not sufficient to make the counterfactual plausible. We should also ask if the proposed *ceteris paribus* condition is *empirically tenable*, meaning that the data show a *covariation* of the included regressors that allows us to imagine that Bangladesh's level of corruption could be like Uruguay's, *with all other covariates referring to Bangladesh (approximately) unchanged*. This is the core of Fearon's claim that the "frequency or magnitude of association across actual cases" provides "support for a hypothesized causal connection."

A simple example further clarifies this important question. Consider a regression where a measure of economic activity, y_i, is explained by two regressors only, one of which, X_{1i}, relates to some characteristic of governance other than corruption, while X_{2i} is a measure of corruption:

$$y_i = \beta_0 + \beta_1 \cdot X_{1i} + \beta_2 \cdot X_{2i} + u_i \tag{4.1}$$

Suppose that the assumptions of the linear regression model are all satisfied, so that the estimated coefficients are unbiased and admit a causal interpretation. Figure 4.1 depicts two thought experiments, each represented by an arrow, whose starting point is within an ellipse that encloses all sample observations of the two positively correlated regressors, that is, their observed range of covariation. A certain country (as it would be Bangladesh in Paolo Mauro's example) is characterized by levels of the two regressors that correspond to the starting point of each arrow. The counterfactual considered is: Suppose that corruption, X_{2i}, was lower, as indicated by the point of the arrow, but everything else (in the present example, just X_{1i}) is the same.

The arrow at the bottom depicts a legitimate thought experiment as it proposes a hypothetical world combining values of X_{1i} and X_{2i} that are observed in the sample, even if not precisely (as per Fearon's "frequency or magnitude of association across actual cases"). The arrow at the top proposes instead a country whose combination of lower corruption level and unchanged X_{1i} is not observed in the sample, rising doubts about its existence, or that if it existed it would still be in the actual world and not in an incommensurable one – as is the case of the partisans in Vilnius having nuclear weapons.

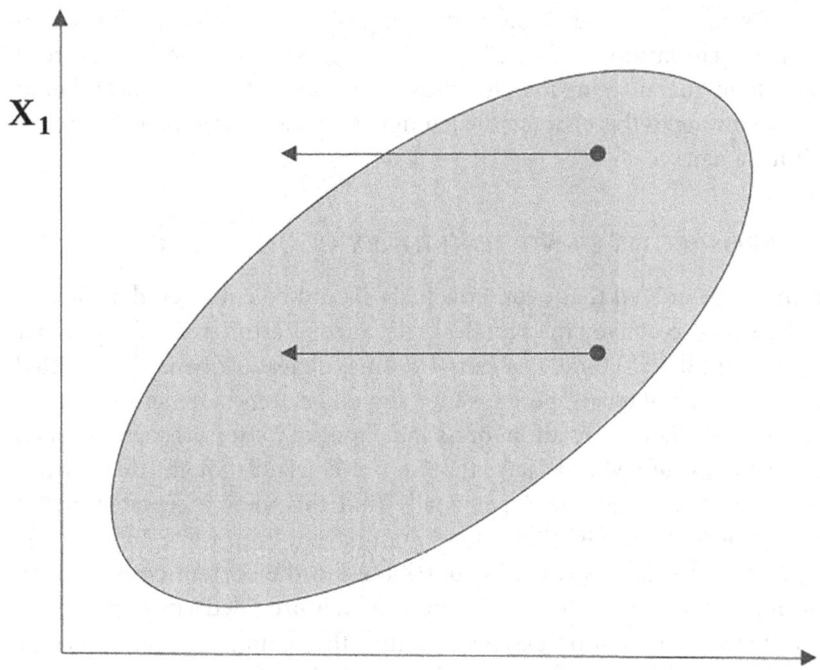

Figure 4.1 Observed covariation and the problem of external validity
In the simple bivariate model of Eq. (4.1), X_1 and X_2 are the two regressors, where X_2 is the regressor "of interest." The elliptical shape indicates the covariation of X_1 and X_2 observed in the sample. The top arrow indicates an effect of a change in X_2 that falls outside of the observed range of covariation of the sample data. The bottom arrow shows that for a different country the same change of X_2 may fall inside the sample covariation range.

In his article, Paolo Mauro does not clarify whether the observed covariation in the data can support the existence of a country similar to Bangladesh but with levels of integrity as Uruguay. We know however that variables indicating different aspects of governance tend to offer a consistent message. For example, measures of political rights and freedom of the press are highly correlated with measures of corruption and economic activity.[35] Hence, it is unlikely that a country with a markedly lower corruption level but with similar characteristics as Bangladesh would still be considered "Bangladesh" or be in the same metaphysical world as ours.

[35] See Table 3 in Escresa and Picci 2020.

Adoption of the regression model *imposes* a causal reading of the data's mutual relationships. Unbiased and consistent estimated coefficients are of no help in guaranteeing that, to return to Abraham Maslow's metaphor at the beginning of this chapter, the hammer that we decided to use is indeed hitting a nail.

PROSPECTIVE AND NONBINARY COUNTERFACTUALS

It might be argued that counterfactuals should be considered as rhetorical devices to convey the practical relevance of estimated effects, rather than being taken literally as causal claims. Instead of being interpreted in strictly causal terms, perhaps they should be seen more as a reflection of a multivariate correlation, or as that "tool of pattern recognition and construction of stylized facts" that Steven Durlauf thought that growth regressions had become. I personally find this view acceptable, but it should be acknowledged that we cannot have it both ways. Interpreting regression results casually has contributed to the current consensus on the high economic costs of corruption and has provided a powerful rationale for anti-corruption policies. On the other hand, the results become significantly less interesting once they are interpreted only as multivariate associations of variables. Once it is stated that high corruption is associated with other bad outcomes, such as weak institutions, little transparency, and mediocre economic conditions, then perhaps the conclusion that bad things tend to happen together would follow, and invoking estimated parameters with their standard errors would not make such a platitude less so.

Another possible line of defense of counterfactuals in corruption levels may be understood through a historical example, which is also a well-known instance of counterfactual reasoning. In 1919, the Treaty of Versailles imposed harsh conditions on defeated Germany, leading to resentment and potentially contributing to the rise of Nazism and to World War II. Germany was imposed an unbearable burden, being asked to repay what amounted to 250% of its 1913 national income or 350% of its lower 1919–1921 level. The argument goes that if the four main victorious powers – France, Great Britain, the United States, and Italy – had been less vindictive, Nazism may not have emerged. Imposing harsh war repayments was common in that epoch also because of a dominant proprietarian ideology, adding to the difficulties to accept anything but a robust compensation from Germany, which besides having lost the war was also perceived to be its initiator. Severe war repayments were moreover considered normal, as France had also had to pay a very large sum to Germany after its defeat in 1871. For these reasons, the counterfactual of a more magnanimous Versailles Treaty might well be unjustified, despite the fact that many recognized its impracticability, as did John Maynard Keynes in his "Economic Consequences of Peace."[36]

However, there is a sense in which the thought experiment of a more magnanimous Treaty of Versailles could be saved, if we see it as referring not to the world of 1919, but to a future one where a broader consensus has formed about the short-sightedness of overly harsh peace treaties. The thought experiment could then be viewed as expressing a historical lesson that was taken to heart after the next world war, leading to agreements that were less punitive toward Germany, Japan, and Italy, whose responsibilities were both clear and heinous. This outcome emerged in a different time and context, but it can be argued that learning from the "lesson of Versailles" was one of the factors that resulted in a change in understanding of how victors should treat the defeated after a major war.

We could also apply a similar thought process to interpret counterfactuals about corruption, such as the one proposed by Paolo Mauro. The "if" clause would then be understood as follows: If corruption in Bangladesh were as low as it is in Uruguay, the expected increase in GDP growth would occur not in the present world but in a future one where the relevant historical lesson has been learned. This lesson may refer to the current understanding of corruption and anti-corruption policies. However, to the extent that such a lesson derives from a causal interpretation of those estimated coefficients, such a line of reasoning would possess an element of circularity.

We should also consider that counterfactuals may propose modest changes from reality. Most people do not have a prophetic view of human affairs and do not anticipate a radical transformation of society resulting in the complete eradication of corruption and would likely be satisfied with even partial improvements. This would result in "nonbinary counterfactuals", such as when Paolo Mauro imagines a substantial, but still only partial, reduction of corruption in Bangladesh. The difference between reality and the imagined counterfactual is important, and counterfactuals that

[36] Keynes 2017 [1919]. See Sharp 2015, chapter 1, for a summary both of events and of the debate, and Piketty 2020, 473, on the conditions of the Versailles Treaty, and 120–125, on proprietarian ideologies. Condensing the years between the end of World War I and the accession of Hitler to power into the historical fetish of the Versailles Treaty is acceptable only as an illustrative device. For an account, see Tooze 2007, chapter 1.

are not too far from reality have less consequential implications for the alternative worlds they envision. Referring to Figure 4.1 again, if the top arrow were shorter, its endpoint would fall within Fearon's "frequency or magnitude of association across actual cases," and the thought experiment it represents would be less controversial. However, these local alternatives are also less interesting in practice. For instance, any increase in GDP resulting from a minor decrease in corruption would likely be modest.

The distinction between small and big changes in levels of corruption is relevant in the context of the debate on "big bang" anti-corruption policies. According to this perspective, corruption should be viewed as an equilibrium, where there may be more than one of them (with different levels of corruption). Modest anti-corruption efforts would be short-lived because the system would eventually revert to the previous equilibrium. In contrast, a large policy shock might result in a permanent shift to a lower-corruption state. However, the presence of these threshold effects, which are intrinsically nonlinear, obviously cannot be inferred using a linear regression model. This is especially true if, as previously discussed, its results are only interpreted causally for modest changes of the regressors. In conclusion, regardless of the approach we take to examine the empirical evidence from multivariate regression models, it also fails to provide support for big bang anti-corruption policies.[37]

THE LINEAR AND ADDITIVE VIEW AND OTHER QUANTITATIVE METHODS OF INQUIRY

The empirical evidence on the causes and the effects of corruption steeped into the growth regression tradition didn't only contribute to the shelving of preexisting more nuanced interpretations of corruption. It also framed the debate at a more general level, by promoting a view where corruption can be isolated from other variables and may be considered as something that, admitting counterfactual considerations, can cause other factors or be caused by them. Widespread use of the linear regression model also assured that its implied linear and additive view of history was taken for granted.

It is a view that also leads to the historical fallacy whereby observed events are seen as almost inevitable. In fact, due to linearity and the rarity of outliers, even if one of the variables (regressors) had been slightly different, the observed outcome would only have changed modestly. Another

[37] For a critique of the internal logic of big bang anti-corruption reforms, see Stephenson 2020.

framing effect of the regression model (or any other parametric model for that matter) arises from some of its maintained hypotheses. These hypotheses imply the presence of parameters that are constant across space and time, or, viewed from a different perspective, they assume the presence of a true and stable relation that applies to the reference population.[38] A high-level maintained hypothesis is that there exists an *underlying true model*, a type of law that researchers are trying to uncover, and that it applies to all countries and at all times within the time horizon under consideration.

Considering the debate on growth regressions once more, Robert Solow expressed strong doubts that they could adequately describe the intricacies of economic growth, affirming that they were "too vulnerable [...] to the recurrent suspicion that the experiences of very different national economies are not to be explained as if they represented different "points" on some well-defined surface."[39] The case of corruption is also one where there can hardly be found such a well-defined "surface," corresponding to a situation where, out there, there are some true coefficients that are just waiting for the researcher's estimations to be rescued from oblivion. At a more general level, and not only in the domain of corruption research, we may live in a "dappled world," as Nancy Cartwright[40] describes it, where scientific "laws" – be them in the hard or in the social sciences – are more elusive of what we would like to think. In particular, in a contest not unlike ours, Cartwright notes that coefficients of economic models are "supposed to exist and be fixed [...] as though laid out by the hand of God in the Book of Nature," and questions "why should we think that there is any such law-like association." She contrasts this approach with a different one that she exemplifies with an instance when Amartya Sen considered that "each of the countries studied has a different socio-economic structure constituting a different socio-economic machine that will generate different causal relations true in that country and concomitantly different probability measures appropriate for the quantities appearing in these relations."[41] With such "different socio-economic machines," we are back to the idea of a dense historical matrix, which calls for paying a heightened attention toward the

[38] Parameters might be allowed to change both across time and space, but with cross-country datasets that are not "big" in the current sense of the word, such degrees of freedom must be assigned parsimoniously.

[39] Solow 1994.

[40] Cartwright 1999.

[41] Cartwright 1999, 154–155.

many relevant contextual factors and their interactions. This is precisely what I will attempt in Part II of the book, when considering the cases of Russia, Brazil, and the United States.

I have focused on the regression model as it has greatly influenced our current understanding of corruption. However, its epistemological view is shared more widely and it is reflected in what Angus Deaton – partly coinciding with Nancy Cartwright's position discussed earlier – defines "a long-standing practice in economics to treat elasticities as constants, as in 'the' elasticity of labor supply of prime age men, or 'the' price elasticity of bread."[42] When considering statistical methods of inquiry, a similar critique also applies to randomized controlled trials (RCTs), which have been widely used in the last few decades, though to a lesser extent in researching corruption. Randomized controlled trials are sometimes touted as the epitome of scientific rigor, but they have received various criticisms, one of which is the transportability of results to different settings and specifically, the implications of scaling up treatments.[43] For instance, consider a widely cited study by Benjamin Olken. He found from a randomized field experiment in Indonesia that "increasing the probability of external audits substantially reduced missing funds" in projects, while "increasing grassroots participation in monitoring reduced missing expenditures only under a limited set of circumstances."[44] These results don't necessarily show what works and what doesn't in reducing corruption, but more likely something else. They indicate the presence of institutions that allowed accountability in those particular Indonesian villages where the experiment was carried out, as well as the information quality of the data collected, which permitted the rejection of the null hypothesis of irrelevance of the variables of interest. They also reveal that local authorities did not feel threatened by those experiments, or at least not enough to impede them. The results give us insights into the contextual factors that were relevant on that occasion but say little about corruption in general. The extent to which these results are relevant in other situations remains unknown. In this sense, RCTs produce less ambitious results than

[42] Deaton 2020.

[43] See Deaton and Cartwright 2018, and Deaton 2020. Deaton 2020 directs my same accusation of "high modernism" (to the applications of the regression model that I described), to RCTs: "I see RCTs as part of what Bill Easterly 2013 calls the "technocratic illusion," that is, the original sin of economic development, an aspect of what James Scott 1998 has called "high modernism" that technical knowledge, even in the absence of full democratic participation, can solve social problems."

[44] Olken 2007.

cross-country regressions, which are meant to provide insights into factors that affect corruption on average across all countries considered.[45]

When discussing solutions to corruption, the issue of scaling of treatments is especially important. Increasing external audits in just a few villages is one thing, but doing so on a larger scale may represent a completely different story. In the former case, there may be no significant resistance – particularly so if the experiment is part and parcel of an aid package by some foreign agency, which, we should recognize more often, is a case of "distributive politics." However, scaling up the treatment could trigger the reaction of important stakeholders of the status quo. For example, in considering the case of Russia, I will argue that relatively high levels of transparency, which empowered a visible anti-corruption movement, led to a vicious reaction that resulted not in less corruption, but in a successful repression of the anti-corruption movement and ultimately in less transparency.

Conclusions

In this chapter, I considered the conceptual framework, part of the current prevailing view on corruption, that sees it as being causally linked to other factors. I argued that this view has been influenced by the adoption of the linear regression model, as part of a tradition of inquiry that goes under the name of "growth regressions." Even if their use fell out of fashion, the results that they produced contributed to a crystallization of beliefs about the causes and consequences of corruption. Also, they framed the problem of corruption in causal terms thus emphasizing the possibilities of human agency in combating it. To paraphrase Abraham Maslow's quip cited at the opening of this chapter, after repeated use of a hammer, everything started to look as a nail.

We need a different conceptual model to study corruption. One that allows the "soft edges" of the current debate that I considered in Chapter 2 to come to the fore. One that admits non-linearities in historical processes and that is more careful about the treatment of counterfactuals and causality. Providing such framework, and readying us for the consideration of the three case studies that await us in Part II of the book, is the task of Chapter 5.

45 On the greater generality of the econometric causal model, with respect to the "'treatment-control' framework," see Heckman and Pinto 2022, also for a general discussion of causality in the context of econometric modeling.

5

What We Talk about When We Talk about Corruption

Some Methodological Considerations

It was to Rome's great happiness that those kings became corrupt quickly, so that they were driven out before their corruption passed to the bowels of that City.

Niccolò Machiavelli[1]

This chapter introduces the methodological lenses to interpret the three country case studies of Russia, Brazil, and the United States. First, we look further back in time at the history of ideas on corruption, to briefly consider a recurrent interplay between two distinct points of view: One that sees it as a problem of the "body politic" and the other prevailing today that focuses on individual behaviors and the duties of public office. This understanding leads to a general characterization shared by all definitions of corruption as a phenomenon: They all imply a distance between an observed reality and a normative point of reference. Later in the book, such characterization will lead us to consider definitions of corruption different from the prevailing one.

Further, I discuss the important distinction between the two levels of analysis of corruption that I summarized in Chapter 1: as a phenomenon and as a social construct. When analyzing corruption as a phenomenon, we are in a familiar territory where corruption is often defined based on human behavior. For instance, corruption may be equated with the related crime, or more broadly, it may correspond to actions representing an "abuse of entrusted power for personal gain," as per the widely accepted definition. "Corruption-as-phenomenon" refers to specific definitions of corruption, regardless of their content, and this level of

[1] Machiavelli 1996 [1531], 48.

analysis is marked by the existence of numerous proposed definitions of what constitutes corruption.

The social construction of corruption represents the debate about different ideas of corruption as a phenomenon. When examining the vexed question of what defines corruption, at this level of analysis (of corruption as a social construction) what defines corruption the best is the fact that it cannot possibly be defined once and for all. Corruption is a concept that cannot be defined conclusively, and it is an "essentially contested concept" in the sense discussed in Chapter 1. I will briefly consider the societal actors that participate in the social construction of corruption.

I propose a view of historical change that takes stock of the discussion of Chapter 4 and does not suffer from the shortcomings of a linear view of history. The framework consists of two interconnected systems: the "lower subsystem," which includes more observable events, and the "higher subsystem," which is characterized by more historical latency. The former is characterized by a nonlinear, nonadditive mode of work: History occasionally accelerates to produce "historical junctures." The latter, characterized by slow motion in time, is where we can observe at play the necessity of a political system to guarantee control in government and to maintain political order, possibly with the help of corruption. I will consider the two subsystems separately before discussing their mutual relationships.

With the methodological compass presented in this chapter, we will have at our disposal all the tools to draw the pertinent lessons from the country case studies awaiting us in Part II of the book.

CORRUPTION-AS-PHENOMENON: A CONCISE HISTORY

We considered the decline of sociological functionalist interpretations of corruption and, starting in the 1970s, the rise of a view based on a principal–agent framework of analysis. These intellectual developments represent but a small part of the history of the concept of corruption in Western political thought, which dates back millennia. This history has been explored elsewhere. In an epic book for breadth and length, Thomas Noonan examined the ideas of corruption that have appeared in written records from Sumerian times and how they have evolved to modern times.[2] More recently, Bruce Buchan and Lisa Hill have argued that two broad general ideas of political corruption can be identified. One views corruption as a degradation of the social body, often within an organic

2 Noonan 1984.

view of society, and the other is the view of corruption in terms of public office, which prevails today.[3]

An important perspective within the first view is represented by the Republican tradition of thought, as exemplified by Machiavelli. He defined corruption as a "generalized process of moral decay, whose beginnings are hard to foresee and its progress almost impossible to resist."[4] Machiavelli believed that the entire citizenry could become corrupt if it lacked the virtues necessary for a republic to function properly.[5] Once corruption has spread within the social body, it is difficult or even impossible to cure. Machiavelli's view also left ample space for the role of historical junctures that I will discuss later in this chapter, as is also exemplified by the accelerationist flavor of his citation reported at the beginning of this chapter: Rome was lucky that early on there was much corruption, so that it could stamp it out before it was too late. His view of corruption does not align with the definition of "abuse of entrusted power," although it could be argued that in Machiavellian republicanism every citizen is a sort of public official, holding a responsibility that has been entrusted to her by the Republic.

The public office view of corruption, which is widely accepted today, has a venerable tradition, and it can be discerned, for example, in debates on corruption in ancient Greece and Rome.[6] However, it was during the early modern era that a series of significant developments led to the prevalence of a public office view of corruption, so that, by the end of the eighteenth century, "the term had become more closely aligned with the rationalities of emergent liberal democratic governance and political economy."[7] Today's consensus view on corruption represents the apex of that process.

3 Buchan and Hill 2014. Other broad classifications of ideas of corruption have been proposed. For example, Mark Philp distinguishes between definitions which are "public-interest centered, public office centered, and market definitions," while noting that "public opinion and legal norms have also been cited, but they can be subsumed under the other cases […]" (Philp 2002, 44). A more thorough discussion of such broad classifications is in Picci and Vannucci 2018, 15–39.

4 Pocock 1975, 204. In Machiavelli, "The corruption that destroys civil and political life is the corruption of the customs, of the habits of citizens, their unwillingness to put the common good above private or factional interests" (Viroli 1998, 131).

5 Dobel 1978 considers "corruption of the body politic" in the works of Thucydides, Plato, Aristotle, Machiavelli, and Rousseau, summarizing that "corruption is defined as the moral incapacity of citizens to make reasonably disinterested commitments to actions, symbols and institutions which benefit the substantive common welfare."

6 Buchan and Hill 2014, 17–19, and references therein.

7 Buchan and Hill 2014, 7, and see also Engels 2017, 169–175. The reasons explaining such transition have been recounted elsewhere and have to do with the overall process of autonomization of the economic sphere. A nuanced historical account of this process in England is provided by Knights 2022.

Albert Hirschman considers the "semantic trajectory" of the term "corruption," to note that in eighteenth-century England it was still used to indicate "deterioration in the quality of government, no matter for what reason it may occur" (as for Polybius and Machiavelli). Hirschman adds that in eighteenth-century England, the "monetary view" of corruption, which identified it with bribes, that is, with a form of public office corruption, "drove the nonmonetary one out almost completely."[8] Such a claim is exaggerated: While a public office view of corruption has prevailed, both views are still present in today's debate, reflecting a "soft edge" of the current consensus on corruption.[9]

Consider the widespread use of the cliché image of corruption as a cancer, which has been used to condemn corruption by prominent figures such as Barack Obama, Joe Biden, and Pope Francis. Such metaphor is based on an organic view of society or government, with the implicit message that if we successfully remove the cancer, the body politic will return to a state of health. What has changed with respect to medieval organic views of corruption is the type of disease invoked. In those days, the rotting of flesh was incurable once it got hold (as it would have been for Machiavelli's Rome in the quotation opening this chapter), while in the age of antibiotics the attention has shifted to a more contemporary disease.[10] There is another indicator of the persistent relevance of organic views of corruption, which is evident in the focus of modern anti-corruption movements not so much on individual behaviors by officeholders, but on a perceived need to cleanse society. Brazil's presidential candidate Jânio Quadros, to whom I will return, carried a broom in his public meetings to theatrically indicate his intention to sweep corruption out of Brazil. More recently, Donald Trump professed his intention to "drain the swamp" in Washington, DC. Similar images of societal cleansing and purification are recurring. The extent to which contemporary measures of corruption may promote a narrative of national culpability, a theme explored in Chapter 3, provides a glimpse of how persistent is the view that corruption reflects an almost intangible quality that is inherently social and collective, rather than corresponding to individual behaviors and responsibilities.

8 Hirschman 1977, 40.

9 See also Buchan and Hill 2014, 15, who affirm that both "have characterized discourse on political corruption until comparatively recently," and Engels 2017, 169.

10 Knights 2017, 184, notes that "the idea of "purging" the state of corruption, still prevalent today, was commonplace in the seventeenth and eighteenth centuries, when satirists depicted corrupt figures vomiting and purging the religious and political impurities in their bodies." He further adds that the phrase "cancer of corruption" in fact is quite old, and traces its origins in the 1590s.

These two broad views – public-office-centered and as a disease of the body politic – have represented the two main poles of gravitation of the intellectual history of the concept of corruption. We are about to observe that all competing definitions, be them according to one view or the other, have something in common: They all propose a normative view of society, or at least they propose a standard of action.

CORRUPTION-AS-PHENOMENON: A DESCRIPTION OF DEFINITIONS

The evolution of the concept of corruption in history reflects different ideas of corruption as a phenomenon, and many definitions have been proposed.[11] Regardless of their mutual differences, all definitions of corruption as a phenomenon have three elements in common:

1. They specify standards of action that may form part of a wider normative view of society.
2. They suggest an idea of what deviates from that normative reference.
3. They map that deviation onto a scale of negative values.

For example, in a public-office-centered view that focuses on individual behaviors, the normative reference may correspond to the absence of bribes. If we observe them, we would conclude that this distance from the stated ideal is "corruption." Similarly, a degenerative conception of corruption would occur when we observe a distance between an ideal, such as a virtuous citizenry in the Machiavellian sense of the term, and an observed reality where such virtue is deemed to be wanting. The distance between the chosen point of reference and reality as it is observed would reflect different judgments on how much corruption, as defined, is present. All views of corruption are idealistic because they assume the conceptual relevance of their paragons, when not their practical possibility.

A spatial metaphor is appropriate to consider item number two, which implies a "geography of distances" between an ideal state of society and

[11] For example, Buchanan and Hill 2014, 2, note that "the meaning of corruption […] has always been tied to a range of other concepts related to the ever-changing patterns of argument within and between established and emergent political discourses," and Dincer and Johnston 2020a consider that it is "an old and perennially contested political and analytical concept. Far from having a fixed and natural interpretation, the idea has gone through a variety of meanings and reinterpretations." Mark Philp also repeatedly stresses the contested nature of definitions of corruption. See Philp 1997, 2002, 2014, 2017, and David-Barrett and Philp 2022.

an observed one. Reference to a spatial metaphor, in indicating the possibility of a geography, also invites to propose new ones, something that in fact we will contemplate at the outset of Part III of the book, in Chapter 9. Also relevant is the mapping of the distance observed between reality and the normative ideal, onto evaluations of corruption (item three in the list). For instance, we might hold a view that considers bribes intrinsically evil, almost regardless of their amount. Alternatively, we could adopt a more practical perspective and conclude that a bribe of one dollar is to be judged less corrupt than one of a million. These different positions correspond to different mappings, as per item three. The same applies, for example, to the earlier functionalist view stating that corruption could have desirable functions, tempering today's more unambiguously negative opinion.

In passing, I note that distinct judgments could apply to the same behavior if observed in different contexts. For example, and to anticipate a case to be discussed in Chapter 10, an American citizen might be appalled by learning of bribes to local public officials, but consider the same practice acceptable when bribes are disbursed to foreign officials to secure the safety of US troops abroad.

All three items in the list imply choices and values that, as researchers, we should transparently acknowledge when participating in the debate on corruption-as-phenomenon.[12] This debate is animated by different actors, to be considered next.

THE ACTORS IN THE SOCIAL CONSTRUCTION OF CORRUPTION

Defenders of a particular definition of corruption implicitly promote a normative view of society, as outlined in item one of the list of all definitions of corruption. Moreover, corruption is judged negatively (item three), so that there is interest in attributing the label of corrupt to one's adversaries.

[12] As far as I know, the characterization of all definitions of corruption that I propose is novel, but it has parallels with previous ones. Philp 2014, in particular, notes that "definitional disputes about political corruption are linked directly to arguments about the nature of the healthy or normal condition of politics," which echoes item one in my list, and adds that "corruption is a term of appraisal: in calling something corrupt we attach negative connotations to it – or, at the very least, we report it in terms to which those involved would attach negative connotations." From these premises, he proposes a "tentative definition of corruption." What I propose is instead a description of definitions of corruption, which is something quite different. See also Buchan and Hill 2014, 7, and Kroeze et al. 2017, 3, who note that "corruption is not only a type of malpractice, but also a basic thread of intellectual discussions about ideal forms of good government."

There is a wide variety of actors who, whether knowingly or unknowingly, participate in the social construction of corruption and, in doing so, contribute to its politicization. Some have been assigned social responsibilities of one type or another in this regard and may be viewed as "guardians of corruption" – including judges, preachers, and even academics researching corruption. Grouping these vastly different figures together may be seen as a provocation, particularly for academics. I do it to emphasize that anyone who publicly speaks about corruption inevitably proposes, if not imposes, the normative views that come with the chosen definition of corruption.

The citizenry at large contributes by publicly criticizing certain behaviors or participating in public demonstrations against politicians they deem to be corrupt, as it happened in Brazil during the *Lava Jato* investigations. Civil society and political organizations also participate, as we will see in Russia in the case of Kremlin opponent Alexei Navalny, who characterized the United Russia ruling political party as the "party of crooks and thieves." The branches of government play a significant role in defining corruption. The legislative branch determines the legal definition of corruption that the judiciary interprets. For instance, we will discuss the US Supreme Court's 2010 "Citizens United" ruling, which (*inter alia*) circumscribed the definition of corruption to quid-pro-quo exchanges. Meanwhile, the judiciary not only adjudicates corruption cases but also selects which cases to hear. In Russia, we will consider the case of former Minister of Economic Development Alexey Ulyukaev, who was sentenced for corruption while many other certainly corrupt officials have not been indicted.

A political party might be more or less effective in arguing that their adversaries are corrupt, and other actors, including civil society organizations, might influence public opinion both by promoting a definition of corruption and by clamoring that more attention should be given to corruption. More generally, and to conclude, different societal actors have at their disposal very different tools and levers to promote a view of who and what is corrupt. But regardless of who they are, and of what their instruments allow them to do, all the actors involved have something in common: With respect to the description of definitions of corruption of the previous section, they all are promoting a given view for items one, two, and three of the list that I provided, before they eventually apply those views to particular cases. They are all actors in the struggle to affirm an idea of how society should be and of what and who, seen as deviating from that idea, deserves to be called corrupt.

A NARRATIVE OF HISTORICAL CHANGE: THE LOWER SUBSYSTEM AND THE HIGHER SUBSYSTEM

Chapter 4 disputed a causal interpretation of relationships involving corruption. It also questioned the conceptualization of corruption as a phenomenon emerging from processes characterized by linearity, within a view of the world which is "additive, multi-factor, none too big." Building on these considerations, here I present a more flexible interpretative framework that will guide the analysis of Part II of the book.

The framework permits to consider corruption within a dense historical matrix, where the counterfactual of significantly less corruption is problematic. It admits that corruption may be the norm rather than the exception and helps clarify the hurdles facing human agency when it attempts to address it. The interpretative framework is composed of two interdependent subsystems: the "lower subsystem," where the more observable events take place, and the "higher subsystem" characterized by the workings of institutions that display a greater degree of persistence. The two subsystems and their mutual relationships are meant to be a narrative device. Each subsystem reflects the working and mutual interactions of institutions, but it would be wrong to identify one or the other with a particular institution.[13]

Within the lower subsystem, societal actors and institutions interact and produce change, which may exhibit nonlinearities in the form of "critical junctures." These are periods of time when more visible change occurs, compared to other times when history is characterized by a more gradual pace. I interpret these developments while adopting a historical institutionalist approach, which posits "a dual model of institutional development characterized by relatively long periods of path-dependent institutional stability" that are "punctuated occasionally by brief phases of institutional flux – referred to as critical junctures – during which more dramatic change is possible."[14] Critical junctures, in turn, are "moments of relative structural indeterminism" when actors have more agency than in normal circumstances, so that their decisions may influence historical developments in the long-run.[15]

13 Or with particular types of institutions, for example, as in Roland 2004, where a distinction between fast-moving and slow-moving institutions is proposed. See Picci 2024, where I further discuss the conceptual framework proposed here and argue for its applicability beyond the case of corruption.

14 Capoccia and Keleman 2007. On critical junctures, and more generally on the "temporality" of institutional analysis, see Jupille and Caporaso 2022, chapter 2.

15 Mahoney 2001, 7.

The changes that take place during critical junctures are particularly difficult to predict and may result in a significant redistribution of resources. An important question regards how societal actors who benefit from the status quo (e.g., through the regular receipt of bribes) may eventually lose out. In particular, we would like to interpret the reasons of actions that, leading up to a critical juncture, with hindsight would appear to have been strategic mistakes. These occurrences are particularly pertinent to the study of corruption that can result in the unexpected downfall of individuals and organizations. For instance, in Chapter 7, we will discuss a series of reforms that took place in Brazil after the return of democracy in 1985 and eventually led to the *Lava Jato* judicial operation, which punished some of the very actors who had initiated these reforms, including Lula and his political party.

The effects of events precipitating a critical juncture are difficult to predict. Uncertainty derives from ignorance on other actors' strategies and their complex interactions, and increases during a critical juncture when both agency and circumstantial events have a greater impact. At a higher level, there is also ambiguity about which regime is relevant at a given time, whether it is a routine situation or an approaching critical juncture when individual agency matters more and overall uncertainty is heightened. Furthermore, exogenous shocks also tend to have a greater impact during critical junctures.

The challenge of understanding an intricate strategic environment, especially during critical junctures when uncertainty is the highest, has significant implications for institutional reforms, whether aimed at reducing corruption or otherwise. The potential outcomes of institutional reforms are often difficult to predict as they vary greatly depending on context. As an example, consider the impact of electoral rules on corruption. In proportional representation systems, open lists can lead to more electoral competition compared to closed lists, which gives more power to party elites in choosing candidates. This increased competition can provide voters with a better opportunity to remove corrupt officials by voting them out of office, making open lists inimical to corruption. However, open lists can also result in intense intra-party competition to secure campaign resources and win clientelist support, leading to more corruption, as was the case in Italy prior to the "*Mani pulite*" ("Clean hands") corruption crackdown in the early 1990s. The outcome of these effects can also be influenced by the size of the electoral colleges, which affects the degree of competition. In an ideal scenario, the polity would be well informed about all these effects and perhaps choose an electoral system based on the available empirical evidence on its effects on corruption. Not surprisingly, the available empirical evidence on this question is not conclusive,[16] and predicting the effects of electoral reforms on levels of corruption is a difficult task.

What is very uncertain ex-ante is better readable as it happens. The same actors who struggle to predict the future and the potential consequences of institutional reforms are more confident in interpreting the present that they observe and experience. Consequently, actors who are satisfied with the current situation will be cautious of changes whose outcomes are uncertain. Meanwhile, those who are dissatisfied, when considering alternative options will face the cognitive difficulties that I described. Additionally, those who advocate for change must build consensus around a reform plan while overcoming the challenges of collective action.

These reasons tend to support the status quo, making it easy to understand why history can seem static away from critical junctures. However, as time goes on, seemingly insignificant events accumulate, bringing about gradual and incremental changes that are difficult to predict – as it happened in Brazil in the years leading to *Lava Jato*. The actors who were previously satisfied with the status quo may accept these incremental changes, or even promote them, as necessary to the consensus that maintains their power. In conclusion, the interplay between forces that support change and those that resist it creates a dialectic tension in the lower subsystems. This relationship is influenced by the asymmetry between the ability to understand the present and uncertainty about the future and its accelerations and junctures.

How consequential are the historic changes that we observe within the lower subsystem is however an open question, to address which we need to consider the higher subsystem. It represents historical dynamics that are rather stable in time and that constrain the changes that take place within the lower subsystem. Their stability derives mainly from the presence of daunting problems of collective action. One important aspect of these constraints relates to guaranteeing control in the choice and execution of policies and political order, and distributive politics, broadly defined, is essential in order to achieve these ends. Corruption, as I argue more broadly in Chapter 10, is one important case of distributive politics and, also for this reason, it is a tool of government. It is at the level of the higher

16 On *Mani pulite*, see della Porta 2001 and della Porta and Vannucci 2007. Golden and Picci 2008, 2015, consider intra-party competition in Italy before *Mani pulite*, its determinant and effects. On the characteristics of electoral rule and corruption, see Chang, Eric CC. 2005; Chang and Golden 2007; Kunicova and Rose-Ackerman 2005; Persson et al. 2003.

subsystem that the political system addresses (to the extent that it does) the problem of control that I mentioned in Chapter 1, thereby ensuring political order. The manner in which this issue is managed evolves over time, but only gradually.

The two subsystems interact with each other. The higher subsystem constrains the working of the lower one, while changes occurring in the lower subsystem, particularly during historical junctures, lead to tensions in the higher subsystem and may contribute to changes in its slow-moving institutions, and to the emergence of new solutions to the old problem of control. This, for example, we observe in the history of the United States, returning to Robert Merton's considerations about highly corrupt city political machines. They were partly superseded as a result of a series of reforms that finally made available to disadvantaged American public services previously provided by those corrupt organizations.[17]

Changes within the lower subsystem rarely result in new options at the higher level, and most often are followed by some form of backlash that restores the previous state. After a historical juncture, there may be new players and political parties, but the situation may revert to its original form if alternative options haven't emerged within the higher subsystem. This potential for immutability despite apparent change is the basis for cynicism about human history, the attitude according to which *plus ça change, plus c'est la même chose*. Further, it presents the possibility of manipulation when superficial change is presented as real one, as in the Italian *gattopardismo*, defined by the adage that "if we want everything to remain the same, it is necessary that everything changes."[18] When discussing Dilma Rousseff resignation as president of Brazil in 2016, I will suggest that she may have served as a sacrificial victim for others to "cross the river" unscathed. Almost in a ritualized fashion, apparent change may be served to satisfy the multitude.

CONCLUDING REMARKS

In this chapter, considerations of the long history of ideas on corruption provided the necessary distance to propose a characterization of the elements that are present in all definitions of corruption. They may be

[17] With reference to our discussion in Chapter 2, see Wallis et al. 2006, and Cuéllar and Stephenson 2020. I will reconsider this theme in Chapter 8.

[18] A sentence pronounced by Prince Tancredi in Tomasi di Lampedusa's novel "The Leopard" (in Italian, Il Gattopardo, hence the adjective *gattopardismo*), in the aftermath of Italy's unification. Tomasi di Lampedusa 1958. See also Picci 2024.

represented using a spatial metaphor, thus introducing the possibilities of charting new geographies of corruption. We will take up this possibility in Chapter 9, when, with reference to the concept of legal corruption, we will discuss ideas of corruption that refer explicitly to this spatial metaphor.

With this understanding, I further proposed a distinction between two different levels of analysis of corruption: One regarding particular definitions of the phenomenon and the other focused on the competition among different definitions, resulting in the social construction of the concept. When we focus on a specific definition of corruption, interesting questions regard its measurement, causes, consequences, and the possibilities that are present to fight it. Different types of questions may be asked when we concentrate on the social construction of corruption. For example, we would like to understand the conditions of the competition among different definitions of corruption, why certain actors may prefer to promote one type of definition of corruption over another, and why they may be more or less interested, in general, in bringing up corruption as a relevant political issue. We will return to these questions repeatedly in the rest of the book.

Moreover, the two levels of analysis are interdependent. For example, a shared perception that legal corruption is widespread among the elite would perhaps lower the ethical resistance of low-level bureaucrats to bribe-taking. A question that regards "bribes to public servants" (corruption-as-phenomenon), that is, would receive different answers depending on the state of play of the struggle among competing definitions of corruption (corruption-as-social construct). The distinction that I proposed between corruption as a phenomenon and as a social construct will be of great importance and lead us to the conclusions that corruption is a tool of government and anti-corruption of politics.

Further, I have presented a conceptual framework to interpret historical change as it pertains to the problem of corruption. It consists of two subsystems. The lower one contemplates historical change that may come in fits corresponding to historical junctures. A higher subsystem reins in these changes, to the point that their effects may be of little consequence in the long-run.

We now have a methodological compass to analyze the three country case studies, the subject of Part II of the book.

PART II

THREE CASE STUDIES

6

The Carrot and the Stick

Systemic Corruption in Russia

Today, in Russia corruption is the most important problem.

Anti-corruption Foundation (ФБК)[1]

Taking bribes [in Russia] is indissolubly interlaced with the whole system and political life.

Pavel Berlin[2]

On June 16, 2014, General Boris Koleshnikov, former deputy chief of the anti-corruption and Economic Crimes Directorate (GUEBiPK) at Russia's Interior Ministry, died after jumping from the sixth floor of the Moscow headquarters of the Federal Investigative Committee. He had been held in Lefortovo prison in Moscow for nearly four months on charges of extortion and running a criminal ring, which arose from a sting operation, known in Russia as a "torpedo." Fully armed with a bag of tempting money, the torpedo was meant to sink an allegedly corrupt official of the Federal Security Service (FSB), the successor of the Soviet KGB. The FSB runs the Lefortovo prison, where Koleshnikov suffered serious skull fractures the month before his death, reportedly after falling from a stool.

The sting operation did not go as planned. As a GUEBiPK agent delivered the money to incriminate the FSB official, FSB agents raided the restaurant where the transaction was taking place. It appears that a "double sting" occurred: an attempt by GUEBiPK to trap the FSB but also, at a higher and more successful level, the other way around. The chief of GUEBiPK, General Denis Sugrobov, was eventually sentenced to 22 years in prison, later reduced to 10 years, which he is currently serving. The FSB counter-operation was overseen by General Oleg Feoktistov, who two

1 Anti-corruption Foundation 2020.
2 Berlin 1910.

years later was in charge of another controversial sting operation against Minister of Economic Development Alexey Ulyukaev. Ulyukaev, also a published poet, peppered his defense speech at his trial with literary references,[3] but to no avail. He was sentenced to eight years in prison following accusations of attempting to extort two million dollars from the Rosneft oil company. General Feoktistov retired from his post at the FSB in the same year and became the head of security at Rosneft. The director of Rosneft is and was the all-powerful Igor Sechin, with whom Ulyukaev reportedly had a falling out.[4]

This brief story should be enough to convince the reader that studying corruption in Russia is not for the faint of heart. It also highlights that the country hardly aligns with the stereotyped image of being an extension of the will of the Kremlin or of its leader Vladimir Putin. The story illustrates that Russia is filled with intra-elite conflicts that do not play along the lines not only of the democracy playbook, but also, of any simplistic view of how autocracies work. These conflicts are aimed at securing resources of one type or another, in the context of a very unequal distribution of income and of wealth. Some have characterized Russia as a kleptocracy,[5] a simple thesis that would facilitate our task of interpretation by naming as the culprit of corruption a lucky and naughty minority going about to grab all that it can. However, competition for the distribution of resources is intense in all countries, and we observe levels of inequality not unlike those of Russia in countries that we would be wary to define kleptocracies, such as the United States.[6]

3 Amos 2017.

4 The description of the GUEBiPK operation as a "double sting" is from Yaffa 2015. General Denis Sugrobov was appointed chief of GUEBiPK in June 2011 by then President Dmitry Medvedev (BBC-Russian Service 2011) and was reputed to be one of his protégés. Medvedev and Sechin were considered to be on opposite sides, with the latter eventually winning the fight. On Denis Sugrobov's jail sentence, see BBC-Russian Service 2017b. On Oleg Feoktistov's involvement in the Ulyukaev affair and on his appointment at Rosneft, see BBC-Russian Service 2017a. Ulyukaev's arrest "has widely been seen as Sechin's revenge for Ulyukayev opposing Rosneft's takeover of another oil company" (Walker 2017). Ulyukaev was granted parole in April 2022 (BBC-Russian Service 2022).

5 See, for example, Dawisha 2015.

6 See also Treisman 2018: "[…] calling Russia a kleptocracy does not help much in understanding its politics. Many key decisions – such as the intervention in Syria or the support for insurgents in Donbass despite the risk of Western sanctions – make little sense in terms of Kremlin bigwigs' mercenary interests." I add to the list the 2022 invasion of Ukraine. On the United States *not* being a kleptocracy, there are dissenting opinions (see, e.g., Chayes 2020). The moral overtones intrinsic in the interpretative category of "kleptocracy" should make it dispensable in general.

I propose a more nuanced view that recognizes the ambiguity between the apparent anarchy of the observed conflicts in Russia's society and the centrality of the state, the Kremlin, and President Putin. I first present background information on Russia's economy since the collapse of the Soviet Union, with a focus on distributional issues. I then discuss a series of existential struggles that the state has faced and examine what is known about corruption in Russia. I anticipate my broad conclusions. For the Russian state, corruption has been a crucial tool in addressing its existential struggles and a highly contested political arena. The theme of anti-corruption has been utilized by both reformers and the Kremlin for their own purposes.

RUSSIA AFTER THE SOVIET UNION: FROM CATASTROPHE TO RESURGENCE

Russia is considered an upper-middle-income country with an average per capita income in US dollars slightly above that of Brazil and China (as shown in Table 6.1, which includes other countries discussed in the book). The population of Russia exceeds 140 million, mostly residing in its European region. The metropolitan areas of Moscow and Saint Petersburg account for more than 15% of the total population. The significance of these two cities in the country's demographics, combined with the vastness of the land and other historical factors, contributes to a notable divide between the main urban centers and the rest of the country.

After the fall of the Soviet Union, the Russian economy underwent a severe contraction, which official figures on GDP per capita (Figure 6.1) exaggerate, both because of overreporting in the late Soviet period and underreporting of the emerging private economy.[7] The downturn was

Table 6.1 *GDP per capita and population, year 2019*

	Russia	Brazil	United States	China	Italy	Spain
Population (millions)	144.4	211.8	325.3	1407.7	59.7	47.1
GDP per cap. US $ (thousands)	11.53	8.84	65.12	10.14	33.67	29.58
GDP per cap. US $ (PPP) (thousands)	30.07	15.30	65.12	16.65	45.80	43.07

Source of the data: The World Bank.

[7] I am grateful to Daniel Treisman for a discussion of this question.

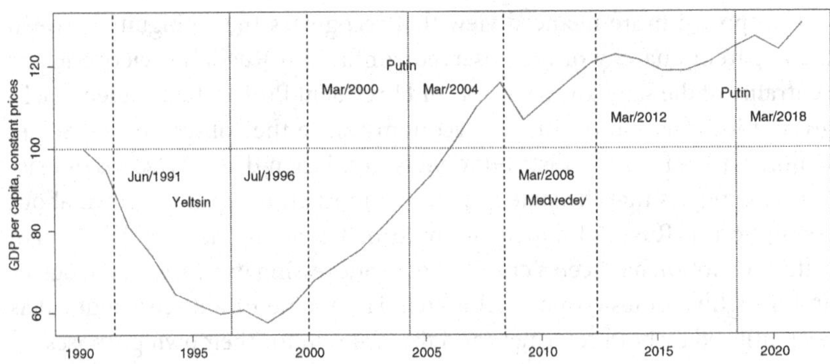

Figure 6.1 GDP per capita at constant prices (Russian Federation)
Source of the data: The World Bank. GDP per capita at constant prices has been set equal to 100 in the year 1990. The vertical lines correspond to presidential elections. Vladimir Putin first became acting President following Yeltsin's resignation on December 31, 1999.

however severe and persisted through the 1998 financial crisis, at whose end official figures of GDP per capita were at only 60% of their level a decade earlier. The economy began to improve toward the end of Boris Yeltsin's second term as president and during the decade that ended in 2007 GDP per capita nearly doubled in real terms. The financial crisis of 2007–2009 took place mostly during Dmitry Medvedev's presidency, and the subsequent recovery was short-lived. Vladimir Putin's third term was marked by economic stagnation, also following the sanctions imposed after the Russian annexation of Crimea in March 2014. The period leading up to the 2020 coronavirus pandemic saw moderate economic growth, and the long-term economic impact of Russia's ongoing invasion of Ukraine is difficult to predict.

The exploitation of natural resources has played a significant role in Russia's economy. Following the 1998 financial crisis, the share of rents from natural resources increased sharply, reaching more than 20% of GDP and over 50% of exports already at the beginning of the new century (Figure 6.2), also following a steep increase in prices (Figure 6.3). Exports of natural resources led to a high value of the Ruble, making imports more accessible and allowing a significant portion of the population to rapidly alter their consumption pattern. These advantages are a key aspect of the social compact of Putin's presidency, to be discussed further.

During the last two years of Yeltsin's presidency, as the economy began to grow, state revenues started to increase also as a share of GDP. They

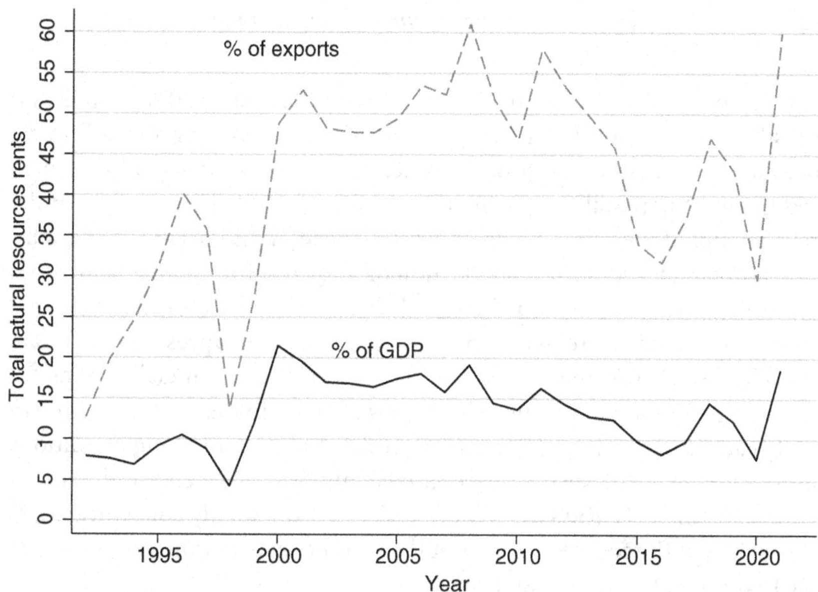

Figure 6.2 Natural resources rents, as a percentage of GDP and of exports (Russian Federation)
Source of the data: The World Bank. Total natural resources rents (production value minus costs) as % of GDP and of total exports.

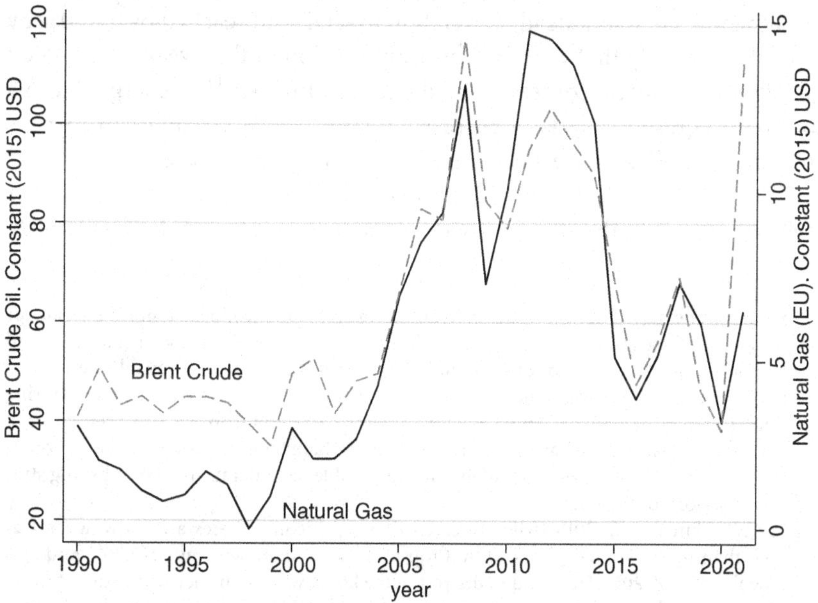

Figure 6.3 Prices of oil and natural gas, constant US dollars (Russian Federation)
Source of the data: IMF Primary Commodity Price System. Prices of Brent Crude Oil and of natural gas (Europe) are at constant 2015 US Dollars. The price of Brent crude is used as the reference price for the Urals variety produced in Russia.

rose from around 20% of GDP in 1998 to approximately 30% in 2002 and mostly stayed around that level or slightly lower during the following decade. The increase in resources available to the state allowed for a quick reduction of national debt, which was almost entirely held abroad, and a rebalancing of the relationship between the center and periphery, which I will address later. Only a small portion of these resources came from taxes (between 10% and 15% of GDP), and the relative share of taxes in total revenues actually decreased during Putin's first term as president. Overall, the macroeconomic management of Russia has been financially sound.[8]

Average per capita income, which grew robustly in the decade starting in 1998, can be misleading as a measure of the evolution of living conditions in Russia due to the vast increase in inequality since the end of the Soviet Union (Figure 6.4). Russia's income and wealth are highly concentrated, at levels that, at the top 1% and 10% of the income distribution, are comparable to those of the United States.[9]

Inequality increased dramatically during the first half of the 1990s. By the mid-1990s, the top 10% of the Russian population earned about 40% of total income, and by the end of the decade, the top 1% reached a share of a quarter of total income. During Putin's first two terms as president, private wealth grew relatively steady in relation to GDP and reached over 400% by the late 2000s. By that time, a significant portion of that wealth, estimated at 74% of national income, was held outside of Russia.[10] The large outflow of financial resources that it represents is believed to be linked to corruption and provides indirect evidence of its widespread nature.

Seen together with the significant decrease in average income during the 1990s (Figure 6.1), the sharp increase in inequality meant that for a majority

[8] Source of the data: The World Bank. In 2001, a tax reform introduced a single flat rate for personal income at the low level of 13% which is still in place. See Ivanova et al. 2005 and Lamberova and Sonin 2018. Starting in 2004, part of the resources available were saved into a sovereign fund, which helped buffer the economy during subsequent crises. During Putin's first two terms, the Minister of Finance was Aleksei Kudrin, who then served, until the end of 2022, as the Chairman of the Accounts Chamber of the Russian Federation. It is not uncommon of autocracies to give leeway to able technocrats in accomplishing strategic missions of the state.

[9] See Novokmet et al. 2018 (who conclude that top income shares are "now at least as high than in the United States, with a top 1% income share around 20–25%") and also Novokmet et al. 2017. Here and in the rest of the book, when considering the distribution of income and of wealth I refer to data drawn from World Inequality Database, which "aims to provide open and convenient access to the most extensive available database on the historical evolution of the world distribution of income and wealth, both within countries and between countries" (World Inequality Database n.d.).

[10] Novokmet et al. 2017 and 2018.

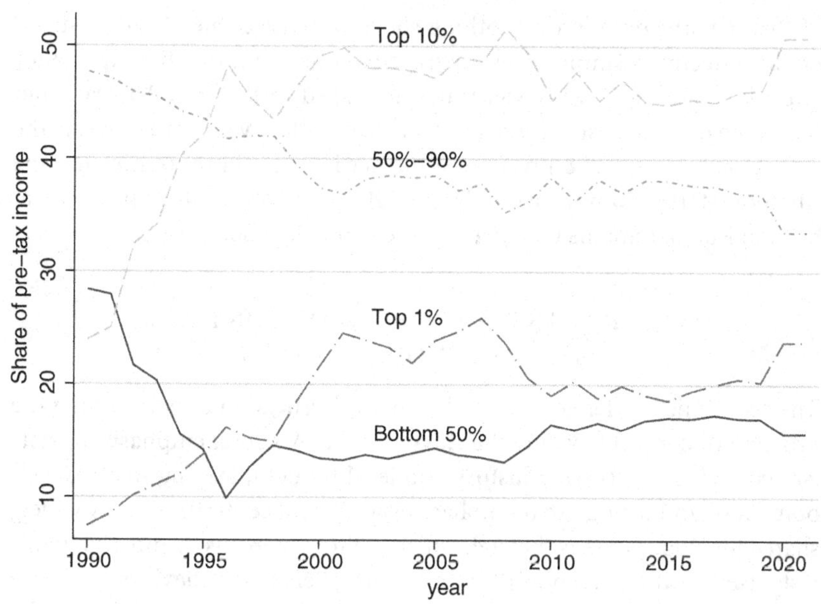

Figure 6.4 Shares of pretax income (Russian Federation)
Source of the data: World Inequality Database n.d. See Alvaredo et al. 2018.

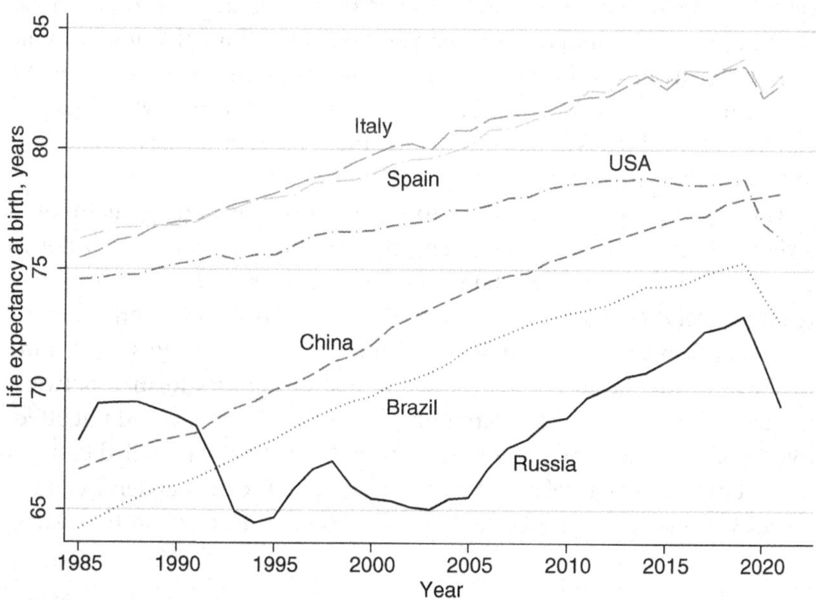

Figure 6.5 Life expectancy at birth
Source of the data: The World Bank and United Nations Population Division.

of Russians the decade was nothing short of catastrophic. A single statistic that effectively summarizes the tragedy of those years is life expectancy at birth (Figure 6.5). In Soviet times, it peaked in 1987 at 69.5 years, but plummeted by almost 5 years by 1994. After a few years of recovery, the economic crisis in 1998 preceded a further increase in mortality, and the situation started to improve only after 2003. However, life expectancy at birth in Russia remains the lowest of the countries considered.[11]

STATISM AND A PROBLEM OF CONTROL: A TUMULTUOUS 30 YEARS

The economic challenges outlined earlier are crucial in understanding the problem of control faced by the Russian state. A strong emphasis on statism characterizes Russian history and legal thought, leading to the development of an ideology that emphasizes unity and centralization. A widely shared ideology is a lens through which reality is perceived, and also manifests itself in the perception that a set of beliefs and behaviors are to be expected in others. The idea that salvation can only be found within the confines of the statist ideology has been reinforced by two instances in the twentieth century where the principle of state unity was challenged, in both cases leading to chaos: the events between the resignation of Czar Nicholas II on March 2, 1917, and the Soviet revolution,[12] and those that followed the end of the Soviet Union. These shared experiences and perspectives make it difficult to imagine a successful Russian political leader who does not adhere to these beliefs and expectations, and reform proposals should take this reality into consideration.

The problem of control refers to the need of the state to maintain a level of supervision over its citizens, territories, and policies in order to ensure political order. Any state, when push comes to shove, will act and react as decisively as it can to guarantee its survival, and modern states have significant resources to do so, even in times of crisis. Push did come to shove in Russia during 1991, when a dual power was formed between Gorbachev and Yeltsin. The Kremlin soon realized that it could not effectively contrast the growing forces of decentralization. The failed coup in August of that year accelerated events, leading to the formal demise of the Soviet Union on December 26, 1991. The Russian Federation then faced

[11] See Men et al. 2003. Russia's life expectancy suffered a particularly severe drop following the coronavirus pandemics, as is evident from Figure 6.5.

[12] See Pomeranz 2019, 68–69.

the risk of falling apart as some of its republics sought greater freedom or independence. This struggle between the central government and peripheral regions continued as the country's economy declined and income inequality increased.

Despite these challenges, the Russian Federation managed to remain intact and, years later, even to assert itself on the international stage. This relative revival came after a crucial struggle for its survival, on three main fronts. The first regards the concentration of power. Two key moments in this battle are the adoption of the 1993 Constitution and, seven years later, Putin gaining control of the Duma.[13] The second front of this struggle relates to the relationship between the central government and its territorial units. In the aftermath of the Beslan terrorist attack in 2004, the decision was made to appoint rather than elect governors of the republics, signaling a shift toward centralization. The third front pertains to the evolving relationship between the political and economic spheres, with the arrest of oligarch Mikhail Khodorkovsky in October 2003 serving as a turning point.

Vladimir Putin emerged victorious in all these struggles, and one can meaningfully distinguish a period "before Putin" from one "during Putin" when considering Russia's recent history. But this observation comes with important qualifications. The state's centrality was reestablished, but it was accompanied by frequent and sometimes rough intra-elite conflicts, bureaucratic inefficiency, and corruption. When we examine the sphere beyond the state, and what is commonly referred to as "nonsystemic opposition" to the Kremlin, we see a civil society that has been suppressed by state repression. The relationship between the state and civil society represents a fourth contested area of significance. These themes are closely interrelated, and I will discuss them in turn.

THE STRUGGLE FOR THE CONTROL OF THE STATE: FROM THE 1993 CONSTITUTION TO PUTIN'S CONTROL OF THE DUMA

As the Soviet Union crumbled, Russia was left with the 1978 Constitution of the Russian Soviet Federative Socialist Republic (RSFSR).[14] Boris Yeltsin, who had been elected as the chairman (speaker) of the RSFSR

[13] The Federal Assembly of the Russian Federation, and lower chamber of Parliament.
[14] It was a derivative of the 1977 Constitution of the Soviet Union, which however had undergone significant amendments during Gorbachev's years (Pomeranz 2019, 115).

Supreme Soviet in May 1990, and finally as the president of Russia the following year, was faced with an inchoate hierarchy of legislative sources and a rudimentary division of powers. Drawing on a centuries-old tradition, Yeltsin was granted broad emergency powers by Congress in November 1991, and he used them extensively, particularly to implement economic reforms. A power struggle ensued over the relative influence of the presidency and parliament. In April 1993, a popular referendum failed to reach the required quorum but indicated a preference for strong presidential powers. The showdown came in September of that year, when Yeltsin dissolved the Duma and called for new parliamentary elections. On October 3, a violent confrontation around and inside Moscow's "White House," the seat of the Duma, resulted in almost 200 deaths and a victory for Yeltsin.[15]

These events led to the Constitution of 1993, which was very statist in nature and granted vast powers to the president of the Russian Federation, with the Parliament serving as the major counterweight to those powers.[16] However, Yeltsin was unable to fully take advantage of the centrality attributed to the presidency because, even after he was reelected in 1996, he never gained sufficient control of the Duma.[17] In an effort to secure the viability of his presidency, he made compromises with the periphery and the emerging class of oligarchs.[18] However, his health declined and his ability to make compromises also weakened. The economy improved after the 1998 financial crisis, but it was Yeltsin's successor, Vladimir Putin, who capitalized on a sustained period of high oil and gas prices and rapid economic growth.

It was during Putin's first term that we witness the "successful taming of what had been for more than a decade a raucous and recalcitrant parliament," accomplished "through a combination of 'party construction' and favoritism in electoral administration."[19] The reference to "party construction" indicates a typical feature of authoritarian regimes (we will also observe it in Brazil) and is highly sophisticated in Russia. The main party, named "Unity," was formed at the end of 1999 to support

15 Pomeranz 2019, 101 and 118.

16 The Parliament was given the "right to approve all federal laws, including laws related to the federal budget, taxes, international treaties, and peace and war." Pomeranz 2019, 124 and 126. The constitution was adopted by popular referendum on December 12, 1993.

17 See Zygar 2016.

18 On the oligarchs – who they were, how they gained control, and on the economic performance of their firms – see Guriev and Rachinsky 2005.

19 Huskey 2009, 216.

Putin's candidacy as president in 2000 and was later renamed "United Russia" following a merge.[20] These "technopolitical" initiatives, as they are referred to in Russia, preempt opposition activities by forming so-called systemic opposition organizations and act as instruments of co-optation.[21]

The distinction between two modes of government operation is often made in Russia. Institutions may follow their course, within the precinct of a highly formalized administration. This is what happens in the great majority of cases, with outcomes that "are determined by an often vicious competition between bureaucratic factions, business actors, regional elites, and powerful individuals."[22] However, occasionally Putin gets involved in what is called "manual control" (*ruchnoe upravlenie*), implying a top-down management, particularly of issues and projects that are seen as strategic. This method also does not guarantee results and is fraught with difficulties and conflicts of its own. Use of manual control partly arises from frustration with the perceived lack of results of the normal mode of operation. Also, its manifestation indicates to all that it is possible to select issues on which formal rules might be bypassed, a fact that will play an important role in my interpretation of corruption in Russia. Manual control is an option also available to other actors, such as governors in the regions, in a context where "no one quite knows who has the president's special authorization and for what. The constant sense of urgency and the injection of *siloviki*[23] into civilian policy leads to a contradictory mix of rash decisions and defensive inactivity."[24]

The characteristics of manual control have evolved, with an increased relevance in more recent years of para-constitutional practices, such, as we will see, in the use of proxies of government.

[20] Petrov and Nazrullaeva 2018.

[21] We observe this tendency both with respect to political parties, as part of a vast array of broadly defined para-constitutional practices, and of astro-turfed civil society organizations. See Sakva 2010, and, for more recent developments, my discussion later.

[22] Treisman 2018.

[23] *Siloviki* (da *silo*, in Russian meaning "force") identifies members, or ex-members, of the FSB (the former KGB) and, more broadly, of security and law enforcement agencies. On their political role, see Soldatov and Rochlitz 2018.

[24] Treisman 2018. The distinction between a normal mode of operation and manual control is one of degree more than of kind, considering that the former entails informal practices, and "every written decision […] requires a special overseer to walk from door-to-door pushing for its implementation […] informally known as the policy's "legs" (*nogi*) [without which] a decision risks being delayed or forgotten, even if it originated at the highest level" (Ananyev 2018).

CENTER-PERIPHERY RELATIONS

Boris Yeltsin was a strong advocate of decentralization while he opposed Gorbachev. However, as he took federal power, he soon had to confront the same centrifugal forces that plagued the last years of the Soviet Union, as they came to affect the Russian Federation, which consists of autonomous republics, territories, districts, and regions. Although Soviet law did not grant them the right of secession, some were demanding greater autonomy. The use of treaties to deal with the diversity within Russia's vast territory has been a tradition since Czarist times, and Yeltsin continued this approach. On March 31, 1992, the Federation Treaty was signed, resulting in a highly asymmetric federalism.[25] Over the course of Yeltsin's presidency, further compromises were made and significant autonomy was granted to the country's regional leaders in exchange for support in federal politics.[26]

Boris Yeltsin's presidency was marked by the challenge of decentralization and the rise of regional political leaders. Unlike in the Soviet era, local leaders were now rooted in their regions and had become local strongmen. Elected and legitimized, they were able to attract federal territorial workers into their patronage networks and created a dual subordination in the provinces, where federal agencies had to answer to both regional governors and their superiors in Moscow.[27] The first Chechen War, which lasted from December 1994 to August 1996, was a vivid expression of the struggle for control in the periphery and resulted in a significant defeat for Yeltsin. The de facto independence of the Chechen Republic after the war sent a signal of weakness to other potential breakaway republics.

This risky situation was to change under Putin's presidency, when the relationships between the center and periphery underwent significant changes.

[25] Pomeranz 2019, 117.

[26] Huskey 2009 notes that "Russian officialdom operated in a turbulent political environment in which lines of authority were contested and ministries and regions took advantage of weak presidential leadership to champion their own departmental and local interests." See also Pomeranz 2019, 130, according to whom Yeltsin "stretched the historic idea of the unified state to its absolute extreme in order to keep the country together." The situation that Eltsin inherited was itself the outcome of previous compromises. In the formative years of the Soviet Union in particular, treatment of nationalities had been influenced by the dire necessities of the Civil War, and "the Bolsheviks' adept handling of the nationality question helped them to build alliances with non-communists and win the civil war" (Hirsch 2005, 66).

[27] Dual subordination of state agencies had been a characterizing pattern also of Soviet time, but with the "party first secretary in the region" as the other pole of attraction besides the ministry in Moscow (Huskey 2009, 223).

In 2004, an administrative reform inspired by New Public Management criteria was launched, although its effects were inconclusive.[28] Additionally, the creation of the United Russia party brought together central and local elites in a single organization. This also marked the end of regional leaders promoting their own political parties, which had previously allowed them to pass favorable legislation in the Duma.[29] The judiciary also underwent attempted reforms, which will be discussed separately.

Other changes that took place at the beginning of the decade weakened the position of governors and regional legislative chairs. They culminated in the already mentioned decision, made in the wake of the Beslan tragedy in September 2004, to appoint governors rather than have them elected. Together with transformations that were already underway, this decision altered the balance of power between the center and the periphery.[30] At the same time, the fiscal reforms of that period significantly reduced the resources that were retained locally. These changes, together with the increase in rents from natural resources that we have discussed, expanded the funds accruing to the center and weakened the influence of local interests on federal workers stationed in the regions. To further these changes, in 2005 direct mayoral elections were canceled in half of Russian cities, a process that continued in subsequent years to include the majority of cities.[31] These changes were accompanied by Putin's "cadre policy," which used administrative personnel for political and economic positions and marginalized elite groups perceived as a threat.[32] Despite these developments, the relationship between the center and periphery remained complex, with occasional shifts, such as the reintroduction of governor elections following the 2011 protests, of which I will say more.[33] Occasionally, the actions of talented local politicians and civil society movements have influenced this dynamic, but the center's superiority over the periphery has not been seriously questioned nor tested anymore.

Despite the appearance of success in restoring the central government' power over the regions, there are indications of ongoing conflicts and competition among the elites, including local elites. The conflict in Chechnya is the most notable case. The second Chechen War started in

28 Huskey 2009, 215 and 219.
29 Petrov and Nazrullaeva 2018.
30 Huskey 2009, 224. See Pomeranz 2019, 145 and 146, on the consequential centralization reforms that had started immediately after Putin's inauguration in May 2000.
31 Petrov and Nazrullaeva 2018.
32 Huskey 2010, 187.
33 Petrov and Nazrullaeva 2018, and Aburamoto 2019.

August 1999 during Vladimir Putin's tenure as Prime Minister and lasted for a decade, resulting in a nominal victory for Moscow. The Chechen Republic, led by Ramzan Kadyrov, has been given a significant degree of autonomy, and Chechen actors have played a unique and murky role in Russian internal affairs.[34]

THE RELATIONSHIP BETWEEN THE ECONOMY AND THE STATE

The transition from socialism to capitalism was fraught with difficulties. The early 1990s saw the privatization of state assets in a situation where property rights were unclear and there were no established institutions to regulate the economy. This process gave rise to the creation of extremely wealthy "oligarchs," who would play an important role in the years ahead.[35]

The climax of this process was the 1995 "loans for shares" scheme, which allowed a small group of individuals to acquire control over some of the country's most valuable assets.[36] Mikhail Khodorkovsky's bank, Menatep, arranged the auction of a state oil company that Khodorkovsky himself won. Vladimir Potanin took control of the metal giant Norilsk Nickel, and Boris Berezovsky acquired the oil company Sibneft. These deals provided Yeltsin with the resources he needed for his reelection in 1996, in a clear case of state capture, and highlighted the difficulties that there may be in distinguishing between illegal and legal forms of corruption. The oligarchs had the means to finance political aspirations, pay for their own security through a network of former security personnel and thugs, and bribe cash-strapped public officials and politicians. These were the "wild 1990s," known for the proliferation of mafia-like criminal groups offering protection, in competition with the state, where the line between law enforcement and criminal activities was often blurred.[37] The relationship between oligarch Boris Berezovskii, who also owned an important television channel, and Yeltsin's inner circle, known as "the family," was a prime example of the close connection between politics, money, and media power during these years.

[34] Consider Zygar's 2016, chapter 19, account of the killing of Boris Nemtsov, on February 27, 2015, practically on the Kremlin's doorsteps.

[35] Huskey 2009. The debate on Russian economic reforms of the early 1990s is vast and occasionally acrimonious. In the background, we observe the intense sufferings of a large part of the Russian population.

[36] Pomeranz 2019, 135.

[37] Varese 2001, and Volkov 2002.

Once the oligarchs were established, they had a vested interest in strengthening the legal framework and property rights to secure their wealth. Mikhail Khodorkovsky, who controlled the largest oil company and was the richest man in Russia, was the most prominent representative of this tendency and in the early 2000s presented himself as a philanthropic tycoon. This situation did not last long, as President Putin, early in his first term, clarified that he expected oligarchs to stay out of politics, or else.[38] This message was brought home to all when Khodorkovsky, who appeared to politically challenge Putin and had accused him of tolerating corruption, was arrested on October 23, 2003, on charges of fraud, tax evasion, and other crimes. He was sentenced and remained in prison for ten years, while his holdings in Yukos were effectively confiscated by the state.[39] The Khodorkovsky case was the high point of what became known as "Basmanny Justice," named after the Moscow court where his and other high-profile cases were judged. This term came to indicate politically motivated high-stakes court decisions, an important issue in my analysis of corruption in Russia that I will address later. Additionally, the Khodorkovsky affair marked the affirmation of state control over the strategically important oil industry, which had been dominated by private actors after the 1990s privatizations. The state-controlled Rosneft, led by the powerful Igor Sechin, benefited from Yukos' assets.[40]

Events that took place during Putin's first term transformed the relationship between the state and the economy. However, it would be misleading to say that Russia transitioned from a situation where business captured the state to one where the opposite occurs. In reality, the distinction between the state and the economy has evolved to become increasingly blurred. Although the overlap of careers in business and politics was already visible during the Yeltsin years, by the start of Putin's presidency, "careers in state administration – rather than elective politics or private industry – had become both the dominant path to political power

[38] Berezovsky, along with another media tycoon, Vladimir Gusinsky, was disciplined soon after Putin took office as President. In the late 1990s, Gusinsky controlled the media group "Media Most" and the influential private television network N.T.V. After a brief period in jail, he agreed to sell his media holdings to the gas giant Gazprom and left Russia in 2000. Berezovsky, on the other hand, emigrated to London and eventually committed suicide after losing a costly lawsuit with another oligarch, Roman Abramovich, who was also part of Yeltsin's "family" and had a higher sense of survival. See Cobain 2014 and Zygar 2016.

[39] Rankin 2014.

[40] The gas industry came to be consolidated and controlled by the state earlier, through state-controlled Gazprom. For a summary of the evolution of the oil and gas industry in Russia during the last decades, see Mitrova 2022.

and an important training ground for business elites."[41] The revolving door has been used as a tool to reward the faithful and to marginalize adversarial elites.

The Kremlin gradually took control of the private media by ensuring that ownership was in friendly hands, and the nationalization of industries accelerated, especially after major private enterprises were bailed out following the financial crisis of 2007–2009.[42] The result was an increase in the possibilities of patronage. Additionally, the expectation has grown that the oligarchs will perform tasks at the Kremlin's call, including contributions to societal objectives. For instance, following the annexation of Crimea in March 2014, plans were quickly made to construct a bridge spanning the Strait of Kerch to connect Crimea to the Russian mainland. The construction of the bridge, which was an important project in both practical and symbolic terms, was awarded without a public tender in January 2015 to Mostotrest, a company owned by oligarch Arkady Rotenberg (a childhood friend of Putin) and his brother Boris. It was reported that the company would not make any profit from the project.[43] However, whether this is true or not might be a moot point, considering that the Rotenberg brothers had received approximately $7 billion in contracts for the Sochi Winter Olympic Games.[44] This case highlights a general trend observed in Russia, where the Kremlin assigns important tasks to individuals who are not state employees and are often entrepreneurs, as part of its "manual control mode." In recent years, tasks outsourced by the Kremlin have included some core functions of the state.[45] At least until Russia's invasion of Ukraine in 2022, such

[41] Huskey 2010, 185. See also Lamberova and Sonin 2018, 140, who note that "being a business person or a politician is not an innate personal characteristic but an occupation of choice. The same people who started their private businesses in the early 1990s ran for governorships a decade later and joined the government or state-controlled companies in the Putin years."

[42] Lamberova and Sonin 2018.

[43] Vlasov 2019. The firm was sold in 2019 "reportedly to companies affiliated with the state-owned gas giant Gazprom" (Radio Free Europe 2020).

[44] United States Department of the Treasury 2014. On their extreme cost, see Müller 2014, who notes that it was "the second-most expensive Olympics ever in terms of sports-related costs and the most expensive Olympics in terms of cost per event." See also Giannakopoulou 2020.

[45] A notable example is provided by Yevgeny Prigozhin, the former head of "Wagner group," a paramilitary organization active in several conflicts around the world (and with high prominence, in the ongoing invasion of Ukraine), and who according to the US Treasury Department, "financed an internet troll factory that deployed social media campaigns in an attempt to influence the 2018 US midterm elections" MacFarquhar 2018). Two months after having staged an armed rebellion, on August 23, 2023, Prigozhin died in an airplane crash.

"proxying" also allowed Russia to deflect responsibilities abroad by allowing it to claim plausible deniability, but it also reflects a perceived inability to accomplish them in the normal mode of operation.

CIVIL SOCIETY AND THE STATE

The Constitution of 1993 outlined civil rights and liberties that reflected the liberally inclined public attitude of the early 1990s, that however faded quickly as Russians came to desire more order and centralization as an antidote for the deteriorating situation.[46] During Putin's first two terms as president, he delivered both order and centralization along with robust economic growth. The implicit agreement between the Russian people and the state was summarized by the ironic phrase "sausages instead of democracy." The state presented itself as a modernizer, guiding Russia through a transition to a market economy and bringing the country up to speed with technology and organizational forms adopted abroad. With the delivery of economic growth and stability, which was highly valued after the difficulties and uncertainties of the 1990s, the Kremlin believed that Russian society would be satisfied with the authoritarian version of democracy it was offering. This has largely proven to be the case, as Putin has consistently received high approval ratings.[47]

All relevant media outlets have been made to enter the Kremlin's fold, either through direct control or through control by proxies, such as the state gas company Gazprom, or Putin's associate Yuri Kovalchuk through his businesses.[48] Such domesticated media have played a significant role in creating a perception of Putin as an inescapable force in Russian politics, best summarized by the words of Vyacheslav Volodin, speaker of the Duma: "without Putin there is no Russia."[49] It is a perception that has been reinforced through the suppression of alternative political projects and the persecution of any nonsystemic opposition that might arise. This is achieved through a combination of media control, regulation of the political space by means of "technopolitical" activities, and repression of dissenting voices. The result is a climate in which Putin's authority is seen as unassailable, further strengthening his grip on power.

46 Rogov and Ananyev 2018.

47 Levada Center n.d.

48 Lipman et al. 2018. A niche of independent media outlets remained until it was summarily disposed of in the aftermath of Russia's invasion of Ukraine in 2022.

49 Lenta.ru 2014. On Volodin, an architect of Putin's reelection in 2012 and of the ensuing conservative turn, see Zygar 2016, chapter 15.

However, among the urban elites who benefited from the country's economic growth and modernization during Putin's first two presidential terms, dissatisfaction grew over time. Widespread fraud in the December 2011 legislative elections, and Putin's decision to run for a third (nonconsecutive) term as president, resulted in massive protests in several cities. The largest of them, taking place in Moscow's Bolotnaya Square on May 6, 2012, was violently repressded.[50] In response, the Kremlin embraced social conservatism and promoted the image of traditional Russian values under attack from an imagined "collective West."[51] A 2012 law required nongovernmental organizations, media organizations, and individuals receiving funding from outside Russia to register as "foreign agents," sharply limiting their freedom of action. The annexation of Crimea in 2014 marked a shift toward overt nationalism and anti-West rhetoric.[52] The fateful decision to invade Ukraine in 2022 further amplified authoritarian tendencies that were however already clearly in sight.

The Internet has been a source of relative freedom in the past, but it has become increasingly regulated in recent years. It has served as an important tool for Russia's nonsystemic opposition, particularly for an able activist, Alexei Navalny, who led various initiatives such as the "Foundation against Corruption." Navalny utilized digital technology effectively to expose cases of high-level corruption and paint the ruling party, "United Russia," as a group of "crooks and thieves."[53] Also thanks to its tech-savvy users, Russia has sometimes shown unexpected levels of transparency, which has been aided by corruption that has made illegal databases such as vehicle registration plates and commercial flight lists available. These resources have allowed for high-quality investigative journalism that has at times greatly embarrassed the Kremlin.[54]

50 Amnesty International 2014.

51 Pomeranz 2019, 156, quips that "Since Putin could not be loved, he decided on the next best thing: To be feared."

52 See Rogov and Ananyev 2018, who also note the success of such maneuver in terms of Putin's approval rate.

53 A moniker that Navalny first proposed in 2011. See Zygar 2016, chapter 13, and in particular Dollbaum et al. 2021. The FBK was closed by the Russian authority on August 31, 2021. See Interfax 2021.

54 Such as on the attempted murder of Alexei Navalny, on August 20, 2020; see Dollbaum et al. 2021. State-sponsored reforms (particularly during Medvedev's presidency) also contributed, for example, in making available as open data detailed information on public purchases. These enabled a series of anti-corruption activities, most noteworthy those by Navalny and his associates.

CORRUPTION IN RUSSIA

Corruption has been a crucial factor in allowing Russia to overcome its existential threats. We now assess its pervasiveness that by all accounts is extensive.

Perceptions of corruption in Russia are extremely high, as indicated by the TI-CPI. In 2019, Russia ranked 137th out of 180 countries on the list. Figure 6.6 illustrates the changes in these perceptions over time, using the same methodology applied in Chapter 3 for Spain (refer to Figure 3.3). The rankings are based on continuous coverage of a group of countries. At the beginning of Putin's first term, coinciding with a period of reforms, there was a noticeable improvement in the perception of corruption. However, this progress was short-lived, and perceptions worsened significantly after 2004, likely due to the high-profile Khodorkovsky case. During Medvedev's presidency, the fight against corruption was given greater priority, and perceptions of corruption improved. In recent years, there has been no significant change in perceptions.

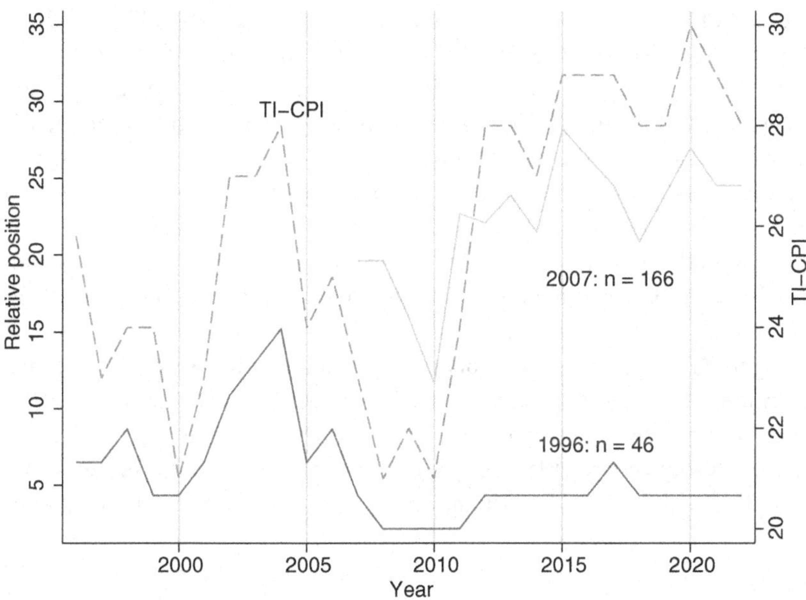

Figure 6.6 TI-CPI and its relative position (Russian Federation)
Dashed line: TI-CPI (right axis; values before 2012 are multiplied by 10). Relative positions (left axis): Percentiles, relative to group of countries (of size *n*) continuously present from a given date. Higher relative positions (and values of the TI-CPI) correspond to less perceived corruption. See Escresa and Picci 2016 for further details.

Perceptions of high levels of corruption are corroborated by other data. When surveyed, Russians report frequent personal experiences with bribes.[55] Cases of corruption exposed by the opposition media and investigative journalism are also informative. Although caution must be exercised when analyzing individual cases, they often provide insight into the general patterns and mechanisms behind corruption. Experts on Russia widely agree that corruption, embezzlement, and other illegal forms of appropriating public resources are rampant among the ruling elite. For example, Alena Ledeneva describes a "system" (*sistema*) that "represents common, yet not articulated, perceptions of power and the system of governance," it includes forms of corruption, and affirms that "the whole economy operates in the mode of 'legal nihilism', so that everyone is bound to disregard at least some laws."[56] The evidence of corruption among members of the elite, including the top tier, is abundant, and it includes the presence of vast offshore wealth, mentioned earlier, and the exorbitant costs of high-profile public projects, such as the 2014 Winter Olympics in Sochi (see note 44). Occasionally, members of the elite are sentenced for corruption or other white-collar alleged crimes, as we saw in the case of former Economy Minister Alexey Ulyukaev in 2017.

Corruption is covered under Articles 290 and 291 of the penal code, respectively, for bribe-taking and bribe-giving. In theory, for every bribe received, one is handed out. However, bribe givers can be exonerated if they cooperate with the prosecutors,[57] and as we have seen bribes can also be offered as "torpedos" in entrapment operations. These are likely the two main reasons why the number of cases under Article 291 (bribe-giving) is fewer than those under Article 290 (bribe-taking). In 2016, Federal Law No. 324-FZ introduced a distinction between petty bribes and those exceeding a certain threshold.

Figure 6.7 indicates the number of criminal cases that were sent to court. They are considered to be resolved and represent the outcome of a decision by the prosecutor to move forward with the case after conducting an investigation.[58] From 2010 to 2016, the number of recorded crimes for bribe-giving, regardless of the amount, was in the range of 5,000 to 6,000. The total number

[55] Levada Center 2017.

[56] Ledeneva 2013, 1 and 14.

[57] According to Art. 291 of the Penal code of the Russian Federation.

[58] See Institute for the Rule of Law n.d. These cases are the bulk of so-called solved cases. Once these cases go to court, they most often result in sentencing. I am thankful to Dmitriy Skougarevskiy for help in clarifying these and other aspects of Russian judicial statistics and criminal procedure.

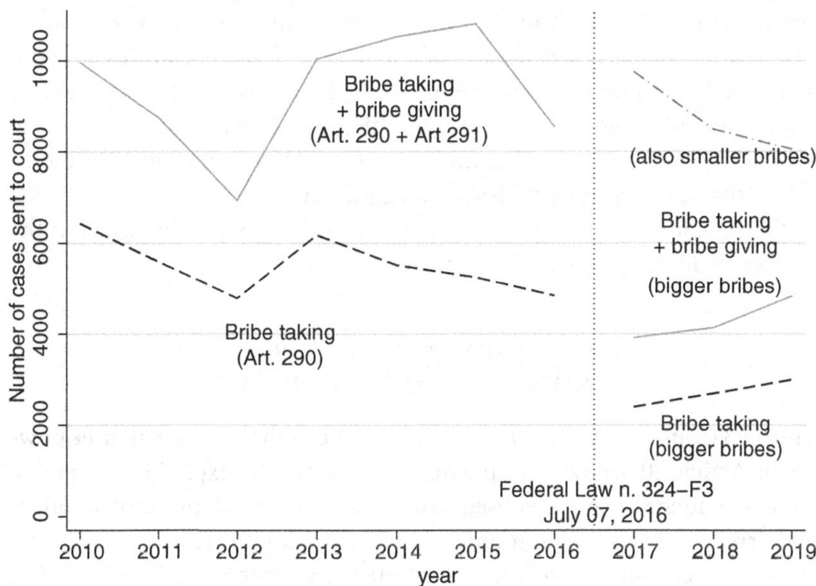

Figure 6.7 Corruption crimes (Russian Federation)
Source of the data: My elaborations of data from Federal Procurator of the Russian Federation. n.d. Number of criminal case files received by courts. "Bribe taking" and "Bribe giving" refer, respectively, to Art. 290 and Art. 291 of the Penal code of the Russian Federation. Crimes under Art. 291.1 ("mediation in bribery"), which in 2019 accounted for 541 cases sent to court, have been ignored.

of recorded crimes, including both bribe-taking and bribe-giving, reached its highest point in 2015 with 10,806 cases and declined in subsequent years.

The numbers of recorded crimes related to bribery in Russia are high,[59] and the penalties for these crimes can be quite severe. Statutory penalties are of interest also because criminal law, besides providing deterrence, represents a "system of moral education and socialization,"[60] which attempts to change or construct "social meanings of a certain act, affecting social norms and inducing stigma."[61] In Russia and the former Soviet Union, corruption has long been considered a very serious crime. The baseline statutory penalty for bribe-taking has been decreasing since 2011 and is currently set at a maximum of three years in prison. However, there are

[59] For a comparison, the number of convictions for corruption in Italy (with a population which is slightly less than half that of Russia) is in the order of 500 every year (see Picci and Vannucci 2018, 47) or one-tenth of the bribe-taking crimes observed in Russia.

[60] Coffee 1991.

[61] Faure and Escresa 2011.

circumstances that can lead to a longer prison sentence, with up to 15 years in jail for particularly serious acts of corruption.[62] The law in Russia is not lenient when it comes to corruption, and the severity of the law reflects public attitudes toward corruption. Although Russians may be cynical about the extent of corruption, they do not condone it and consider it to be one of the most serious problems facing the country.[63]

The penalties for corruption are meted out by the judiciary, which is the final element that we need to consider.

THE JUDICIARY: ACCUSATORIAL BIAS AND A WEAPONIZED JUSTICE

The 1993 Constitution lists the judiciary as one of the traditional three powers in Article 10, one of its opening provisions, and explicitly recognizes its independence,[64] while subsequent legislative provisions granted judges with irremovability and immunity. These provisions were accompanied by a series of reforms aimed at transforming the former Soviet justice system to align more closely with the practices observed in liberal democracies. In particular, in the following years judges' salaries were increased, jury trials were reintroduced, and new civil and criminal codes were promulgated. While the results of these reforms have been dubious, and despite the judiciary's many shortcomings, its services are frequently used. The commercial courts, in particular, have outperformed other areas of the justice system, but their role and independence have diminished, particularly after the decision to merge them with regular courts in 2014.[65] In recent years, there has been a regression in the progress that took place until the end of Medvedev's presidency.

62 The relevant statutes are available in Sistema Garant n.d.

63 According to a survey by Levada Center which started in 1998, between 30 and 40% of Russians think that it is one of the most worrying problems, within a list provided where more than one choice is possible. It is the fourth most frequently chosen option, behind inflation, unemployment, and poverty. See Levada Center 2020.

64 In Article 120. The provisions in the 1993 Constitution were partly based on the 1992 document titled "The Conception of Judicial Reform in the RSFSR," which was approved by the Russian Supreme Soviet. This document presented a liberal viewpoint and advocated for the appointment of judges for life, an adversarial system, separation of investigators from the prosecution, and the implementation of trial by jury. Solomon 2015a.

65 Hendley 2017. The Higher Commercial (Arbitrazh) Court (one of the distinct high courts that were originally established under the constitution, together with the Constitutional Court and the Supreme Court) was also abolished in 2014, in what also represented an ominous message to the traditionally slightly recalcitrant Constitutional Court (see Pomeranz 2019, 159).

Corruption is a crime, and the functioning of the criminal justice system is of particular interest to us. The system is characterized by a strong accusatorial bias. The presence of very low rates of acquittal in itself does not prove bias, in case prescreening of cases gets rid of most of those having little merit. However, this is not the case in Russia, where prescreening is modest at best.[66] Corruption of judges or investigators, or intimidation, may lead to flawed justice. The pressure on judges is reminiscent of the Soviet practice of "telephone justice," where verbal political orders from above, rather than legal norms, may dictate the outcome of a case. The result of such practices however may be both the imprisonment of innocent individuals as the unjust release of criminals, so they are not sufficient to explain the observed marked accusatorial bias in criminal justice. This in fact is due to several reasons, including the use of metrics to evaluate judges based on their "hit rates," together with the deference they show to law enforcement interests. Despite reforms, Peter Solomon notes that "judges remained career officials whose continuation in office and promotion depended upon the good will of the chairmen of their courts," and "the evaluation of judges on the basis of rates of reversal ('stability of sentences') and the power of long-serving chairmen of courts made it dangerous for judges to act creatively, let alone as mavericks."[67]

Solomon succinctly summarizes the strong accusatory bias in the criminal justice system by stating that "once a case with serious charges has been initiated, it is nearly impossible for the accused to avoid conviction."[68] The consequences of this bias are significant when considering corruption in Russia. The individuals with the power to initiate a criminal case are often successful in sending their target to prison, creating a weaponized justice system. Those powerful actors who use criminal justice as a powerful tool for discipline have no incentive to reform the system, which may be considered to be at equilibrium.

[66] As Solomon 2015b notes, "other countries like Canada, Germany, The Netherlands, and France also have low rates of acquittal without the perception of bias." The key difference between these countries, and Russia, "lies in the presence or absence of pretrial screening – through the withdrawal of charges, diversion, and/or dispositions imposed by prosecutors."

[67] Solomon 2015a. The importance of these broad factors is recognized by several researchers besides Solomon. See, for example, Pomeranz 2019, 137–138, and Paneyakh and Rosenberg 2018. Solomon also underlines the historical persistence of accusatorial bias in Russia, noting that starting from the late 1940s "acquittals were stigmatized as failures of investigators (*sledovateli*) and procurators (*prokurory*) and judges were discouraged from giving them," while similar attitudes continued in the post-Stalin period: "by 1970, judges risked not only censure but, even, the loss of their job if they gave more than the occasional acquittal" (Solomon 2015b).

[68] Solomon 2015b.

CONCLUSIONS: CORRUPTION AS A TOOL OF GOVERNMENT

After the dissolution of the Soviet Union, Russia faced a series of challenges representing a triple problem: reestablishing the control of the state, redefining the relationship between the center and periphery, and establishing a working relationship between the state and the economic sphere. These were existential threats to the state, and they are crucial to my interpretation of corruption in Russia, which Chapter 10 considers in more detail. Russian elites are plagued by widespread corruption, where everyone is "bound to disregard at least some laws."[69] This means that everyone is vulnerable to a weaponized justice. The stick, which is the credible threat of being targeted by the justice system, is paired with the carrot, which takes the form of bribes and other incentives for individuals, their families, and associates. These incentives are especially important in a country with pronounced inequalities, making exclusion from privilege particularly painful. In such a dire situation, corruption is a tool that helps the government function, and it is in fact an institution of government, as dysfunctional as it is.

The question is open on whether similar traits of corruption can be found in other places and contexts, and I will begin to address it by examining the case of Brazil. Corruption is also a tool of government in Brazil, but with important differences compared to Russia.

[69] Ledeneva 2013, 14.

7

Corruption as the Glue of the System

The Case of Brazil

We won't cover anyone, regardless of who may be involved. I say that we will cut into our own flesh, if necessary.

Luiz Inácio Lula da Silva, June 7, 2005,
on accusations of corruption against his own party.

June 7, 2005, was a complicated day for President of Brazil Luiz Inácio Lula da Silva. The previous day, the influential newspaper Folha de São Paulo had published a revealing interview with Federal Deputy Roberto Jefferson. Jefferson, who was the president of the small *Partido Trabalhista Brasileiro* (PTB) and a supporter of Lula, had been accused of corruption in a scandal involving the Brazilian postal service (Correios). In the interview, Jefferson hit back by claiming that Lula's political party, the *Partido dos Trabalhadores* (PT), paid a number of legislators to sway their votes an illegal monthly allowance from the advertising budgets of state-owned companies. Jefferson directly implicated President Lula, stating that he was aware of these illegal payments.[1]

The paying of politicians was not a novelty in Brazil,[2] but the timing of the "*Mensalão*" (monthly payment) scandal, as it was to be known, was unpropitious to Lula because presidential elections were to be held the following year. The scandal seriously impacted his reelection prospects, and in a July survey, 78% of respondents believed that his government was involved in corruption, up from 32% in March 2004.[3] Lula's approval

[1] Lo Prete 2005.

[2] See Da Ros and Taylor 2022, 28.

[3] Folha de São Paulo 2005. The same opinion poll however indicated that Brazilians thought that the situation had not been better during the mandate of Lula's predecessor, Fernando Henrique Cardoso. According to 48% of respondents, there had not been changes in that respect, while 24% believed that corruption had decreased, and 22%, increased.

ratings deteriorated significantly from Spring to Summer 2005, and by August of that year, an opinion poll indicated that he would lose to his opponent, José Serra, if the elections were held at that time.[4]

However, on that particular day, President Lula faced a more pressing problem with the news of Jefferson's allegations dominating the news cycle. Ironically, he was scheduled to deliver the opening address at the *IV Global Forum on Fighting Corruption* in Brasília. The event had been planned in advance also as an occasion for the Brazilian government to showcase its commitment to integrity.[5] Lula arrived at the luxury hotel hosting the meeting with a significant delay, to deliver a bold speech in which he directly addressed the accusations of corruption. He acknowledged that corruption in Brazil was a *doença crônica*, a chronic disease, but emphasized that the Congress was not for sale and that his government would thoroughly investigate the allegations "until their ultimate consequences."[6]

Despite the political setback, Lula recovered and was easily reelected in 2006. Many Brazilians believed that his government was corrupt, but they may also have thought that, according to the Brazilian catchphrase, "he steals, but gets things done" ("*Rouba, mas faz*"). And the Lula government did get things done, during a tenure coinciding with a period known as the *milagrinho*, or "little miracle,"[7] because of fast-paced economic growth. Nevertheless, the *Mensalão* scandal marked a turning point. For the first time since the return to democracy, it would show that powerful politicians could be held accountable and set the precedent for the more significant corruption scandal of the following decade, *Lava Jato*.

On that day in Brasília, Lula employed powerful language to assure the audience of his government's dedication to combating corruption, declaring that every measure necessary would be taken, even if it meant "cutting into our own flesh."[8] This phrase proved to be prophetic, as some of the reforms aimed at increasing transparency and accountability, implemented by both Lula and his successor, Dilma Rousseff, set the stage for the *Lava Jato* scandal that was disastrous to them and their party.

4 See Datafolha 2005.

5 According to the United Nations' Secretary-General, the Forum was to be "an important contribution to the global fight against corruption." See United Nations 2005.

6 Jungblut 2005. My account is also based on my personal recollections as a participant to the event.

7 With reference to the *milagre* years that occurred during the dictatorship (see later in this chapter and Luna and Klein 2014).

8 Jungblut 2005.

The aftermath of *Lava Jato* highlights the unpredictability of anti-corruption campaigns and reforms. These changes occurred at the lower subsystem of historical change (with reference to Chapter 5) and did not challenge the use of corruption as a tool of government. In this regard, Brazil shares similarities and differences with Russia. In both countries, there is a close, often corrupt relationship between political power and state-controlled enterprises, such as the Brazilian state-run postal service in the *Mensalão* scandal and Petrobras in the *Lava Jato* case. In contrast to Brazil, the anti-corruption movement in Russia has not only failed to seriously challenge the government but also has been confronted by brutal repression. Unlike in Russia, Brazil's judiciary has been highly proactive. Moreover, the Brazilian government's hosting of an important international conference on corruption in 2005 highlights its participation to the anti-corruption global regime, which in the case of Russia has been lukewarm at best.

I aim to find a balance between the possibility of making useful generalizations and the need to consider the unique context of each case. To start, I will provide a comprehensive overview of relevant facts, with a focus on the economy and the distribution of economic resources. This understanding will be crucial in examining the role of corruption in the political landscape of Brazilian society, which is marked by pronounced inequality.

BRAZIL AFTER THE DICTATORSHIP: A FEW STYLIZED FACTS

Brazil is a federal republic with a population, in 2019, of approximately 210 million, living in an area slightly smaller than the United States. It is divided into 26 states and the Federal District of Brasília. The population is primarily concentrated in the more economically dynamic South, particularly in the states of São Paulo and Rio de Janeiro, which occupy only 3.5% of Brazil's surface but account for almost 30% of the country's population and 42% of its GDP.[9] The North-East of the country, particularly the states of Alagoas, Sergipe, and Pernambuco, also have substantial population densities. With the exception of the well-inhabited state of Minas Gerais and the Federal District of Brasilia, only a small fraction of Brazil's population lives in the vast areas outside of the coastal states between the Northern state of Pará and the state of Rio Grande do Sul bordering Argentina.

9 Source of the data: IBGE 2017.

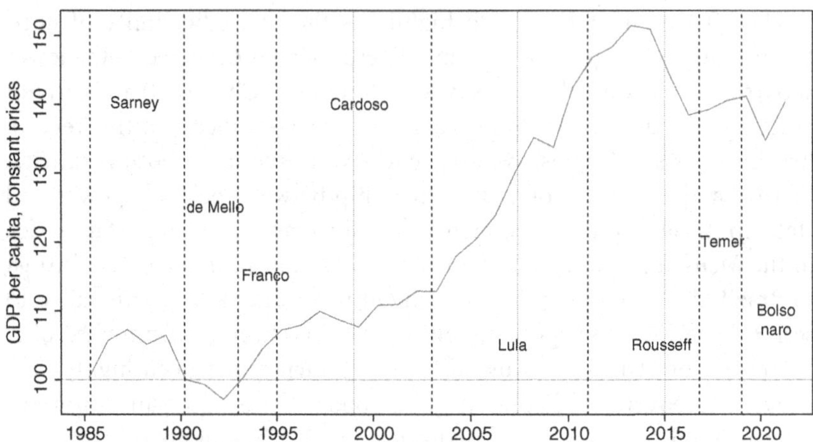

Figure 7.1 GDP per capita at constant prices (Brazil)
Source of the data: The World Bank. GDP per capita at constant prices, set equal to 100 in the year 1990. The vertical lines correspond to presidential elections.

Brazil is classified as an upper-middle-income country (as shown in Table 6.1 on page 89). After a period of sustained economic growth, known as the "*milagre*" or miracle, that ended around 1980, a severe economic downturn helped mobilize opposition to the dictatorship and ultimately led to its downfall in 1985. It wasn't until around 1993, during the presidency of Itamar Franco, that there was a significant increase in economic activity: Brazil's "lost decade" of the 1980s and its painful continuation into the next decade had finally come to an end (as shown in Figure 7.1). Franco's presidency also marked a turning point in regard to inflation, which had been a persistent problem. In the last years of the dictatorship, yearly inflation rose from around 100% in 1980 to 226% in 1985.[10] During Sarney's term as President, inflation had morphed into hyperinflation, making prices difficult to interpret and obscuring public accounts. These were the years of the *doleiros* (black-market money changers), "one of the many *malandros* (rascals or rogues) that make up the folkloric tapestry of the Brazilian underworld,"[11] appearing frequently in Brazil's corruption scandals. Fernando Collor de Mello's attempt to curb hyperinflation was plagued by corruption, and the resulting "Collorgate" scandal led to his resignation as president.[12]

[10] The source of the data is the World Bank, and the inflation rates that I report refer to the consumer price index.

[11] Da Ros and Taylor 2022, 23 and 53, on the obfuscating effects of hyperinflation.

[12] Schwarcz and Starling 2018, 572–573.

It was under the presidency of Itamar Franco and the implementation of the "Real Plan" in 1994 that hyperinflation was finally brought under control.[13] This success paved the way for Franco's Minister of Finance and former academic, Fernando Enrique Cardoso, to run as the presidential candidate of the *Partido da Social Democracia Brasileira* and in October 1994 to win the presidential election, defeating Lula. After Cardoso's two terms in office, Lula finally became president in 2003, marking the opportunity for his Workers' Party to be tested.[14] His two terms were characterized by steady economic growth, with the global financial crisis of 2007–2009 only making a minor impact on Brazil's GDP. The *milagrinho* ("little miracle") had more than one cause, including Lula's prudent financial management, which continued Cardoso's legacy and created a stable and confident environment for investors.[15] Additionally, along with other South American countries, Brazil was positively influenced by low US interest rates and high commodity prices, fueled by the increasing demand globally, particularly in China.[16]

Brazil is rich in natural resources, although their relative importance to the economy is smaller than in Russia. From the mid-1990s until the 2008 crisis, the share of natural resource rents steadily increased in relation to both exports and GDP (Figure 7.2). Considering also the concurrent rapid growth of GDP (Figure 7.1), the absolute increase of these rents was very pronounced. They funded ambitious social programs, the most politically consequential of which was a package of conditional cash transfers known as *Bolsa Familia*. They also financed a spending spree on new infrastructure. However, these resources also presented governance challenges, which were laid bare by the various scandals of the decade, including the climax of *Lava Jato*, among whose corporate protagonists was the state-owned oil company Petrobras, which was flush with money at the time.

Robust economic growth characterized the first two years of President Dilma Rousseff's first term. However, the situation rapidly deteriorated, leading to a deep recession in 2014. Rousseff was barely reelected in 2014, but the political situation soon spiraled out of the government's control

13 Inflation fell from 66% in 1995 to 16% in 1996, and has remained at single digit since 1997, except for a brief period in 2003 when it approached 15%.

14 Lula was elected President on October 27, 2002, and took office on January 1 of the following year.

15 Lula famously sent a "Letter to the Brazilian People" before the 2003 elections that "effectively meant continuity of economic policy whatever the outcome of the election, a factor that was reinforced by the partial institutionalization of the letter through a new IMF standby agreement and the promise of a constitutional amendment to facilitate the independence of the Central Bank" (Wylde 2012, 148–149).

16 See the discussion in Campello 2015.

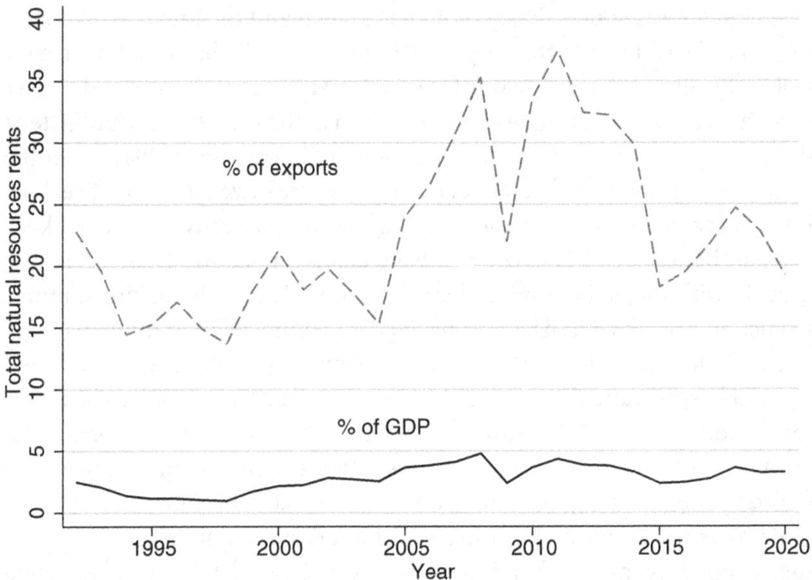

Figure 7.2 Natural resources rents, as a percentage of GDP and of exports (Brazil)
Source of the data: The World Bank. Total natural resources rents (production value minus costs) as % of GDP and of total exports.

concomitantly with the explosion of the *Lava Jato* scandal. She was eventually impeached on allegations of manipulating the budget and removed from office on August 31, 2016. The years leading up to the COVID-19 pandemic in 2020 saw only a partial recovery in economic activity with respect to the peak levels recorded in 2013.

ECONOMIC INEQUALITY IN BRAZIL

Inequality is deeply rooted in Brazilian society, and discussions about inequality, race, and racism are often intertwined. Slavery was only abolished in 1888 in Brazil, and questions of race and racism are central to the country's identity. Two perspective observers offer a concise synthesis: "Although there is no legal form of discrimination, the poor, and above all black people, are the most harshly treated by the justice system, have the shortest life span, the least access to higher education and to highly qualified jobs. The indelible mark of slavery conditions Brazilian culture; the country defines itself on the basis of gradations of skin colour."[17]

[17] Schwarcz and Starling 2018, xix. See also Telles 2014.

Brazil is also a country with very significant levels of economic inequality. In 2014, the top 1% of earners received 24% of total income, and the top 10% received 59%, implying levels of inequality higher than in Russia and the United States.[18] During the presidencies of Lula, there was a decrease in inequality. The bottom 50% improved its condition and increased its share of total income by almost 2% during Lula's two terms as president. It was a period of sustained economic growth, so that the absolute gain of Brazil's poor was of particular significance. Under President Cardoso, a conditional cash transfer program was already in place, but it was during President Lula's administration that this type of policy was expanded with the *Bolsa Familia* program. This program marked a shift from the past, as it distributed relatively large resources and was based on objective rules for disbursement, breaking away from the previous discretionary and clientelist systems.[19]

The share of the top 1% of income earners also increased under the Lula presidency, despite fluctuations caused by the financial crisis of 2007–2009 which primarily impacted capital income, while the share of the top 10% was almost unchanged. However, the Brazilian middle class saw a relative decline compared to both the poor and the very rich. Specifically, the middle 40% saw a decrease in their share of income from 2001 to 2015.[20] As Laura Carvalho notes, "what for some was an income increase, for others was inflation," which "was felt mostly by those whose salaries were growing less – those at the middle of the pyramid," and they "started to complain about the increased cost of domestic work, hairdressers, construction."[21] A discontent middle class played a significant role in the wave of unrest that began in June 2013, leading to the impeachment of President Dilma Rousseff in 2016 and eventually to the election of Jair Bolsonaro as president in 2018.

Redistributive policies in Brazil also influenced the country's political landscape. Historically, the North-East region was considered underdeveloped compared to the more modern South and was known for its clientelist politics.[22] In Brazil, clientelism should be understood in the context of the long-standing tradition of "*coronelismo*" during the First Brazilian Republic (1889–1930). This term refers to a system of power

[18] World Inequality Database n.d.

[19] Ansell and Mitchell 2011, and Wylde 2012.

[20] Source: World Inequality Database n.d. See Alvaredo et al. 2018. On the "squeezing of the middle class," see Gethin and Morgan 2021, Figure A16.

[21] Carvalho 2018, 40.

[22] Geddes and Ribeiro Neto 1992.

that originated at the municipal level, where vote trading played a crucial role. These political machines were largely based on power structures that were, and still are, more pronounced in regions of Brazil that have experienced less industrialization and modernization. During the years of the dictatorship, the northeastern part of the country showed the most support for the dictatorship, and it was not a coincidence that it was overrepresented in the Brazilian legislature.[23] During Lula's presidency and especially during his second term, the North-East saw a significant shift to the left, following a reorientation of social policies such as the flagship *Bolsa Familia* program, and of the Workers' Party itself, that in the same years was being abandoned by a disappointed middle class.[24] The result was visible in the runoff of the 2018 presidential elections, when the North-East, which was the poorest region of the country with a per capita income barely above half of the national average, was the only region where the losing candidate, Fernando Haddad, received a majority of the votes. This region also leaned decisively in favor of Lula in the presidential election of 2022.

As a final observation on the advancements made in Brazil since the return of democracy, life expectancy at birth has significantly improved over the years, rising from around 64 years in 1985 to over 75 years in 2019, only slightly less than in the United States (Figure 6.5 at page 93).

BRAZIL'S "ANTI-PARTY SYSTEM"

On January 15, 1985, Tancredo Neves was elected president of Brazil, along with his vice president, José Sarney. The election was indirect and followed the rules set by the dictatorship, but it also marked its termination. The beginning of democracy was marred by tragedy: On the day before his inauguration, Neves was rushed to the hospital and after a series of unsuccessful surgical operations, he died on April 21. Sarney, who had supported the 1964 coup d'état, became president in his place.

The biographies of Tancredo Neves and José Sarney are cases of parallel lives that illustrate important long-standing traits of Brazilian politics. Prior to the dictatorship, Neves was a prominent leader of the *Partido Social Democrático* (Social Democratic Party, or PSD), which, despite its name, was a relatively centrist party. The PSD was established in 1945 by President Getúlio Vargas as he navigated the transition from his

[23] See Geddes and Ribeiro Neto 1992, Table 5.
[24] Avelar 2021, 107.

dictatorial "Estado Novo" regime to democracy, along with another party, the *Partido Trabalhista Brasileiro* (Brazilian Labor Party, or PTB), that was meant to cover the left flank of the PSD. After being ousted from power in 1945, Vargas was elected president in 1951, but in August 1954, amidst scandals and political unrest, he took his own life.[25] The alliance between these two parties, the PSD and PTB, proved to be unbeatable against their main adversary, the conservative *União Democrática Nacional* (National Democratic Union, or UDN),[26] until the advent of the dictatorship in 1964 changed the political landscape. In the mid-1950s, José Sarney began his political career with the UDN.

The creation of the PSD and the PTB under the leadership of Getúlio Vargas was a political strategy aimed at appealing to different groups of voters with the same goal of securing Vargas' political future. This type of party building, not unlike what we have observed in Russia, is common in autocratic regimes that seek to imitate democracies, and in Brazil, it is rooted in a tradition of political parties that are highly opportunistic. In 1965, all existing parties were banned and two new parties, the *Aliança Renovadora Nacional* (National Renewal Alliance, or ARENA) and the *Movimento Democrático Brasileiro* (Brazilian Democratic Movement, or MDB), were created. ARENA was the ruling party, while the MDB was meant to play the role of the opposition, that in the minds of the top military brass in power had to be very well behaved, or else.

Some of the trappings of democracy were preserved, and the military went to great lengths to maintain a veneer of legitimacy. However, the regime was indeed dictatorial, especially after the passage of the "Institutional Act No. 5" in December 1969, which suspended all constitutional protections. The military was responsible for widespread repression of opponents, including torture and extrajudicial killings. Politicians "who wanted to remain in politics and had not been arrested or had their mandates revoked, were forced to choose a party."[27]

[25] In what was his "final political triumph" (Schwarcz and Starling 2018, 467), considering that he left in disarray an opposition that was already savoring victory.

[26] The UDN did formally support Jânio Quadros, who was elected president in 1960, who however was a populist outsider on whose figure I shall return.

[27] Schwarcz and Starling 2018, 525. On the appearance of legality, see Schwarcz and Starling 2018, 522–523; Pereira 2005, chapter 2 in particular, and Skidmore 1988, 52–101. Much has been written on the reality of the dictatorship and on repression. For a vivid account of the key years of 1974 and 1975 in the ABC region (the industrial area nearby São Paulo, of which I will say more), and of the tragic consequences for the direct victims of repression and their families, see French 2020, chapter 10.

Many politicians from the pre-dictatorship UDN joined the ARENA party, including José Sarney, the son of a wealthy landowner from Maranhao in the Northeastern region of Brazil. Sarney incarnated the way the business of politics was – and to a degree, still is – conducted in Northern Brazil, pervaded by forms of clientelism, nepotism, and corruption. He was a successful politician during the dictatorship years, serving as the governor of his home state and later as a senator. Many politicians from the PSD joined ARENA for refuge, while the more progressive ones migrated to MDB, including Tancredo Neves. He was a seasoned politician and an expert negotiator, first elected as a federal deputy in 1950. He later served as a minister in Getúlio Vargas' last government and held the position of prime minister briefly.

During the dictatorship, Tancredo Neves was a federal deputy, then a senator for the MDB. In 1982, he was elected governor of Minas Gerais.[28] In 1984, he played a crucial role in the "*Diretas Já*" campaign, which demanded direct presidential elections, propelling him to run for president. In short, both Tancredo Neves and José Sarney flourished politically during the dictatorship years, but in different ways. Neves was less submissive, aligning himself with the MDB, a political party that served as both a tool of the dictatorship and a vehicle for change. On the other hand, Sarney thrived with ARENA, which came to be known as the "yes, sir" party.

These historical antecedents reveal key characteristics of the Brazilian party system that still persist today. With the notable exception of the PT, contemporary political parties tend to be nonideological, artificially created, and highly opportunistic, to the point that some of them are referred to as "parties for rent." The characteristics of such an "anti-party system," as Giovanni Sartori defined it,[29] have significant implications for understanding corruption in Brazil. To interpret it, it is crucial to examine certain key aspects of the transition to democracy that took place in the mid-1980s.

A TRANSITION TO DEMOCRACY AND TO CONSOCIATIVISM

During the dictatorship years, the presence of a limited but official channel for political debate had a significant impact on the future. The two officially recognized political parties, ARENA and MDB, served as the

[28] Direct elections for governors were reinstated in 1982 and for the president only with the democratic Constitution of 1988.

[29] Sartori 1993 (cited in Desposato 2006).

primary platforms for political activity, with politicians like Tancredo Neves and José Sarney continuing their careers despite the regime changes of 1964 and 1985. In the latter years of the dictatorship, attempts to challenge the boundaries of what was allowed grew bolder. The top tier of power gradually became aware of the inevitability of a transition to some form of democracy, as the economic crisis of the early 1980s undermined the regime's popularity and provided support for stronger forms of opposition.[30] The process of gradual re-democratization, known as "*abertura*" (opening), also expanded the political landscape beyond the two sanctioned parties.

Industrialization paved the way for stronger and more independent trade unions, particularly in São Paulo and the neighboring region comprised of the municipalities Santo André (A), São Bernardo do Campo (B), and São Caetano do Sul (C), known collectively as "ABC." It was in the ABC where a young Lula, a skilled metalworker, honed his skills as a trade unionist. A very gifted deal-maker, he rose to national prominence by leading a series of successful strikes in 1978 and 1979. In this environment, the PT was founded in 1980 as a coalition of forces that included trade unions, Catholic progressives, and traditional Marxist groups.[31] The PT established a new political tradition in Brazil, represented a turning point as it was programmatic, and had a strong identity, eventually to both attract and repel, creating a divide between "*petistas*" (PT supporters) and "*anti-petistas.*"

The result of various strategies enacted during the late 1970s and early 1980s led to a democratic transition that was partly managed by the military regime. Although the military's control over the democratization process diminished over time, especially after the popular and enthusiastic "*Diretas Já*" campaign in 1983 and 1984, which called for the direct election of the president and saw collaboration between the officially sanctioned MDB and other opposition forces such as the PT, no single political entity had the power to dictate the agenda. There was no winning coalition that could come together to form a comprehensive plan beyond a shared desire for the return of democracy. The transition ultimately resulted in a political compact that comprised strong democratic institutions, but also

30 The dictatorship was also taking a toll on the military. See Schwarcz and Starling 2018, 537–538, who note that "the bureaucracy created to administer the violence had taken over the armed forces and become the source of power in the military hierarchy," which in turn created frictions.

31 French 2020.

maintained a political representation based on clientelism and a disturbing level of impunity for military personnel responsible for serious human rights violations.

The compromise that was reached was reflected in the new constitution, which was approved in October 1988. The country was to be a federal presidential republic, and significant consideration was given to defining the powers of its main institutions to ensure their stability. Important powers were granted to the presidency, in response to its ineffectiveness during the previous democratic period. However, the new constitution and accompanying legislation led to an increase in party fragmentation and incentivized the formation of new parties. Additionally, the overrepresentation of Northern regions, where vote-buying was prevalent and support for the dictatorship had been stronger, became even more pronounced.[32] In conclusion, the political landscape that emerged after the transition was marked by significant and sometimes subtle continuities with the past. The presence of numerous small political parties offered opportunities for maneuver to established elites that had both the resources and the inclination to forge mutually beneficial arrangements.[33]

Collusive fragmentation was also facilitated through a separate channel. During the drafting of the new constitution, the lack of strong parties and the absence of a clear winning coalition resulted in many principles being given constitutional protection, while they would typically be addressed through ordinary legislation in other democracies. The Constitution, with its 250 articles, is lengthy and highly detailed, leading to frequent needs for modifications. While most of the approximately 130 amendments that have been approved to date may have been relatively noncontentious, there has been an incentive, and at times a need, to secure not just a simple

32 The increased fragmentation that followed the 1985 democratization was already evident to Geddes and Ribeiro Neto 1992. See their Table 3, offering a summary of the Chamber of Deputies elections from 1946 to 1991, and also their Table 4, on changes in party registration rules and number of parties, from 1945 to 1992 (when there were 37 of them). On the overrepresentation of north, northeast, and center-west, their Table 5 reports that their aggregate percentage of seats held by deputies actually increased, to reach 49.4% in 1988, "despite substantial population shifts toward the more developed south." They also provide examples of incentives to form new parties.

33 On the "rhetoric of pacts" in Brazil, see Avelar 2021. See also Marcos Nobre's considerations on what he calls "Pemebedismo" (from PMDB, a centrist political party), "a closing of the political system against society" which took advantage from the "lack of a unified route and of a party (or coalition of parties) which could channel reformist aspirations" (Nobre 2013, 11).

majority for legislative approval but also the supermajority required to amend the Constitution. This further increased the need for political bargaining, patronage, "pork-barrel" spending and outright corruption to reach consensus.[34]

Considering the 2018 elections, when a total of nine parties received more than 5% of the votes,[35] Octavio Amorim Neto notes that they delivered "the most fragmented legislatures in the history of post-1945 democracy," and that legislative fragmentation, and increasingly weak parties, "mean that presidents' coalitional necessities have been growing."[36] An increased need for political maneuvering is in sharp contrast with any hopes for societal cleansing that may have arisen from the *Lava Jato* investigation.[37]

***

I summarize the factors that will be key to my interpretation of corruption in Brazil. There is a multitude of political parties, none of which is very large, and which tend to be highly opportunistic and weakly programmatic at best. This fragmentation requires presidents to find ways to gather the necessary votes to pass legislation. The difficulty is compounded by the level of detail of the 1988 Constitution, which often requires the formation of supermajorities to amend it. This situation is intertwined with a long-standing tradition of clientelism perpetuated during the dictatorship and maintained after the transition to democracy, serving the interests of elites. Elites in Brazil have been structurally powerful over time, as evidenced by the persistent levels of economic and social inequality, and their structural power can be seen as the backdrop for the equally structural weakness of political parties.

An important institution that we have not yet considered is the judiciary. Unlike the subservient judiciary in Russia, Brazil's judiciary has undergone significant transformation since the years of the dictatorship and is now a powerful and assertive part of the traditional triangle of power. Its ability to

[34] According to Article 60 of the Constitution, in order to be approved, a proposed amendment has to be debated and voted in two rounds in both the Chamber of Deputies and the Senate, while always obtaining at least three-fifths of the votes. Benjamin Fogel 2019 notes that "by ensuring that any left government would have to deal with a corrupt political machinery if it wanted to get anything done, the military and the bourgeoisie were able to insulate themselves from the dangers of a future left government."

[35] There are currently 31 political parties officially registered at the Superior Electoral Court (Tribunal Superior Eleitoral n.d.).

[36] Amorim Neto 2019, who notes that "a judicious distribution of patronage and pork is a vital aspect of legislative majority building in Brazil."

[37] Pereira and Bertholini 2019.

address high-level corruption also serves as a test of its strength, especially when political actors are involved. To the available evidence on corruption, we first turn our attention.

CORRUPTION IN BRAZIL

Since the transition to democracy, mass media have uncovered many scandals that have gained widespread public attention and contributed to a high perception of corruption. According to Transparency International's Corruption Perception Index, in 2019 Brazil was ranked 106th out of 198 countries, with a score of 35. This places it better than Russia (ranked 137th), but worse than China (ranked 80th) and far behind countries such as Italy (50th), Spain (30th), and the United States (23rd). Over time, perceptions of corruption in Brazil have fluctuated (Figure 7.3). We observe an improvement in perceptions of corruption after 1995, during the presidency of Cardoso. The *Mensalão* scandal in 2005 caused a sharp drop in these perceptions, followed by a brief rebound, before declining again after the *Lava Jato* investigations. Statistics on victimization also support this pessimistic view, with Brazilians frequently reporting personal experiences of corruption.[38]

Bombarded by a litany of high-profile corruption scandals, and themselves experiencing episodes of corruption rather frequently in their daily lives, it is no surprise that Brazilians believe that corruption is a serious problem, as various surveys witness. In particular, public concern about corruption increased in the wake of the *Mensalão* and *Lava Jato* scandals.[39]

When the current Brazilian democracy was only seven years old, Barbara Geddes and Artur Ribeiro Neto observed that "although corruption scandals erupted from time to time during the previous democratic regime (especially during the last year of the Vargas administration and the last year of the Goulart administration), these past episodes lacked the magnitude and pervasiveness of the recent one[s]."[40] If anything, the public visibility of corruption scandals was to increase significantly in the course of the more recent decades. To the several high-profile corruption

[38] Transparency International's Global Corruption Barometer (TI-GCB) reports for 2019 8% of the population declaring at least one experience of corruption in the previous year.

[39] For the years since 2006, see the Latin American Public Opinion Project n.d., and Senters and Winters 2019 integrate different data sources and provide a picture that extends further back in time.

[40] Geddes and Ribeiro Neto 1992.

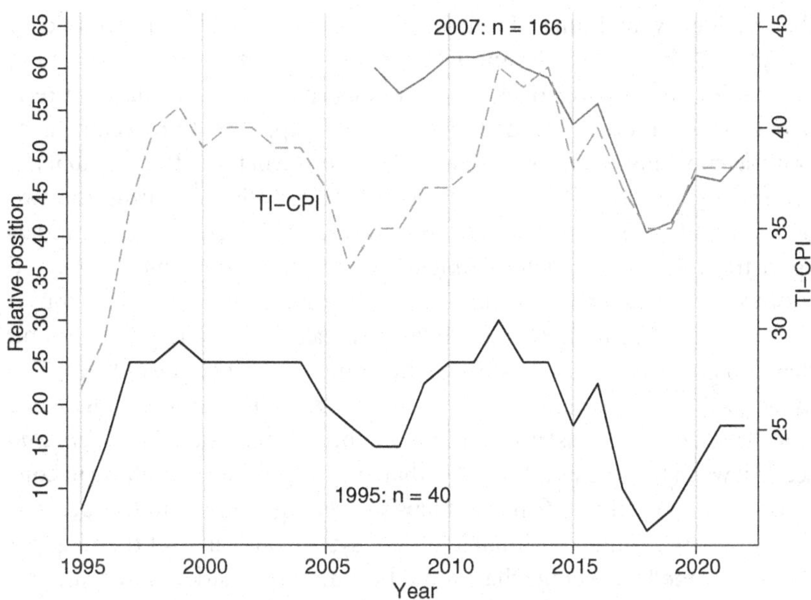

Figure 7.3 TI-CPI and its relative position (Brazil)
Dashed line: TI-CPI (right axis; values before 2012 are multiplied by 10). Relative positions (left axis): Percentiles, relative to group of countries (of size n) continuously present from a given date. Higher relative positions (and values of the TI-CPI) correspond to less perceived corruption. See Escresa and Picci 2016 for further details.

scandals that had taken place before *Mensalão*, the Brazilian slang expression "*acabou em pizza*" ("it ended up in pizza," meaning, in nothing) applies.[41] Some of these scandals lasted for years and eventually fed into later cases, such as the 1987 *Ferrovia Norte-Sul* (North-South Railway) bid-rigging scheme where some of the bidders, including the construction firm Odebrecht, were also involved in *Lava Jato* 25 years later. This intermingling of scandals reflects the deeply ingrained nature of corruption practices in Brazil.

Not all corruption cases in Brazil went completely unpunished. In 1992, the corruption scandal involving President Collor led to a public outcry and his resignation. Another significant scandal, the "Budget Dwarves" during

[41] Da Ros and Taylor 2022, 33. I only consider national scandals and omit those of a more local nature, as important as they occasionally were. I derive information on corruption scandals from several sources, but particularly from Da Ros and Taylor 2022. See also, for a summary of high-profile corruption episodes up to 2010, Power and Taylor 2011, 2–3 and Table 1.1.

the presidency of Itamar Franco, saw several congressmen accused of accepting bribes to alter the annual budget in favor of specific construction companies, but had relatively modest consequences.[42] During the presidency of Fernando Henrique Cardoso, whose appointed prosecutor general was mockingly referred to as the "Shelver-General of the Republic,"[43] several corruption scandals were mostly inconclusive.[44] During the two terms of Lula as president, there were several major corruption scandals apart from *Mensalão*, such as *Sanguesuga* (2006), *Satiagraha* (2008), and *Castello de Areia* (2009), none of which resulted in significant consequences. The *Anaconda* scandal in 2003 revealed a network of corruption that also included judges, leading to the imprisonment of one of them. The same year, the *Banestado* scandal involved *doleiros*, or money changers, who have been a persistent presence in corrupt activities. The *Mensalão* scandal was a turning point in more than one way. Besides resulting in convictions, it marked a shift in the focus of investigations from Congress to a more assertive and coordinated judicial system, and also set the stage for the type of media coverage that would become a hallmark of *Lava Jato*.[45]

Lava Jato broke out in March 2014, during the presidency of Dilma Rousseff.[46] It began with a routine police investigation into the activities of money launderer Alberto Youssef, who had previously been implicated in the *Banestado* scandal and who operated out of a gas station located in the heart of Brasília. The case was handled by a competent and ambitious team of local prosecutor, Deltan Dallagnol, and judge, Sérgio Moro, both based in Curitiba, the capital of Paraná. The judicial offices in

42 Da Ros and Tailor 2022, 226.

43 "*Engavetador-Geral da República*"; interview with former prosecutor general of the Republic Rodrigo Janot, October 29, 2018, Brasília. See also Da Ros and Taylor 2022, 90.

44 In the *Marka-Fonte Cindam* scandal in 1999, a businessman served time in jail, and the 1999 São Paulo Labor Court scandal showed the limitations of accountability due to lengthy judicial procedures and uncertain outcomes. The Judicial Debts of DNER ("*Precatórios do DNER*") in 1999, the SUDAM scandal in 2001, and the Banestado scandal in 2002, also had limited consequences. The "Re-Election Scandal" of 1997, in which two legislators were accused of exchanging votes to support a constitutional amendment allowing for the reelection of prefects, governors, and the president of the Republic (Constitutional Amendment 16/1997) is a clear example of vote-buying, which would resurface in the *Mensalão* scandal. See also Da Ros and Taylor 2022, 227.

45 Da Ros and Taylor 2022, 130.

46 The "seventy-nine numbered phases to Lava Jato in Curitiba between 2014 and 2021" were "a bit of an artificial construct: a phase is merely a series of coordinated actions by police and prosecutors, which may or may not lead to concrete legal actions," while they "clearly evolved in pursuit of distinct targets." Da Ros and Taylor 2022, 104. See also Lagunes and Svejnar 2020.

Curitiba had the jurisdiction to cover the crime-ridden tri-border area of Brazil, Argentina, and Paraguay, providing ample opportunities for them to hone their skills.[47]

The timing of the scandal was unpropitious for President Rousseff, who had been easily elected in October 2010 coat tailing on the popularity of her predecessor. The PT-led government responded to the financial crisis of 2007–2009 by implementing expansionary policies, which helped cushion the economy. However, inflation eventually increased and an overvalued currency began to hurt exports and the trade balance,[48] as it became apparent that the previous fiscal discipline was giving way to creative accounting practices. The *Mensalão* case finally reached the Supreme Federal Court in 2013, attracting widespread public attention. A powerful wave of protests started in June 2013 in São Paulo, initially triggered by a hike in bus fares. The demonstrations were met with a strong police response, which further fueled public outrage.[49] The protesters were mainly left-leaning students, but they were soon joined by members of the middle class. As the *Lava Jato* investigations gained momentum, corruption became the main focus of public discontent.[50]

An email from Alberto Youssef to a high-ranking executive of the state-run oil company Petrobras, Paulo Roberto Costa, was the catalyst for a significant development in the investigation, eventually reaching the Supreme Federal Court, which sided with the prosecutors in its rulings.[51] Jail was used as a means to exert pressure on defendants, a technique that had been used in Italy by the "*Mani pulite*" prosecutors in the early 1990s, closely studied by Sérgio Moro.[52] Pressure on defendants led to further revelations, creating a snowball effect. Pressure on defendants was also made possible by two recent laws allowing for leniency

[47] There, the problems of a multiborder jurisdiction are enhanced by the presence of a free-trade zone, "minimizing regulation and compounding the possibilities for illicit trade" (Shelley 2014, 149). See also Da Ros and Taylor 2022, 104, who describe the state of Paraná as a "hotbed of smuggling and money laundering," and Deltan Dellagnol's reference to his learning how to investigate money laundering schemes in Curitiba, in Lagunes 2020a, 120.

[48] Brazil had run sizable trade balance surpluses between 2002 and 2007, and in 2008 started running deficits until 2015. The biggest deficit, of 2.22% of GDP, occurred in 2014. Source: The World Bank.

[49] Benson and Levine 2013. See also Winters and Weitz-Shapiro 2014, and Avelar 2021.

[50] Da Ros and Taylor 2022, 114. The cost overruns associated with the 2014 World Cup and the 2016 Olympics, both hosted by Brazil, as well as the perceived mismanagement of the Zika virus outbreak starting in 2015, were to contribute to discontent in the years that followed.

[51] Da Ros and Taylor 2022, 134–135.

[52] Lagunes 2020b.

agreements that reflected a belated attempt by President Rousseff to fend off public demands for further anti-corruption measures.[53] In contributing to her political downfall, these measures demonstrate how strategies can sometimes backfire within the "lower subsystem" described in Chapter 5. Illegal leaks to the press generated media coverage, which was then used as evidence in court in an almost tautological manner. Capitalizing on the wave of public support, the press coverage further fueled the anti-corruption movement.[54]

Accusations to Petrobras executives were used to reach other culprits, in particular, a number of construction firms, uncovering a colossal bid-rigging scheme where "only 7 cartel-companies carved up between 55 and 75 percent of all government contracts between 2003 and 2014."[55] Following these successes, and mounting public support, Curitiba's task force felt confident enough to step into political terrain by targeting former congressmen, together with the elites of the most important construction firms, Odebrecht among them, which was to be involved in several spin-off investigations in many Latin American countries.[56] By August 2015, the scandal moved close to Lula, with the arrest of his former head of staff, José Dirceu, who had also been involved in the *Mensalão* case 10 years earlier. Other associates and political allies of Lula were involved, such as former finance ministers Guido Mantega and Antonio Palocci, who were both arrested in September 2016. These arrests signaled that Brazil's institutions were better equipped, and ready, to investigate and prosecute corruption at the highest level, and that any claim by the PT to be "different" was becoming difficult to sustain.[57]

The government's response to what had become the perfect storm was inadequate. It decided spending cuts, contradicting its previous narrative of successful intervention into the economy during the *milagrinho* years, and

[53] Law 12.846 of August 1, 2013, and Law 12.850 of August 2, 2013. The threat of jail became more credible following a ruling by the Supreme Federal Tribunal (STF) in 2016, with Habeas Corpus n. 126.292 which made it possible to jail convicted defendants without, as it had been, waiting until all appeals had been exhausted. The decision was to be reverted by the STF in November 2019 (Glezer 2020), within a wider backsliding that I will discuss.

[54] See Avelar 2021, and in particular, in chapter 5, the section significantly titled "The tautological rhetoric of Lava Jato."

[55] Valarini and Pohlmann 2019.

[56] See the account in Gaspar 2020. On the corrupt reverberations in Latin America of Odebrecht's activities, see also Wahrman 2020.

[57] Michener and Pereira 2016. These progresses were however rather circumscribed geographically: The great majority of Lava Jato indictments and convictions occurred in the trial courts of Curitiba and Rio de Janeiro, with São Paulo a very distant third. See Da Ros and Taylor 2022, 153.

it proposed unconvincingly more anti-corruption reforms. As it had been the case in Italy during the early 1990s *Mani pulite* scandal, the successes of the judges granted them a popularity which shielded them from retaliation and allowed them to achieve even more victories. The accumulation of events ultimately led to the impeachment of President Dilma Rousseff on August 31, 2016. The impeachment was not directly related to Lava Jato but instead was due to allegations of creative accounting practices. She would not have been impeached for such a mundane trifle had it not been for *Lava Jato*, but the spirit of those months was well summarized by what a Minister of the Rousseff's government, Romero Jucá, was recorded saying in a leaked telephone conversation that took place in March 2016. A change in government was needed to "stop the bleeding," and it would need a "great national alliance," or whatever help could arrive, "from the Supreme Court or from any quarter."[58] Dilma Rousseff served as what in Brazil is known as the "*boi de piranha*" ("ox for the piranhas"), as when in order to cross a river infested by piranhas, an ox is pushed into the water to satisfy the carnivorous fishes, so that the others – here, the other politicians, and members of assorted elites that *Lava Jato* had targeted – may cross to safety.[59]

Rousseff's impeachment and subsequent resignation was the high point of *Lava Jato*. Its task force "played at cat and mouse for much of 2016 and, especially, 2017"[60] with the next president, Michel Temer, until he too was engulfed in scandals. As for former President Lula, in July 2017 he was sentenced by Moro's trial court for allegedly having received a beach-side apartment from a construction firm as a corrupt gift. He entered jail in January 2018, and in August of the same year, the Supreme Federal Court ruled that, according to the Clean Slate Law of 2010 (see later in this chapter), he could not run in the presidential elections to be held in October.[61] John French notes that Lula, the former metalworker, "even at the pinnacle of his prestige […] had never fooled himself into believing that he had been honestly, definitively accepted by those on Brazilian society's upper floors."[62] *Lava Jato* also was a decisive action for the re-establishment of a conservative social order.

These were the conditions that led to the election of Jair Bolsonaro, with a robust majority of Brazilians ready to try change or just to punish

58 Valente 2016.
59 See Pedlowski 2016, and Da Ros and Taylor 2022, 143.
60 Da Ros and Taylor 2022, 144.
61 Da Ros and Taylor 2022, 144.
62 French 2020, 360.

a political elite that was perceived to be utterly corrupt. In terms of corruption, the years of the Bolsonaro's presidency were no better and perhaps worse than those preceding it. But before proceeding further in time, we examine what we can learn from the long string of scandals that I briefly summarized. They are not representative of corruption in Brazil, but they provide a "core sampling"[63] that is helpful in uncovering its regularities.

First, we observe the wide scope of the cases. They were not the cabal of a few criminals, but involved complex networks that included politicians, administrators, intermediaries, and important firms. The extent and sophistication of these networks, as well as the presence of intermediaries with recurrent roles, indicates the presence of a stable demand for the services they offered. Corruption has been systematic, and this conclusion is reinforced by the fact that the same names often appear in more than one scandal, sometimes over the course of several decades. Second, it is noteworthy that publicly controlled firms were involved in corruption scandals in Brazil. For example, Correios was involved in the *Mensalão* case and Petrobras was involved in the *Lava Jato* scandal. Furthermore, many privately owned firms, such as those involved in the *Ferrovia Norte-Sul* episodes of corrupt bid-rigging, also had close connections with the political sphere.[64] Last, most of these scandals "ended up in pizza," until when they didn't. Some of these corruption cases, such as the Collorgate in 1992, had significant political repercussions, leading to the resignation of its eponymous protagonist. The *Mensalão* case, on the other hand, marked a departure from the previous pattern of judicial impunity and set the stage for the more far-reaching consequences of *Lava Jato*. Finally, we note a shift in the ways in which corruption scandals have emerged. Initially, such scandals were often exposed through accusations made by political allies or even family members, as was the case with President Collor's resignation following accusations by his brother. Similarly, the exposure of the *Mensalão* scandal was the result of internal conflicts within the coalition supporting President Lula. Over time, however, the judiciary and investigative authorities became more proactive, utilizing their newfound powers and abilities to uncover corruption, following a series of reforms. We now consider them.

[63] In the spirit of Picci and Vannucci 2018, 71–72.

[64] Malu Gaspar's "The Organization" (Gaspar 2020), a compelling history of Odebrecht from its beginning as an outsider in the rarefied world of Brazil's patrician businessmen, to become one of the most important industrial conglomerates in Latin America, provides a vivid example of the concrete working of such relationships over several decades.

THE JUDICIARY AND REFORMS

Brazil's judiciary system since the end of the dictatorship is a testament to how deep-rooted institutional changes can mask forms of persistence. As previously mentioned, the military regime maintained a façade of legal legitimacy and formally upheld judicial independence. However, the judiciary was timid and subservient during the dictatorship, and the long tenures of judges favored institutional persistence after the return to democracy.[65] The 1988 Constitution provided strong protection to the judiciary[66] and allocated it a generous budget, which in 2014, expressed as a percentage of GDP (1.2%), was approximately three times that of Germany and an order of magnitude greater than in the United States, Great Britain, or Spain.[67] These resources have sustained a massive system where judges, selected on stringent standards, are highly paid and well supported.

These facts must be viewed in the context of the broader agreement that facilitated a smooth transition to democracy, leading to the establishment of several extra-constitutional practices that gave elites significant control. In the political realm, we have discussed the impact of political fragmentation and the persistence of clientelist practices. In the administration of justice, a sprawling and overfed administration has been at the constant risk of collapsing under its own weight, burdened by biblical waiting times and often inconsistent decisions.[68] Additionally, the Constitution of 1988, which permits a wide standing to bring constitutionality suits, has resulted in a large number of players utilizing the Supreme Federal Court as a de facto final court of appeal. This has created a significant workload for the court.[69] Brazil's elites have an advantage in navigating such system, and recurring cases of corruption among judges – of which the São Paulo Regional Labor Court case of 1999 represents but one example – have provided a further possibility, for the privileged few, of obtaining injustice.

The almost proverbial ineffectiveness of Brazil's judiciary has led to widespread cynicism and a disconnect between lofty and progressive principles and the reality on the ground. When considering corruption,

[65] On judiciary subservience in the years of the dictatorship, see Pereira 2005, and Pereira 2010.

[66] Da Ros and Taylor 2017. See also Da Ros and Ingram 2018, and Arantes 2005.

[67] Da Ros and Taylor 2017, Figure 1.

[68] See Da Ros and Taylor 2017 on "so-called 'legal insecurity' ('*insegurança jurídica*') – a widely used, if derogatory, term referring to the unpredictability of judicial decisions."

[69] Da Ros and Taylor 2017.

the situation began to change with *Mensalão*, and the tide really turned with *Lava Jato*. In view was no longer the inefficiency of a self-referential and overpaid machinery of judges who often seemed to be too smart for the good of justice. Those same resources, and that same sophistication, seemed then to be employed for resolute action. For Judge Sérgio Moro, the successes of *Lava Jato* represented a personal triumph and consequent elevation to national and international stardom, with *The New York Times* publishing a "profile" dedicated to him – and to his bid "to clean up Brazil from the bench". As an example of the then prevailing mood, it noted that "outside the courthouse, T-shirts with Judge Sérgio Moro's picture go for $12".[70]

To understand these changes, we must consider the reforms of the years leading to *Lava Jato*. An important institution is the Public Prosecutor's Office (*Ministério Público* (MP)), to which the Constitution of 1988 attributes wide-ranging responsibilities, that some have described as representing a sort of "fourth branch of government."[71] The MP's responsibilities and influence grew over time, with two major developments. In 1993, under President Franco, the MP's duties and prerogatives were clarified[72] and the newly instituted federal attorney general[73] took over the MP's former role as government solicitor, allowing it to focus more on its prosecutorial role. Ten years later, in 2003, President Lula accepted to choose the prosecutor general[74] from a list of three names (the so-called *lista tríplice*) voted by the National Association of Federal Prosecutors (*Associação Nacional dos Procuradores da República*), granting the MP greater autonomy.[75] One of the prosecutor generals chosen according to this informal rule under Dilma Rousseff's presidency was Rodrigo Janot, who played an important and proactive role during the *Lava Jato* years.

To address the widespread dissatisfaction with the judiciary, the Brazilian government made significant reforms with Constitutional Amendment No. 45 in December 2004. This amendment established two oversight bodies, the *Conselho Nacional de Justiça* (CNJ) and the *Conselho Nacional do*

[70] Londoño 2017.
[71] Da Ros and Taylor 2017, and references therein.
[72] Law n. 8625 on MP, and Supplementary Law n. 75 of May 20.
[73] *Advocacia-Geral da União*, instituted with Supplementary Law n. 73 of February 10, 1993.
[74] *Procurador-Geral da República*; the head of the MP, that according to Article 128 of the Constitution is "named by the President."
[75] See the discussion in Da Ros and Taylor 2022, 119. The *Associação Nacional dos Procuradores da República* had first proposed a list of three candidates to President Cardoso, in 2000, who however decided otherwise, confirming Geraldo Brindeiro, whose reputation as a "shelver" I have mentioned.

Ministério Público (CNMP) as well as mechanisms for binding precedents, whose lack had contributed to enormous caseloads.[76] During Lula's tenure as president, the federal police was overhauled.[77] In 2013, civil and administrative liability for corporate corruption was established,[78] in line with the global trend emphasizing compliance with organizational standards that I discussed in Chapter 2. A new law on organized crime was also introduced, which spelled out penalties for racketeering.[79] The laws also provided guidelines for leniency agreements with companies and for plea-bargaining ("*colaboração premiada*"), which was previously an option but lacked clear standards. As we have seen, this latter tool was crucial in the *Lava Jato* investigation.[80]

To combat corruption, various laws were enacted.[81] In 2001, the federal executive branch established the anti-corruption agency (*Corregedoria-Geral da União*), which superseded previous anti-corruption units within individual government departments.[82] The criminal code was reformed in 2003, resulting in longer jail terms for bribery.[83] Public procurement, which is often associated with corruption, has been a target of multiple reforms since the transition to democracy.[84] Additionally, money laundering was

76 These were the "*súmula vinculante*" and "*repercussão geral.*" "The first is a mechanism of binding precedent in constitutional questions that have been settled repeatedly by the STF" (Da Ros and Taylor 2017); the second is "an analogue to the U.S. procedural device of certiorari by granting the STF the power to refuse to hear extraordinary appeals which lack general repercussions" (Rosenn 2014). The practical consequences of these reforms however were limited by well-organized corporatist interests of the judges.

77 As Judge Sérgio Moro himself acknowledged "the merit of the government of former president Luiz Inácio Lula da Silva in strengthening mechanisms for the control of corruption, including prevention and repression, especially the investments made in the Federal Police during the first term, the strengthening of the Comptroller General … and the preservation of [prosecutorial] independence …" (July 12, 2017, in a sentence; cited in Da Ros and Taylor 2022, 47). On the same question, see also Glezer 2020.

78 Law 12.846 on anti-corruption law (or "Clean Companies Law") of August 1, 2013.

79 Law 12.850 of August 2, 2013.

80 See Da Ros and Taylor 2022, 119.

81 Engelmann and de Moura Menuzzi 2020, Table 1, list a total of 13 "anti-corruption laws" between 2000 and 2019.

82 Provisional measure n. 2.143-31. Its creation represented "an important breakthrough, pulling many of the previous anti-corruption units out of the different ministries they oversaw and into one central agency" (Da Ros and Taylor 2022, 58). Its powers were expanded in 2003 with Law n. 10.683 on Cabinet reform.

83 Law n. 10.763.

84 Starting from Decree-law n. 2.300 of 1986, which in 1993 was replaced by the *Lei de Licitações* (public bidding) n. 8666, that followed the *Collorgate* (see Gaspar 2020, 91–92), and then, in 2002, by the "Pregão" Law n. 10.520. In 2011, Law n. 12.462 further intervened on the matter.

criminalized in 1998, with a significant impact on the "doleiro" figure that was prevalent in Brazil.[85] Overall, accountability improved gradually over time, in terms of both vertical and horizontal institutions, as the governance structure became denser and more interconnected.[86] Other measures targeted the political sphere in an attempt to control political financing, although with limited success.[87] The most impactful change was the 2010 Clean Slate Law (*Lei da Ficha Limpa*), which prohibited politicians who have been convicted on appeal from running for office.[88] I mentioned that it was under this law that Lula was forbidden from running in the 2018 presidential election.

The cumulative effect of these incremental changes in accountability enabled the *Lava Jato* investigations, which implicated the same political forces – most notably, the PT – that had either promoted or accepted many of these changes. In Chapter 5, I presented a model of historical change that features a lower and an upper subsystem, also allowing for the interpretation of the paradox of why the PT, in particular, promoted reforms that ultimately led to its political downfall. In the lower subsystem, change can occur incrementally, almost unnoticed, as in Brazil, until it reaches a critical point, as it happened with *Lava Jato* and its huge political fallout. I will delve further into this issue in Chapter 11, where I will discuss the intrinsic unpredictability of the outcomes of anti-corruption policies.

FROM *LAVA JATO* TO THE BOLSONARO'S PRESIDENCY, AND BACK TO LULA

Lava Jato implicated leaders from the major political parties in Brazil and paved the way for the election of Jair Bolsonaro as president in October 2018. In the months before the elections, Bolsonaro successfully created a coalition from different interests and parts of society[89] and campaigned

85 With Law 9.613 that instituted the *Conselho de Controle de Atividades Financeiras* and that followed a 1986 Law (n. 7.492) on financial crimes and one (Law n. 8.021) on taxpayer identification.

86 Aranha 2020.

87 In 1993, with Law n. 8.713, which in fact "permitted campaign from businesses but not labor unions" (Fleischer 1997), to be modified in 1997 by Law 9.504, which introduced new types of electoral crimes, while Law 9.840 of 1999 further criminalized vote-buying. On a "tacit gentleman's agreement among politicians not to question each other's financing too vigorously," see Da Ros and Taylor 2022, 62.

88 Supplementary Law 135 of June 4, 2010. Attempts to regulate conflicts of interests are well represented by Law 12.813 of 2013.

89 Avelar 2021. On the motivations of the Bolsonaro vote, see Rennó 2020.

on an anti-corruption platform, promising to support the country's accountability institutions, the *Lava Jato* Task Force, and to establish "a decent government [that will be] different from all that which has thrown us into an ethical, moral, and fiscal crisis. A government without quid pro quo, without spurious agreements."[90] Days after Bolsonaro's election, Sérgio Moro accepted his offer to become Minister of Justice, which fueled accusations that he had been politically motivated in his work as a judge. Bolsonaro and his family soon became embroiled in allegations of crimes and corruption, leading to tensions with Moro and his eventual resignation in April 2020, after he was allegedly pressured to protect Bolsonaro's son, who had been accused of serious crimes.[91]

A significant blow to Moro's reputation came from the leak by *The Intercept Brazil* of personal digital messages exchanged with chief prosecutor Deltan Dellagnol and others involved in the *Lava Jato* investigations, which suggested that their actions were politically motivated.[92] The ensuing scandal contributed to a change in the political climate, leading to the release of Lula from prison in November 2019, following changes in the rules on prison on appeal that also reintroduced an element of impunity.[93] A free and politically reinvigorated Lula immediately began campaigning for the 2022 presidential election. Sérgio Moro also initially ran as a presidential candidate in the 2022 election, but soon dropped out of the race. He then turned his attention to the Senate and successfully ran for a seat in his home state of Paraná on a right-wing platform, effectively aligning himself with Bolsonaro.[94]

The impeachment of Dilma Rousseff in 2016 marked the high point of *Lava Jato,* with normalization and a reduction in anti-corruption efforts occurring under the subsequent presidency of Michel Temer. The *Lava Jato* investigations were officially ended in 2020,[95] and several accountability

[90] See Lagunes et al. 2021, also for the citation, and in particular Table 3 and 4 on "Candidate Jair Bolsonaro's promises to fight corruption."

[91] See Da Ros and Taylor 2022, 146–147, and Pinheiro da Fonseca 2022, who judges that all of Bolsonaro's career "is marked by corruption and suspicious enrichment of his wife and sons."

[92] The Intercept Brazil n.d.

[93] Da Ros and Taylor 2022, 173. The Supreme Court annulled a corruption conviction against Lula, relating to the beachfront property that he had allegedly received, in March 2021. A federal judge later archived the case, because of the Lula's age. See *Justiça* Federal da 1ª Região 2021.

[94] Veja 2022.

[95] Bolsonaro declared Lava Jato to be over because "there is no more corruption in the government" (Pineda Sleinan 2021). Commenting on this news, Celso Rocha de Barros notes that "ironically, on Wednesday the vice-leader of Bolsonaro's coalition in the Senate was found with about $5,000 in his underwear during a police raid for suspected embezzlement of COVID-19 funds." (Rocha de Barros 2020)

measures were reversed. Bolsonaro broke with the traditional custom of selecting the prosecutor general from the *lista tríplice* indicated by the Association of National Prosecutors.[96] An analysis by Paul Lagunes et al. of the anti-corruption promises made by Bolsonaro during his campaign found that in all cases there had been either a deterioration or no improvement.[97] The new congress returned to its usual ways of bargaining, and an informal coalition against *Lava Jato* was established in Brasília.[98]

In 2021, revelations surfaced of a secret budget used by the government to buy legislative support, which Bolsonaro later justified as a way of "calming down" the Congress.[99] With respect to *Mensalão*, whose monthly payments likely also had a calming effect on the recipients, under the unlikely anti-corruption candidate Bolsonaro, Brazilian politics came full circle.[100] Ominously, in a country that not too long ago suffered the horrors of a military dictatorship, Bolsonaro's flirting with the military has revitalized an antidemocratic sentiment that, in Brazil and elsewhere in Latin America, represents "the politics of antipolitics."[101]

On October 30, 2022, Lula made a remarkable political comeback by narrowly defeating Bolsonaro in the presidential election runoff. Just one week before the elections, Roberto Jefferson, the former small party leader who had sparked the *Mensalão* scandal in 2005 and now a Bolsonaro ally, once again grabbed the headlines. The Supreme Federal Court had ordered his detention after he violated the conditions of his confinement by publicly abusing Justice Cármen Lúcia online (calling her a "witch" and a "prostitute") and spreading false information. Misinformation and forms of violence characterized the presidential campaign. When federal police officers attempted to arrest Jefferson, he fired a rifle and threw grenades at them, but eventually surrendered without causing further harm.[102]

[96] See Da Ros and Taylor 2022, 150. His predecessor, Temer, had chosen the second name in the list.

[97] Tables 3 and 4 in Lagunes et al. 2021. See also Da Ros and Taylor 2022, chapter 5.

[98] Da Ros and Taylor 2022, 142 and 163.

[99] See Da Ros and Taylor 2022, 2, and Cravo and Gullino 2022. A further "calming" effect, not on Congress, but on the electorate at large in view of the presidential elections of 2022, had a very opportunistic and irresponsible expansive fiscal policy. See Ferrari Filho and Bittes Terra 2023.

[100] These developments interacted with a disastrous management of the COVID-19 pandemics. Avritzer and Rennó 2021 consider this broad question in the context of Brazil's "crisis of democracy."

[101] It is based on ideas of national security which include social order and economic progress. In granting the military with such extended responsibility, it practically turns it into a fourth branch of government. See Loveman and Davies 1997, and in particular, Loveman 1997.

[102] Villegas 2022.

The episode of Roberto Jefferson's arrest epitomizes Brazil's rough ride since the start of *Lava Jato* in 2014. Although Bolsonaro's threat to democracy was eventually defeated in the election, the margin of Lula's victory was slim. Brazil is now a divided nation, and the social cohesion that is necessary for a functioning democracy has been significantly eroded.

CONCLUSIONS: BRAZIL'S UNSUCCESSFUL FIGHT AGAINST CORRUPTION

Bolsonaro has not delivered on any hope of cathartic cleansing of Brazil's public life, much like another unlikely president six decades before. Jânio Quadros took office at the beginning of 1961 with the reputation of being an honest administrator, and his rapid rise to power made him appear a relative outsider. He run his presidential campaign on an anti-corruption platform, chastised the apparent waste of public funds for the construction of the new capital Brasília, and preached austerity. Quadros was a talented populist with a strongly anti-political message. He used a broom as a symbol, which was also the protagonist of the official jingle of his campaign titled "Varre, varre vassourinha" ("Sweep, sweep, little broom"), symbolizing his promise to cleanse Brazil of corruption.[103] His candidacy proved to be attractive to a middle class particularly receptive to his moralizing message and promise to fight inflation.[104] Quadros resigned after only seven months in office and with no substantial achievements to show. This led to a period of political turmoil and eventually to the dictatorship.

While Jânio Quadros was not implicated in any corruption scandals,[105] Fernando Collor de Mello, also a populist president who run an anti-corruption presidential campaign, was forced at the end of 1992 to leave office following the "Collorgate" corruption scandal. Like Quadros before him, Collor styled himself as an outsider and as president maintained an anti-party rhetoric.[106] Like Quadros and Collor, Bolsonaro made only lackluster efforts to form a solid majority in Congress and he appeared to prioritize the support of his dedicated followers rather than making strategic political alliances. This is hardly a politically successful strategy under the Constitution of 1988.[107]

[103] Schwarcz and Starling 2018, 490. Quadro's jingle is available on YouTube.

[104] Cardoso 2020, 95.

[105] See, however, Barros de Mello 2009.

[106] Collor fared much better among the poor than among higher-income groups and "did best among the least educated and worst among the best educated" (Amorim Neto and Pimenta 2020, citing Mainwaring 1999: 117).

[107] Amorim Neto and Pimenta 2020, and Lagunes et al. 2021.

These cases illustrate two fundamental issues that affect political projects focused on an anti-corruption discourse. The analytical framework discussed in Chapter 5 provides a perspective to understand how changes that may appear to be significant, such as those of *Lava Jato*, do not necessarily lead to the establishment of new, noncorrupt ways of solving problems of government. In Brazil, structural change has been historically hindered by a social compact shaped by deeply ingrained forms of inequality. Additionally, anti-corruption efforts may not only fail to reduce corruption but also be used as a tool by certain societal actors whose self-interests may be harmful to society as a whole. In the cases of both Quadros and Bolsonaro, the anti-corruption message appealed to a middle class that was fearful of its relative position in the social order, ultimately contributing to an authoritarian turn. Considering once more Lula, the relatively uneducated metalworker turned president, his incarceration by a white upper-middle-class elite of prosecutors and judges served to reinstate a social order that, if seen from a particular angle, *had been corrupted.*

Last, we note that an important component of Bolsonaro's winning coalition was represented by economic interests such as agro-business and mining, which favored an aggressive exploitation of the vast expanses of the Amazon.[108] Such support blurs the distinction between political expediency, illegal corruption, and legal forms of corruption (a theme that Chapter 8, dedicated to the United States, begins to elaborate). At a broader level, corruption emerges once again as a concept that is difficult or impossible to separate from other aspects of governance and politics, within a dense historical matrix. These are important questions that I will revisit in Part III of the book.

[108] Avelar 2021.

8

Legal Corruption in the United States of America

The U.S. is not better than any other corrupt country.

Joaquín Archivaldo Guzmán Loera, known as "El Chapo"[1]

We may have democracy, or we may have wealth concentrated in the hands of a few, but we can't have both.

Louis Brandeis[2]

Shortly before leaving office, the head of state of a former colony officially pardoned a number of political loyalists, one of whom was a close relative who had been sentenced for serious crimes. This act of cronyism did not happen in some African "shithole country" – to quote that very same dignitary. It happened in the United States of America, and the head of state in question was, of course, Donald Trump. Among the individuals he pardoned were Paul Manafort, who briefly served as the chairman of the Trump 2016 presidential campaign and "had been sentenced to seven and a half years in prison for his role in a decade-long, multimillion-dollar financial fraud scheme for his work in the former Soviet Union," and his longtime friend Roger J. Stone Jr., who had been convicted "on seven counts of lying to Congress, witness tampering and obstructing the House inquiry into possible Trump campaign coordination with Russia."[3] Trump also pardoned Charles Kushner, who in 2004 had pleaded guilty "to 16 counts of tax evasion, a single count of retaliating against a federal witness and one of lying to the Federal Election Commission" and "served two years in prison before

[1] BBC 2019b.

[2] Louis Brandeis served as US Supreme Court Justice between 1916 and 1939. On the veracity of this quote, see Campbell 2013, who concludes that "if it is not a Brandeis quote, it is at least a Brandeisian one."

[3] See Haberman and Schmidt 2020 (for all quotations in the paragraph). On Trump's "shithole country" remark, see Hirschfeld Davis et al. 2018.

being released in 2006." Charles Kushner is the father of Jared Kushner, who is Trump's son-in-law and served as Senior Advisor to the President. His daughter, Ivanka Trump, was also named an (unpaid) "adviser."[4]

In getting those persons off the hook, President Trump did not have to engage in any illegal activities such as corruption or extortion of judges. He simply exercised his prerogative, under Article 2, clause 1, of the US Constitution, to "grant reprieves and pardons." The drafters likely had different intentions for the use of this provision, and the outcome we see today is similar to what could have been achieved through illegal means in other countries, such as through corruption or extortion, or other forms of pressure, such as the "phone justice" observed in Russia. But the United States is not a country with below-the-floor ranking in the Transparency International Corruption Perception Index. To the opposite, throughout its history, the country's rise as a powerful nation has highlighted its institutions, which have been emulated around the world. These observations raise questions about how we should view outcomes that in some cases follow crimes such as corruption, but are legal in others, even if they may be considered inappropriate or even scandalous. I refer to these instances as cases of "legal corruption" and explore this theme in Chapter 9. Here I introduce the concept by considering a country, the United States, where illegal corruption is relatively modest while its legal variant is arguably widespread.

In recent decades, as a narrow view of corruption has taken hold, the United States has experienced a significant increase in economic inequality and a decrease in social mobility. Despite the growing public discourse on economic inequality, concerns about the viability of a democratic system in the face of extreme economic inequalities have a long history, as demonstrated by Luis Brandeis' quote that opens this chapter. In recent years, corruption has been frequently invoked to describe the state of American politics, with business corporations and their ultra-wealthy owners indicated as possible culprits. In the United States, the notion that corporations may have a corrupting effect dates back to the early days of the Republic, when it was feared that corporate charters could be granted by state legislatures as rewards for favors or bribes. Today's heightened levels of inequality have only increased the scrutiny on corporations. Opinions similar to that of Salvador Allende that I mentioned in Chapter 2 resurface more often, where corporations are seen as "some of the major drivers of contemporary corruption around the world."[5] The political influence of ultra-billionaires

[4] Yuhas 2017, and Merica et al. 2017.
[5] Teachout 2018.

has also come under increased scrutiny, as in the case of the Koch brothers, who have funded conservative political causes for decades.[6]

The United States also holds a special place in the history of corruption and anti-corruption efforts. The country has played a significant role in shaping ideas about corruption, thanks to its institutions, universities, think tanks, and headquarters of international organizations like the World Bank. The United States is also viewed as a success story in the fight against corruption, which was rampant until a series of reforms were enacted starting in the late nineteenth century and continuing over several decades. We examine this success using the analytical framework outlined in Chapter 5.

GROWING INCOME AND A PROSPEROUS COUNTRY

The United States is undoubtedly impressive in numerous ways, and particularly so when considering its economy. In 2019, its GDP per capita was approximately six times greater than that of China, Brazil, or Russia, or between two to four times greater when accounting for differences in purchasing power (as shown in Table 6.1 on page 89). With a population of 325 million in 2019, the country generates and consumes a truly unparalleled quantity of resources. Since the middle 1970s, GDP per capita in the United States has more than doubled in real terms (Figure 8.1). Some countries have grown faster, most notably China, whose economic catching up has far-reaching implications for the global order. However, these economies had much lower starting points and as they were further away from the world's technological frontier, they had more room for improvement. Despite this, the United States has managed to keep pace with each and every new phase of the industrial revolution over the past century and a half, which is truly remarkable.

The US economy's large output and unparalleled military expenditures allow it to project its power on a planetary scale. The US military budget exceeds China's by a factor of three, Russia's by more than ten, and Brazil's by nearly 30 times.[7] These basic figures provide a fitting starting point for

[6] Mayer 2016. The Kochs brothers are Charles G. Koch (born in 1935) and Frederick R. Koch (born in 1933, deceased in 2020), of Koch Industries, Inc., a sprawling conglomerate headquartered in Wichita, Kansas.

[7] Military expenditure by country, in billions of US current dollars, in 2019 was equal to 734 for the United States, 240 for China, 65 for Russia, and 26 for Brazil. Also in 2019, military expenditures as a percentage of GDP amounted to 3.4% for the United States, 1.7% for China, 3.9% for Russia, and 1.4% for Brazil (SIPRI 2020).

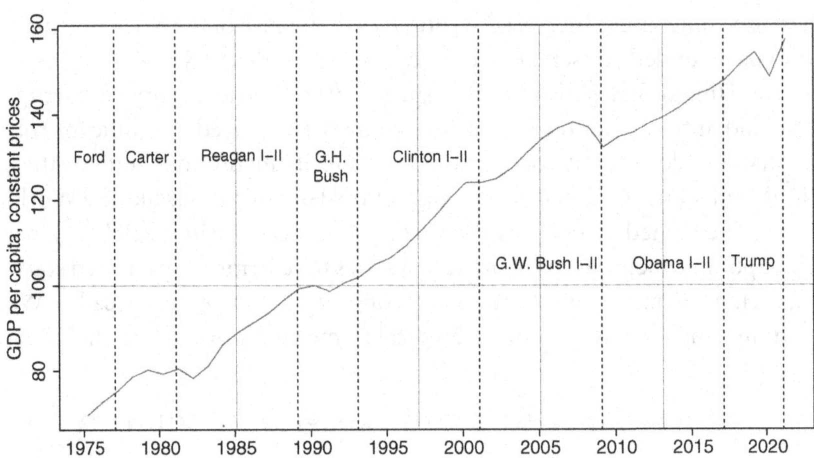

Figure 8.1 GDP per capita at constant prices (USA)
Source of the data: The World Bank. GDP per capita at constant prices, set equal to 100 in the year 1990. The vertical lines correspond to presidential mandates, starting every four years on January 20.

any realist analysis of world affairs, while the uniqueness of the United States expresses itself in many ways beyond its economic and military power. As I write these lines, NASA's Perseverance Mars Rover, after having landed on the surface of Mars, is being photographed by a small hovering helicopter, named "Ingenuity," which it carried with it and which has successfully demonstrated the possibility of "powered, controlled flight of an aircraft on another planet."[8] Such technological capabilities are closely tied to the economic power of the country, as well as to its military interests, which have been a major driving force behind technological innovation in the United States. While the power projected abroad by the United States serves its economic interests in multiple ways, this does not detract from a sense of admiration for the country's ingenuity.

Admirable accomplishments contribute to a "soft" variety of power, which in the case of the United States is interestingly multifaceted. The world's most important media industries, including Hollywood as a major producer of films and television content, project an American vision of the world abroad. Additionally, the rise of US-based internet platforms, which serve as gatekeepers and arbiters of free speech, has profound implications that are not yet fully understood. These media industries, both old and new,

[8] See Gorman 2021 and NASA's tweet: "I spy with my little eye … a rover" (@nasagpl, April 28, 2021).

have taken advantage of the robust defense of extreme intellectual property rights carried out by the United States,[9] showcasing how "hard" and "soft" forms of power can be interrelated. Furthermore, American universities consistently occupy top positions in international rankings.[10] The presence of numerous scientific journals and publishers based in the United States has further contributed to a global influence in shaping the development of ideas, including the idea of corruption and the tenets of the current anti-corruption global regime.

CORRUPTION IN THE UNITED STATES

These successes are commonly attributed also to the presence of an effective and noncorrupt government. Corruption in the United States is perceived to be relatively low, with some evidence of a worsening during the most recent years (Figure 8.2). Measures based on personal experience also indicate that bribing is not a common occurrence in the United States.[11]

There is evidence to suggest that bribery in the United States was significantly more widespread in the distant past. Andrew Jackson, whose administration saw the rise of the "spoils system," was elected President in 1829 on an anti-corruption platform.[12] The sale of state-owned land and selective granting of incorporation rights by states were sources of corruption in the early nineteenth century. Partly in response, the free incorporation movement gained traction in the mid-nineteenth century, as states passed incorporation laws and competed to attract corporations.[13] Despite efforts to reduce corruption, it persisted in the years leading to the Civil War, particularly in relation to investments in infrastructure such as railroads, also at the center of some of the most egregious episodes of corruption during the *postbellum* period.[14] After the Civil War, new forms of patronage became structured around those political machines that Robert Merton considered to be also providers of useful services.[15]

[9] The United States has had a significant role in "coding capital" more generally; see Pistor 2019 and in particular its chapter 9 for the coding of intellectual capital.

[10] See MacLeod and Urquiola 2021.

[11] See, for example, Transparency International 2013.

[12] Wallis 2006, 45, and Cuéllar and Stephenson 2020.

[13] Hennessey and Wallis 2017.

[14] Such as the Crédit Mobilier Scandal. See Cuéllar and Stephenson 2020, and Lamoreaux and Rosenthal 2006.

[15] Merton 1972 [1957]. Such as "help with the law, finding a job, getting a new apartment after a fire, access to coal during hard times" (see Daniel J. Czitrom's intervention in Baker et al. 2019).

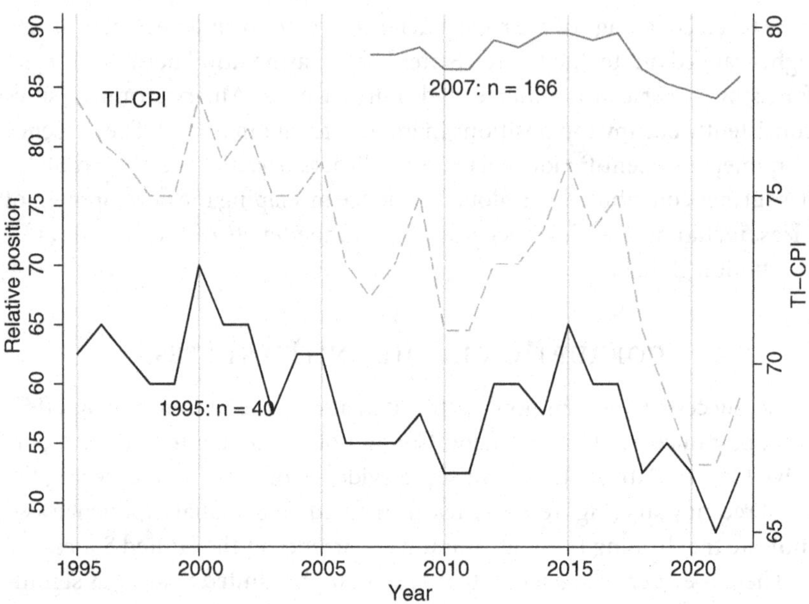

Figure 8.2 TI-CPI and its relative position (USA)
Dashed line: TI-CPI (right axis; values before 2012 are multiplied by 10). Relative positions (left axis): Percentiles, relative to group of countries (of size *n*) continuously present from a given date. Higher relative positions (and values of the TI-CPI) correspond to less perceived corruption. See Escresa and Picci 2016 for further details.

During the late nineteenth and early twentieth centuries, or what is known as the Progressive Era, an emerging consensus for reforms was spurred by the growth of the media industry and muckraking journalism. Reforms took place over a long period starting from the 1890s and took three main forms.[16] First, the principles of a professional and impartial civil service gradually gained acceptance.[17] Second, the introduction of independent regulatory commissions led to the creation of a "regulatory state" with extensive control over corporations. This was driven by

16 Cuéllar and Stephenson 2020 summarize: "A new generation of leaders – at the national, state, and local levels – made anti-corruption central to their agendas and campaigns," and at the national level, "President Theodore Roosevelt made fighting public corruption a defining feature of his presidency." See also Wallis et al. 2006. On the rise of the media, the "Fourth Estate", that took place in those years, see Gentzkow et al. 2006

17 The 1883 Pendleton Civil Service Reform Act introduced competitive examinations and a merit system for hiring public servants, even if for only a small fraction of federal government jobs, later to be increased, particularly so during Roosevelt's New Deal. See Cuéllar and Stephenson 2020.

concerns about the consolidation of corporations and their increased practical relevance, particularly following the decade that started in 1895 during which an intense process of horizontal consolidation took place.[18] Last, the secret ballot was gradually introduced as was regulation of campaign expenditures. In particular, the Tillman Act of 1907 marked the beginning of a series of consequential federal acts and judicial rulings in the field of campaign finance[19] that I will consider in some detail. These reforms faced a setback in the 1920s, but regained momentum during Roosevelt's New Deal, to include the expansion of the government safety net, which was largely administered in a noncorrupt manner and contributed to the weakening of political machines.[20]

An anti-corruption sentiment was certainly present during the Progressive Era, and it was particularly evident in muckraking journalism. However, it should be seen as part of a wider set of social demands. In his landmark 1955 book, Richard Hofstadter notes that the Progressives, who were mainly drawn from the middle class, were concerned about their social status, that they saw threatened by the increasing power of corporations and the social advancements of immigrants, that political machines were facilitating. Condemnation of corruption on one hand, and of the betrayal of a more egalitarian past by the rising corporate world on the other, served their desire to defend their class status.[21] A rich historiographical debate has tempered these conclusions.[22] Fear for one's social and economic status was a relevant preoccupation among at least some of the actors asking for less corruption, and together with different motives it resulted in a complex series of outcomes. The reduction of corruption that we observe cannot be solely attributed to an anti-corruption effort, as it was accompanied by sweeping transformations that introduced new institutions and ways of governance. These changes affected the higher subsystem of historical change, and public policies partially replaced the "latent functions" of

[18] Lamoreaux 1985, 1.

[19] Mutch 2014, 17.

[20] Wallis et al. 2006. Brinlkely 1985 notes that "the New Deal made no effort to combat the political machines; instead, Roosevelt attempted to conciliate and forge alliances with them." The social programs enacted in those years, however, eroded some of the reasons behind political machines. They did not disappear outright and survived well into the post-World War II period.

[21] Hofstadter 1955, 135.

[22] For a nuanced summary, see Brinkley 1985. Granovetter 2007, 165, defends Hofstadter's position and, citing Brinkley, notes that Hofstadter's "arguments about Progressives have generally fared better than those about Populism."

political machines, which also became less necessary as the inflow of immigrants decreased.[23]

As for corporations, corruption was partially replaced by legal forms of political influence, which were facilitated by their greatly increased economic power. These forms took various shapes related to the development of the media, lobbying activities, and other tools such as think tanks, all of which emerged broadly during the same period. Although corporations were eventually subjected to the newly established regulatory state, which gained strength over time, in exchange they were allowed to retain their size and power after the decade of great consolidation that began in 1895.[24]

Gabriel Kolko provides a view of the regulatory turn in the United States where business was the clear winner: "The regulation itself was invariably controlled by leaders of the regulated industry, and directed toward ends they deemed acceptable or desirable." He concludes that "it is business control over politics (and by "business" I mean the major economic interests) rather than political regulation of the economy that is the significant phenomenon of the Progressive Era."[25] My view is perhaps more nuanced, as I underline the *acceptability* of the regulatory turn by corporations, more than their *control* over it. Corporations were able to accept some limitations domestically also because they were able to prosper globally, supported by an increasingly assertive foreign policy that they contributed in shaping through new legal modes of influence. This occurred while Southern white elites and a significant portion of the white population were placated through the marginalization of the black population, as a discriminatory apartheid system was established. In conclusion, corruption in the United States decreased as a result of long-term developments that transformed the country, defined a new political compact, and consequently made bribes less necessary.

While corruption has been partly substituted by legal forms of influence, incidents of corruption still occur in the United States. With regard to those who pay bribes, the criminal justice system has been lenient toward corporate crime in general. As I noted in Chapter 2, criminal

[23] The share of immigrants in the total US population started to decrease approximately in 1910, when it was 14.7%, continuously until 1970, when it reached 4.7%. See Migration Policy Institute n.d.

[24] Or to be recognized as a regulated monopolist, as was the case of AT&T with the 1913 "Kingsbury Commitment," which "sanctioned the most lucrative monopoly in history" (Wu 2010, 59).

[25] Kolko 1963, 3. I will briefly return to this point of view in Chapter 9, when I will consider the debate on regulatory capture.

corporate liability was established in the United States at the beginning of the nineteenth century. However, with the exception of the Enron case in the early 2000s, which resulted in severe sentences and bankruptcies,[26] large corporations have been regarded as "too big to jail" because, as Brandon Garrett notes, "they are considered to be so valuable to the economy that prosecutors may not hold them accountable for their crimes."[27] In fact, when we focus on the most recent decades, this situation has gotten worse over time. Corporate prosecution penalties have decreased,[28] and there has been a reduced tendency to hold individuals responsible for these crimes accountable.[29] In general, the justice system favors those with deep pockets, and both corporations and their managers tend to belong to this category.

INCREASING ECONOMIC INEQUALITY

Having looked at the historical background of corruption in the United States, our attention turns to more recent events and the issue of economic inequality, which has significantly risen over the past four decades.

The New Deal era was marked by a long-term decrease in inequality. The pretax income share of the bottom 50% of the population, which was 13.8% in 1940, reached its highest historical level of 21.3% in 1969 and was at 20.3% in 1979, before experiencing a steep decline.[30] Since 1975, the bottom 50% of the adult population has seen its share of pretax income shrink from over 20% to around 13%, while the rich, and especially the superrich, have become much richer (Figures 8.3 and 8.4). The share of the top 10% has increased from approximately 33% to over 45%, but the most significant change has occurred at the top of the income distribution. The share of

[26] Garrett 2014, 13.

[27] Garrett 2014, 1.

[28] Garrett 2020.

[29] Garrett 2018. During the last years, the Supreme Court has been raising the bar for corruption cases, as part of a more general trend to which belongs the "Citizens United" ruling of 2010, to be discussed soon. See, for example, Barnes 2022, and Eliason 2023.

[30] Source: World Inequality Database n.d. Prominent among the reasons behind these fortunate years for the less well-off, "labor was matched in influence – and even more so in campaign contributions – by sectors of the business class persuaded that their industries would benefit from the full-employment, mass-consumption system of regulated capitalism that the New Deal promised to create." Also, "the communist success in the Soviet Union scared American businessmen as did the influence of communists in the ranks of American labor, inclining them (the businessmen) to compromise with more moderate sectors of the labor movement" (Gerstle 2022, 21).

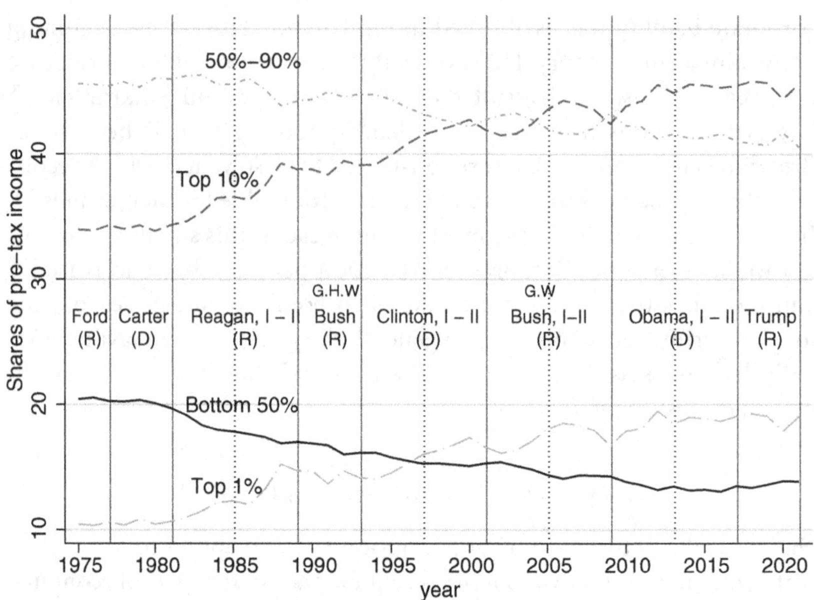

Figure 8.3 Shares of pretax income, all earners (USA)
Source of the data: World Inequality Database n.d. See Alvaredo et al. 2018. Vertical lines indicate presidential inaugurations. "R": Republican Party; "D": Democratic Party.

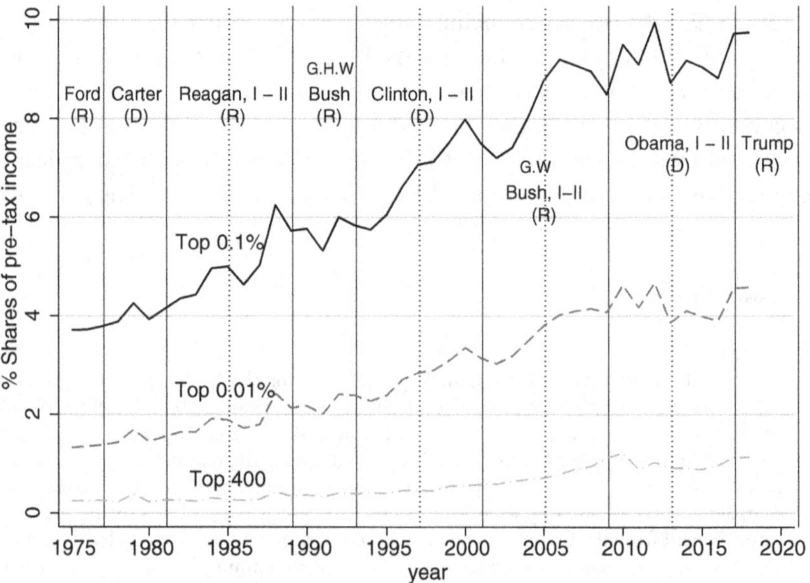

Figure 8.4 Shares of pretax income, top earners (USA)
Source of the data: Saez and Zucman 2019, Table A1. Vertical lines indicate presidential inaugurations. "R": Republican Party; "D": Democratic Party.

the top 1% of earners has nearly doubled, approaching 20%, and the share of total income received by the top 0.1% of earners has more than doubled since 1975, from about 4% to 10% (Figure 8.4). This indicates that inequality has not only increased overall, but also within the top 1% of earners. By 2018, the most fortunate 10% of this privileged group received half of its income, and a share of income overall not much lower than that of the less fortunate half of the population.

The above figures are pretax, which means that they do not take into account the redistribution of income through taxes and consumption of public goods. However, considering transfers would only slightly affect the conclusion about increasing inequality.[31] Taxation, in particular, roughly approximates a flat tax, but it is clearly regressive for the ultra-rich, their average tax rate being in fact lower than that of the poorest Americans. This reality is the result of significant changes in tax rates in recent decades.[32] In 1950, the tax system was progressive, and while it remained so to a lesser degree in 1980, its progressivity had been greatly reduced by 1990. Tax cuts in 2001 and 2003 under the presidency of George W. Bush "dramatically reduced the federal tax burdens of wealthy Americans."[33] Under Trump's presidency, a further regressive reform, the Tax Cuts and Jobs Act, became effective in 2018.[34]

Also, the figures are based on tax receipts, which may be impacted by tax evasion, which has risen significantly in the last few decades, especially among the rich and ultra-rich.[35] They have more ways to evade taxes compared to salaried workers, whose incomes are reported to the tax administration by their employers, and they can rely on a tax-dodging industry that has become more sophisticated, exclusive, and politically influential over the years.[36] At the same time, there has been a decrease in enforcement, for example, of the estate tax, whose statutory rates have trended downward beginning with President Reagan's Economic Recovery Tax Act of 1981, and has all but disappeared in practice. In the meantime, opportunities to shift profits to tax havens and hide wealth in friendly foreign jurisdictions have increased. In 1973, estimated tax evasion was roughly equal across the income spectrum, but by 2018 it was much more prevalent among wealthier Americans.[37]

[31] Saez and Zucman 2020.

[32] Saez and Zucman 2019, Figure 1.3, and Saez and Zucman 2020, Figure 5, whose data are from Saez and Zucman 2019.

[33] Bartels 2016, 5 (with reference to chapter 5).

[34] Clausing 2019.

[35] See the discussion in Saez and Zucman 2019, 59–63, and Figure 3.1.

[36] Saez and Zucman 2019, 62.

[37] Saez and Zucman 2019, 60–61.

Aside from the problem of tax evasion, privileging the rich, regressive reforms that have taken place have shifted the tax burden from capital to labor, so that labor is now taxed more heavily than capital. This is even more so once we consider the cost of employer-provided health insurance, which effectively serves as a regressive tax on labor, and in 2019 accounted for more than 5% of GDP.[38] As the rich derive much of their income from capital, and the poor from labor, this shift in taxation has contributed to an increase in wealth concentration. The relationship between wealth distribution and income inequality is complex, and one particularly relevant question is the extent to which capital and labor incomes are correlated at the individual level. Historically, rentiers in Europe and elsewhere enjoyed their rents without working for a salary, but today, capital and labor income tend to be correlated across individuals and households, with significant implications for wealth distribution and opportunities in society.[39] Considering the current low taxation of capital relative to labor, the increased correlation of incomes from labor and capital creates a snowball effect where wealth generates capital income, which, combined with high labor income, can be easily saved at a high rate due to low taxes, adding to the existing stock of wealth. This in turn generates more income and so on.[40]

In 2014, nearly three-quarters of the wealth in the United States was owned by the top 10% of owners, and 36% was owned by the top 1%. Both groups significantly increased their relative shares since the early 1980s. The bottom 50% of Americans have an estimated net wealth close to zero, meaning that a significant fraction of the population has more debt than assets.[41] Easy access to credit has acted as a temporary solution for rising income inequality, as it has enabled the American poor to maintain a level of consumption that exceeds their means, while also addressing basic needs such as education and healthcare. Inequality in wealth has significantly increased not only overall, but also within the top 1% of the population. Between 1975 and 2018, the top 1% share of wealth increased from 22% to 37%, the top 0.1% share of wealth tripled from 7.8% to 19.2%, and the top 0.01% share of wealth more than quadrupled from 2% to 9.5%. The share

[38] Centers for Medicare & Medicaid Services n.d., Table 5.

[39] See Berman and Milanovic 2020, who note that "In 1985, about 17% of adults in the top decile of capital-income earners were also in the top decile of labor-income earners. In 2018, this indicator was about 30%."

[40] Piketty 2014 discusses at length the mutual dynamic relationships between the distribution of income and of wealth.

[41] Source of the data: World Inequality Database n.d. See Alvaredo et al. 2018.

of total wealth held by the 400 richest Americans increased eightfold and reached 3% of the total in 2018.

The extreme economic insecurity experienced by many Americans is well reflected in popular culture. For example, "Nomadland: Surviving America in the Twenty-First Century," a nonfiction book by Jessica Bruder, describes transient lives in the years following the financial crisis of 2007–2009. LaVonne's van, in which she lives, breaks down, and she has no money for repairs. "Making matters worse, she still owed a few thousand dollars in payments on her now-worthless van, which had died several times before. She decided to stay put and wait on her Social Security checks." LaVonne, who "ended up living in the dead van for nearly a month and a half," finally could afford a tow to the repair shop, where she was quoted $3,000 to fix the engine, more than she could pay. Nearby, "she spotted a nearly new twelve-person Chevy Express on a used car lot. A salesman emerged from the office. He said he could help her get a loan even though she had bad credit. This is not surprising – subprime auto loans have surged in recent years. LaVonne wasn't sure about the terms, but what choice did she have? 'If I didn't get it, I was going to be homeless,' she later told me."[42]

The cause of the observed increase in inequality, in both the United States and other countries, is the subject of debate. Changes in international trade and the impact of technological progress that has favored skilled labor are partly responsible, as is the shift in power that has occurred in American society, and in particular the decline of organized labor. What is certain is that transfers and taxation would directly affect the distribution of disposable income. Policies can be explicit, but also "by omission" when there is no response to exogenous shifts. The changes in taxation that I have summarized are largely due to significant changes in statutory tax rates and the tax code. It is worth noting that the two main political parties are not equally responsible for the significant increase in inequality that has been observed. Inequality has tended to increase more under Republican Presidents, while Democratic administrations have tended to promote redistributive policies.[43]

42 Bruder 2017. The book was adapted into a 2020 film, also called "Nomadland," which won the "*Leone d'oro*" at the 2020 Venice Film Festival, and carried the day at the 2021 Academy Awards. In the film, the van of the protagonist (Fern, played by actress Frances McDormand) breaks down, and she borrows from her estranged sister the money needed for repairs.

43 Bartels 2016, 294, notes that "For most of the past century, when Democrats have controlled the reins of government, they have consistently pursued high employment, high taxes, and economic redistribution from the rich to the poor. When Republicans have governed, they have consistently done the opposite."

A DYSFUNCTIONAL HEALTH SYSTEM

A different perspective to assess the modest progress that most Americans have experienced since 1975 is through examination of the health system and health outcomes.

Per capita spending on healthcare in the United States is more than three times that of Italy and Spain (slightly lower when calculated using purchasing power parity), and ten times higher than in China or Cuba (Table 8.1). Despite the abundance of resources devoted to healthcare, many uninsured or inadequately insured Americans are lacking proper medical treatment. This has led to widespread dissatisfaction with the system, resulting in two major attempts at reform in recent decades. In 1993 and 1994, President Clinton made a significant effort to propose a compromise reform of the health system. However, the plan was met with a significant defeat after the 1994 midterm elections, when the Republican Party gained control of both the House of Representatives and the Senate.[44] Continuing dissatisfaction with the current system, where the number of uninsured Americans was steadily increasing, reaching 16% of the total population in 2009,[45] created the political conditions for the "Affordable Care Act" of 2010, also known as "Obamacare," the landmark achievement of the Obama presidency.

The Affordable Care Act also was a compromise solution, that regulated the existing private insurance markets by implementing a series of complex provisions aimed at increasing coverage and eliminating discrimination based on pre-existing conditions or demographics. As a result, the percentage of uninsured Americans decreased significantly in the years following the implementation of the policy.[46] Along with strengthened Medicare and Medicaid programs (established in 1956 and 1965, respectively), the Affordable Care Act has brought significant improvement to healthcare in the United States. After a rocky start, Americans have become increasingly supportive of the policy.[47]

Despite these improvements, the healthcare system remains highly flawed. Life expectancy at birth increased modestly during the 1980s and

[44] For an analysis of that aborted attempt at reform, see Skocpol 1995.

[45] Or 22% if we consider the 18–65 age interval. See United States Census Bureau n.d.

[46] In 2019, it was equal to 9% for the whole population and to 14.7% for the 18–65 age interval. See Cohen et al. 2021.

[47] Republican leaning citizens are overwhelmingly against it, while Democrats are in favor. Overall, opinion polls have shown a clear majority in favor that has tended to grow over time. See Bowman 2020. On Medicare and, most importantly, Medicaid increased reach, see Jacobs and Skocpol 2016, 92–94.

Table 8.1 *Total health spending, 2019. Percentage of GDP and US dollars per capita*

	United States	Russia	Brazil	China	Italy	Spain	Cuba
% of GDP	16.77	5.65	9.59	5.35	8.67	9.13	11.34
US dollars (th.; current)	10,921	609	853	653	2,905	2,711	1,031
US dollars (th.; PPP)	10,921	1,704	1,497	880	3,998	3,983	2,599

Source of the data: The World Bank. Estimates of current health expenditures include healthcare goods and services consumed, as a percentage of GDP and, per capita, in current international US dollars (also at purchasing power parity), during each year. Capital health expenditures such as buildings, machinery, IT, and stocks of vaccines for emergency or outbreaks, are not included.

1990s (Figure 6.5 at page 93), then reached a plateau, and started to decline in 2014, further widening the gap with countries such as Italy and Spain, whose per capita healthcare expenditure is about one-third that of the United States. Such dismal situation can be attributed to several factors, among which drug overdoses figure high, particularly with respect to white non-Hispanics. By 2014, these "deaths of despair" had become prevalent enough to result in a decline in life expectancy at birth not only among this demographic group, but also overall.[48]

In considering the rise in midlife mortality from 2010 to 2017, Steven Woolf and Heidi Schoomaker concur that "a major contributor has been an increase in mortality from specific causes (e.g., drug overdoses, suicides, organ system diseases) among young and middle-aged adults of all racial groups, with an onset as early as the 1990s and with the largest relative increases occurring in the Ohio Valley and New England." The opioid epidemic has taken a significant toll, contributing to over 70,000 drug overdose deaths in 2019 alone.[49] The opioid crisis has multiple causes, and for those Americans who are poorer and less educated, the distribution of income and wealth and the associated scarcity of opportunities for social and economic advancement play a role. Corruption, occasionally

[48] Case and Deaton 2017, who also note that life expectancy at birth (which represents the number of years that a hypothetical person could be expected to live if it were born today, if current age-specific mortality rates continue into the future) is not very responsive to changes in middle-age mortality rates, which makes the observed decline particularly remarkable. On "deaths of despair" more generally, see Case and Deaton 2020.

[49] With nearly 841,000 deaths reported between 1999 and 2019. These figures refer to deaths caused by overdose of opioids and other drugs, with the former accounting for 70.6% of the total for 2019. See National Institute on Drug Abuse n.d., and Woolf and Schoomaker 2019 for the previous quotation.

petty and sordid, has also been a contributing factor to this disastrous outcome. Literature helps in grasping such reality, as is the case with Stephen Markley's novel "Ohio," which depicts a Midwestern human wasteland punctuated by drug abuse. For Kaylyn, one of the protagonists, the "pill mill worked just fine" thanks to a collaborative doctor, first in exchange for money, and then for sex.[50] At a higher level, but not less sordidly, Patrick Radden Keefe presents an excruciating journalistic account of the Sackler family, who controlled Purdue Pharma, purveyors of OxyContin, one of the main enablers of the opioid overdose crisis. The account details a range of behaviors over a period of decades, including revolving doors for regulators involved in decisions affecting Purdue Pharma, lobbying, and that muscular exercise of the right to defend oneself in court which only the very wealthy can afford.[51] This crisis, characterized by inequality and lack of opportunities, is also reflected in what is known about social mobility in the United States.

SOCIAL MOBILITY, THE EDUCATION SYSTEM, AND OPPORTUNITIES

In the United States, social mobility is low and has decreased over time in parallel with the observed increase in economic inequality. Raj Chetty et al. present a measure of "absolute income mobility," for cohorts born in different years, which expresses the percentage of children who at age 30 earn more than their parents did at the same age.[52] This measure, available from 1974 to 2014, has decreased from 92% in 1975 to 50% at the end of the period under consideration. In other words, individuals who were 30 years old in 1975 were almost certain to earn more than their parents had at the same age, but that probability almost halved for those who were 30 in 2014.

Figure 8.5 shows this measure of income mobility along with a further summary measure of income inequality, the Gini index, and a summary measure representing the "American Dream," to be considered in Chapter 9. Part of the decline in the measure of income mobility observed in the United States is due to the reduction in economic growth since the

[50] Markley 2018, 129–130.

[51] See Radden Keefe 2021, and Cutler and Glaeser 2021, who report that "Two examiners involved in OxyContin's approval by the Food and Drug Administration went on to work for Purdue. When the FDA convened an advisory group in 2002 to examine the harms from OxyContin, eight of the ten experts had ties to pharmaceutical firms."

[52] Chetty et al. 2017a.

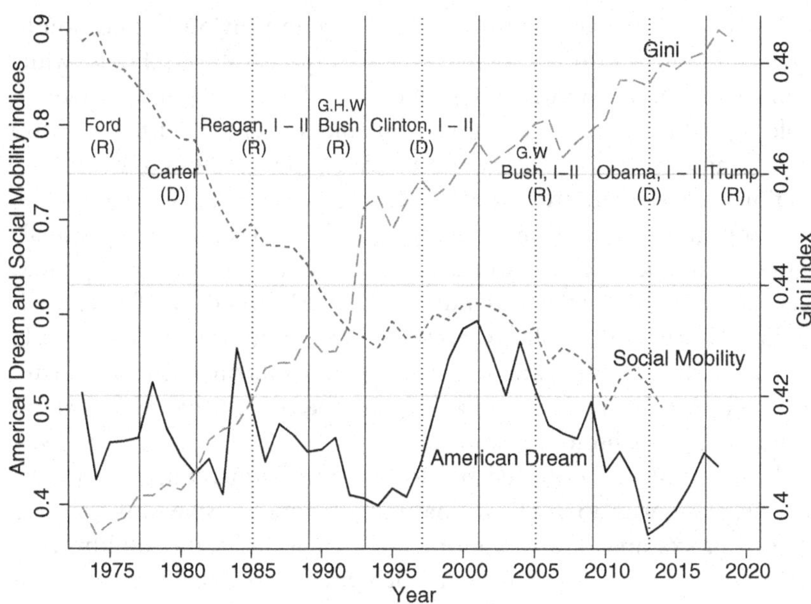

Figure 8.5 Inequalities, social mobility, and the American dream
Source of the data: Social mobility index: Chetty et al. 2017a (cohort mean, as in Wolak and Peterson 2020). Gini: U.S. Census Bureau. Vertical lines indicate presidential inaugurations. American dream index: Wolak and Peterson 2020 (yearly averages).

post–World War II era. However, even if economic growth had remained as strong as it was then, the measure of absolute mobility would only increase to 62%, significantly lower than the 90% observed for individuals who were 30 years old in 1975.[53] This indicates that the decrease in income mobility is a genuine issue and only partly explained by slower economic growth.

Social mobility, of which income mobility is a crucial aspect, is affected by the nature of a country's education system and its ability to act as a "social elevator." In the United States, most top universities are private and the fees they charge have skyrocketed in recent decades, far outpacing the increase in median income.[54] The result is a dramatic rise in student debt, which rose from 2.1% of GDP in 2003 to 7% in 2019.[55]

[53] Chetty et al. 2017a. On decreased social mobility in the United States, see also Davis and Mazumder 2017 [2020].

[54] Milanovic 2019, 59.

[55] My computations, using data from Federal Reserve Bank of New York 2020, data annex.

Rich Americans have a significant advantage in providing education to their children, who often attend expensive preparatory schools, while poor Americans are limited to chronically underfunded public schools.[56] Holding a diploma from a highly reputable university enhances future opportunities in numerous ways. It provides opportunities to build connections, as well as improving one's prospects for finding a suitable mate, as "assortative mating" (the tendency for couples to consist of individuals with similar stocks of capital) has increased over time.[57] These diplomas serve as signals of prestige and indicate that the bearer comes from a well-to-do family with valuable connections. According to Ray Chetty et al., "children whose parents are in the top 1% of the income distribution are 77 times more likely to attend an Ivy League college than those whose parents are in the bottom income quintile."[58]

Great advantages conferred by attending prestigious educational institutions, along with their classist nature, are not exclusive to the United States. For example, Pierre Bourdieu discussed the "state nobility" represented by the attendees of the French *grandes écoles*.[59] In the United States, what is at play is well represented by a high-profile sprawling corruption scandal which emerged in 2019, where standardized test scores were doctored, and sports credentials fabricated, in exchange for money paid by rich parents.[60] This was a case where illegal and legal corruption intersected and reinforced each other, with a legally corrupt system providing incentives for bribery, and bribery reinforcing the social hierarchies inherent in a legally corrupt system. These themes will be discussed in Chapter 9 while focusing on the question of capture of the political process. Political campaign finance is a major issue in this respect, which I address next.

[56] On how access to higher education is "largely determined by parental income," also see Piketty 2020, 535, who concludes that the observed significant decrease in social mobility, "which contrasts so flagrantly with hypothetical talk about 'meritocracy' and equality of opportunity, attests to the extreme stratification of the American educational and social system. It also demonstrates the importance of subjecting political ideological rhetoric to systematic empirical evaluation, which the available sources do not always permit us to do with sufficient comparative historical perspective."

[57] See Schwartz and Mare 2005, and Eika et al. 2019. Increased participation in the labor force by women, an otherwise positive development, augments inequality under assortative mating. See Milanovic 2019, 19.

[58] Chetty et al. 2017b.

[59] Bourdieu 1998.

[60] See Nicholson 2021, and Hartocollis 2023. Arcidiacono et al. 2022, studying admissions at Harvard University, find a very significant effect of preferential admissions in general.

MONEY AND POLITICS: POLITICAL CAMPAIGN FINANCE

In the United States, the issue of the corrupting influence of money has been a topic of critical discourse since the early days of the Republic. The concern over the potential corruption caused by corporations also has a long history, gaining momentum as corporate power grew during the latter part of the nineteenth century. It was in this climate that the first regulations on campaign expenditures were enacted. The Tillman Act of 1907, which was part of the anti-corruption drive during the presidency of Theodore Roosevelt and a product of the Progressive Era,[61] prohibited corporations from making campaign contributions. A series of other measures followed, including a 1910 act mandating disclosure of donor information and amount of money received, and a 1911 ceiling on congressional campaign expenditures.[62] The 1925 Federal Corrupt Practice Act further limited contributions, and the 1940 Hatch Act II introduced limits on contributions and spending in presidential campaigns. In 1943, the War Labor Disputes Act prohibited trade unions from making campaign contributions, leading to the creation of the first Political Action Committee (PAC) by the CIO trade union as a means of sidestepping these restrictions.[63] A PAC is a political committee that raises and spends money to elect and defeat candidates, while being formally independent from them and political parties.

A long period of relative stability in campaign finance laws was interrupted by a new push for reform in the late 1960s, culminating with the passing of the Federal Election Campaign Act (FECA) in 1971. Besides legalizing PACs, it revoked previous contribution and spending limits, but imposed limits on media spending. The 1971 FECA also required greater transparency in campaign finance, which led to the discovery that the Committee for the Re-Election of the President (Nixon) had not disclosed all of its funding sources, as required. The Watergate scandal generated political pressure that resulted in the 1974 FECA (Amendments to FECA), which established more stringent contribution and spending limits,[64] a public funding program for presidential campaigns, and the creation of the Federal Election Commission (FEC), an independent regulatory agency responsible for enforcing the new law and administering the public funding program.[65]

[61] Teachout 2014, 182.

[62] Mutch 2016, 7.

[63] On the 1943 Smith–Connally (or "War Labor Disputes") Act, see Mutch 2016, 62.

[64] On the "campaign finance part of Watergate," see Mutch 2016, 13, and 15, on the FECA.

[65] Mutch 2016, 30–39. The Presidential Election Campaign Fund Act of 1966 had anticipated a similar mechanism, but it had never gone into effect (Mutch 2016, 153).

The 1974 Amendments to the FECA remain the fundamental regulatory framework for federal campaigns to this day, despite undergoing numerous modifications. The Amendments soon faced legal challenges on allegations that the limits on campaign contributions and expenditures violated free speech.[66] This issue, involving questions and jurisprudence about free speech, the rights of corporations, and their intersection, became a central topic of the debate. Subsequent changes to campaign finance were determined not by Congress, but by the courts,[67] particularly the Supreme Court. The Supreme Court's views on campaign finance have increasingly favored the removal of limits, a fact that should be understood in the context of the Court's composition. Since April 1970, it has had a majority of its nine members nominated by Republican Presidents, and currently, six of the nine members are appointees of Republican Presidents.[68] It would be wrong to draw strict conclusions on the leaning of Supreme Court Justices from the party affiliation of the President who appointed them. For example, Harry Blackmun, who was nominated by President Nixon, was known for his liberal opinions, including writing the majority opinion in the landmark Roe v. Wade case, which legalized abortion in 1973. However, polarization in the Supreme Court has increased over time.[69] For example, the 2000 Bush v. Gore case, which awarded the Presidency to Bush, was decided strictly along partisan lines.[70] Jurisprudence shifts during the last decades should more broadly be interpreted under the light of the rise of a conservative legal movement that superseded the previously hegemonic "liberal legal network."[71]

Significant changes in campaign finance, which largely bypassed Congress, actually started in 1976 with the Supreme Court case of Buckley v. Valeo. In this case, the Court upheld the limits on political

[66] Mutch 2016, 16–17, and Gaughan 2016.

[67] With the significant exception of the BCRA of 2002, on which I will return.

[68] See United States Senate n.d.

[69] See Bonica and Sen 2021, who consider Martin–Quinn scores (Martin and Quinn 2002), and note that "prior to the 1990s, voting patterns reveal substantial ideological overlap of justices appointed by Republicans and Democrats. Following the retirement of John Paul Stevens in 2009, justices separated into two distinct ideological voting blocks along party lines."

[70] Roe v. Wade was overturned in 2022, with a 6 to 3 majority drawn along partisan lines. Bush v. Gore represented a historical juncture in US and world history for more than one reason. It later allowed George W. Bush, as President, to nominate Chief Justice John Roberts, who was to concur in the momentous campaign finance decisions that we are about to discuss (2010 Citizens United v. FEC and 2014 McCutcheon v. FEC), and Samuel Alito, who also aligned with the majority in Citizens United and McCutcheon.

[71] Teles 2008.

contributions established by the 1974 Amendments to the FECA Act and its other provisions, but made a crucial distinction between contributions and spending. The Court acknowledged the risk of corruption from political contributions, but determined that political spending had the same First Amendment protection as political speech.[72] Moreover, the Court held that such protection must extend not only to candidates, but also to independent expenditures made on their behalf by citizens and non-party groups without the candidate's authorization, on the basis that the absence of authorization would prevent corrupt quid-pro-quo transactions.[73] From then on, the jurisprudence developed in a direction where corruption was defined as an explicit quid-pro-quo transaction and did not take into account the negative impact that even the appearance of corruption could have in a democracy. The most significant impact of the Buckley v. Valeo decision was in the area of independent expenditures, as it created opportunities to evade the restrictions of the FECA.[74]

In order to comply with the ruling in Buckley v. Valeo, the FECA was further amended in 1976. The number of registered political action committees (PACs) and the amount of business money in elections significantly increased in the late 1970s. During the 1980s, a highly controversial issue arose regarding so-called "soft money," which was money that parties were allowed to raise and spend for party-building activities under an amendment to the FECA in 1979. This was a vague category that provided ample room for interpretation, but was later regulated in 2002 with the Bipartisan Campaign Reform Act (BCRA or McCain-Feingold Act), which remains to these days the most recent legislation focused on campaign finance.[75] The BCRA was defended on constitutional grounds in 2003 in the McConnell v. FEC case, which to date is the last Supreme Court ruling to uphold a campaign finance law.

In 2007, FEC v. Wisconsin Right to Life and in 2008, Davis v. FEC made it clear that the Supreme Court was inclined toward a jurisprudence that did not support strict limitations on campaign finance. The landmark case Citizens United v. FEC in 2010 marked a turning point

[72] Issacharoff and Karlan 1998 summarize the contradiction intrinsic in the distinction between contributions and expenditures (which were not to be limited) with a simile: "The effect is much like giving a starving man unlimited trips to the buffet table but only a thimble-sized spoon with which to eat: chances are great that the constricted means to satisfy his appetite will create a singular obsession with consumption." See also Gerken 2014.

[73] Mutch 2016, 20. Moreover, "The Supreme Court decided that issue advocacy was not political at all" (Mutch 2016, 21).

[74] Mutch 2016, 23. This scenario also condemned the presidential public funding program, which was all but dead by 2012, when both major party candidates opted out of it.

[75] Mutch 2016, 158.

in the history of campaign finance by ruling that corporations and trade unions have a First Amendment's right to make independent expenditures in candidate elections. The importance of the case is not limited to campaign finance. It established a limited definition of corruption, in a major shift from the previous stance taken by the Supreme Court, which had gradually broadened the definition of corruption to encompass more than just quid-pro-quo exchanges.[76]

This ruling opened the door to subsequent decisions,[77] such as SpeechNow v. FEC in 2010, where the Federal Circuit Court for the District of Columbia determined that the 2003 BCRA's ban on all independent expenditures by corporations and unions violated the First Amendment's protection of free speech. As a result, the distinction between contributions and expenditures made in the Buckley v. Valeo's case lost significance, and the entire framework of campaign finance rules that had been established since the beginning of the century with the Tillman Act of 1907 became practically irrelevant.[78]

Certainly, attempts to evade campaign finance rules have been present since their inception. However, the Citizens United and subsequent sentences have created new avenues for political actors to utilize different instruments in an effort to bypass these rules. This has led to an increase in anonymous political donations flowing into American politics, often referred to as "dark money." One of the most significant impacts of Citizens United and SpeechNow was the creation of "super PACs," independent expenditure committees that can accept unlimited contributions from American individuals, corporations, or labor unions.[79] This has allowed the ultra-rich to not only donate to political campaigns practically without limits, but also to become major political players in their own right. Some billionaires even sidestepped political parties to construct their own parallel political machines, as did the Koch brothers who, through their network of donors, have exerted significant influence on the Republican Party. They were involved in crucial functions, such as assembling and

[76] Gerken 2014.

[77] See Kang 2010.

[78] A further relevant Supreme Court ruling was McCutcheon v. FEC, which in 2014 struck down the aggregate limit to the amount anyone could contribute to candidates, parties, and PACs in an election cycle, which had been established in the 1974 Amendments to the FECA.

[79] Their flexibility allowed them to occasionally take over the role that previously had been played by party's exploratory committees (Mutch 2016, 85). Creativity permitted further developments, such as the "hybrid PAC," which is "the grafting of a super PAC onto a standard non-connected PAC" (Mutch 2016, 75).

managing strategic databases used to recruit volunteers and mobilize voters. In describing these events, Theda Skocpol and Caroline Tervo do not mince words when they affirm that the Republican Party was "outflanked by a massive, Koch political machine" to become "a wholly owned subsidiary of ultra-free-market ideologues," leading to a situation where "Republican Party elites were all-in for an unpopular agenda featuring upward-tilted tax cuts and the undercutting of government capacities to redistribute resources and regulate the market economy."[80]

MONEY AND POLITICS: THE DATA AVAILABLE

To complete a broad-brush picture of the evolution of campaign finance in the United States, I present a synthesis of the data available, focusing on the federal-level and excluding state-level politics.[81] Election cycles last two years, ending in even-numbered years, with congressional elections renewing the House of Representatives and a third of the Senate in November. Presidential elections take place at the end of every other election cycle, resulting in higher costs for those cycles. The changes in campaign finance regulations in the past few decades have led to a significant increase in the amount of money being poured into politics, a trend that has been frequently reported in the media.[82] However, if we express campaign expenses as a percentage of GDP, the increase is not as pronounced, showing a modest increase until the 2018 cycle (Figure 8.6; the data series beginning in 1990 is more circumscribed).[83] The 2020 presidential election, which saw Joe Biden defeat Donald Trump, was perceived as an existential struggle and commanded an exceptional effort from both parties, resulting in a sharp increase in expenditures, and data on the 2022 cycle confirm the trend.

The amount of money spent on federal elections in the United States may seem significant, but in the grand scheme of things, it only accounts for a

80 Skocpol and Tervo 2020. Democrats followed suit, in 2005, with the so-called Democratic alliance (Mutch 2016, 100). Gerken 2014, in commenting the rise of dark money subsequent to Citizens United, observes that "The worry […] isn't so much about dark money, but 'shadow parties'-organizations outside of the party that house the party elites." See also Hertel-Fernandez et al. 2018.

81 Aggregating campaign finance data is laborious, and to provide an overall indication I consider data from the Center for Responsive Politics, whose project "Opensecrets.org" serves as a clearing house for data on campaign finance.

82 For example, The Economist noted in 2014 that "with nearly every American election cycle new spending records are broken" (The Economist 2014).

83 The source for this narrower aggregate (Open Secrets n.d.c.), which is based on data from the FEC, also is the Center for Responsive Politics.

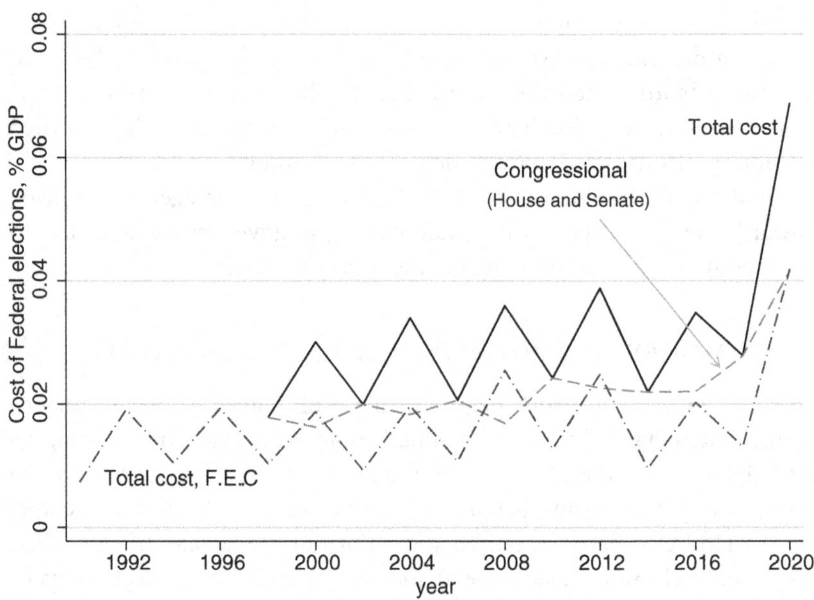

Figure 8.6 Total cost of federal elections as a percentage of GDP
Source of the data: Top two lines: Open Secrets n.d.b., including the amount of money spent by party committees on election activities, so-called "outside" spending such as money spent on issue ads, political action committees' money on overhead expenses. Bottom line: Open Secrets n.d.c.; GDP: The World Bank.

very small portion of the country's GDP, and also of the value of the policies that it may desire to influence.[84] This highlights the idea that there is "little money" in American politics, a topic that will be explored in Chapter 9. It is also important to note that, even if a great share of contributions are from wealthy people, small donors also play a significant role in directly funding candidates.[85] Additionally, PAC money disproportionately comes from

[84] See also Malbin and Glavin 2020, 11. On a yearly basis, these figures should be halved, since they are lumped in two-year electoral cycles. It is worth noting that comparing a category of costs with national product should only be taken as an expository device, since the two variables are incommensurable. Someone's costs are someone else's revenues, which are invariably more than value added. Gross national product, on the other hand, reflects value added. Ansolabehere et al. 2003 noted that "Candidates, parties and organizations raised and spent $3 billion in the 2000 national elections" (approximately as is reported in Figure 8.5), while in the same year "consumption and gross investment of the federal government was $590 billion; and the actual and potential costs of compliance with regulations were surely worth hundreds of billions of dollars, as well."

[85] The preponderance of rich donors confers Republicans an advantage; Bartels 2016, 116 and 280. See Malbin et al. 2020, 7, on the importance of small donors in the 2016 presidential elections.

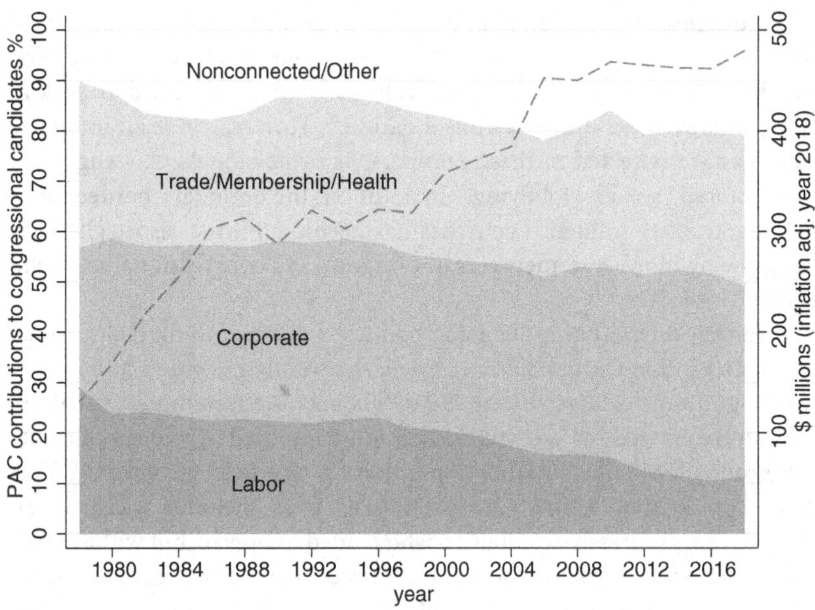

Figure 8.7 PAC contributions to congressional candidates
Source of the data: Malbin and Glavin 2020, Table 2.10. The dashed line refers to the right vertical axis.

moneyed interests. The spending of PACs on congressional candidates has increased four-fold since 1979, reaching $480 million in 2018 (indicated by the dashed line in Figure 8.7). It is also worth noting that the composition of PAC contributions has changed, a fact on which I will return, with labor's relative share decreasing from 29% to 11% and corporations increasing from 27% to 38%.

LOBBYING, THE MEDIA, AND OTHER FORMS OF INFLUENCE

Moneyed interests have more than one way to influence the political process besides campaign finance, be it proactively, by seeking new policies to be approved, be it, perhaps more often, defensively to preserve a status quo which serves them well.[86]

Lobbying is one of these methods. Lobbying expenses are estimated to cost approximately $3.5 billion per year, or less than 0.02% of GDP.

[86] See De Figueiredo and Richter 2014.

These expenses have more than doubled since the late 1990s and reached their current level in 2010, but have not changed significantly since. The number of registered lobbyists has declined by over 20% since its peak in 2007, following an industry consolidation.[87] However, not all influence activities are reflected in these numbers, as professionals may engage in unregistered "shadow lobbying." In addition, the boundary between lobbying and other influence activities has become blurred, especially with the growing number of members of Congress and congressional staff who become lobbyists.[88]

A further method of influencing politics is through think tanks, which originated in the United States in the early twentieth century and underwent significant changes in the 1980s. Thomas Medvetz notes that think tanks were created by "a tenuous coalition composed of two specific elite sub-groups located at proximate positions in the field of power."[89] One group consisted of technocratic intellectuals, while the other was made up of moderate progressive capitalists, who tended to prevail, but within a balancing act which took into account the need to confer a degree of autonomy to the holders of cultural capital.[90] This has been the model that, since the Progressive Era, has accompanied and favored a process of rationalization of the American corporation, presenting itself not only as a tool of shared prosperity, but also, as a good citizen.

The situation changed in the 1980s as a new type of think tank emerged, which resulted from the merging of traditional think tanks with activist organizations, favoring the political right, which, Medvetz notes, effectively took "control of the space of think tanks."[91] These developments also contributed to the active promotion of an intellectual climate where the

87 Data on lobbying are from the Center for Responsive Politics. See Open Secrets n.d.d.

88 On shadow lobbying, see Wedel 2014. For further examples, see Swaine and Rushe 2018, and The New York Times 2012. Ansolabehere et al. 2002 note that lobbying should be seen as linked to PAC contributions, and Mutch 2016, 135, notes that "lobbying and campaign finance have always sustained one another, but in the last decade they have merged to become a single operation." On the revolving door in Congress, see Mutch 2016, 136, who also notes that over time "Congress has strengthened its lobbying regulations," citing the Honest Leadership and Open Government Act of 2007 and, before that, the Lobbying Disclosure Act of 1995.

89 Medvetz 2012, 75.

90 Medvetz 2012, 78

91 Medvetz 2012, 93 and 95, who adds "Think tanks reordered the institutional space of knowledge production and consumption in the United States in a way that prevented the most autonomous social scientists from constituting themselves as effective participants in policy debates" (Medvetz 2012, 210)

poor were increasingly seen as undeserving of welfare,[92] redistributive policies, and even a progressive tax system. Further, the dominance eventually acquired by a conservative legal movement[93] represents the background of the developments in campaign finance that we have considered, and of the affirmation of a strict interpretation of corruption as a quid-pro-quo exchange. At a more general level, the intellectual climate amounted to a "great persuasion," where a particular version of neo-liberalism, lacking the social sensibilities of previous strands of its intellectual tradition, became hegemonic.[94]

Returning to the transformed think tanks that have emerged since the 1980s, they have focused on their relationship with the media, and political messaging has increasingly become a room of mirrors where political and commercial interests reflect into each other. Part of the political messages are communicated through the mass media as paid advertisements, to which is dedicated a significant portion of the campaign expenditures documented. Investment in politics creates content that the media industry is interested in, as it attracts a paying audience. Internet platforms such as Facebook and X (formerly, Twitter) also benefit from the traffic generated by political content. These mechanisms were evident during the 2016 election cycle, when Donald Trump's candidacy received so much media attention that, according to an estimate, it benefited from $5 billion in free advertising.[95] Regardless of the accuracy of this estimate, the value of media coverage in political affairs is substantial. The mass media might be viewed as providing a matching fund mechanism to investments made into politics, as it repackages and sells the content that candidates and parties produce using the money they collect and spend. Any money spent on political advertisements through the media contributes to the visibility and newsworthiness of a political project, which in turn generates free coverage and attracts donors, creating a multiplier effect. This means that the amount of money involved in elections that we have previously discussed is an underestimate of the true amount.

92 See Medvetz 2012, 179, on Charles Murray's 1984 book "Losing Ground," "which argued that the availability of AFDC [Aid to Families with Dependent Children] benefits had created a durable culture of dependency that encouraged illegitimate childbearing, criminal activity, drug abuse, and labor market avoidance."

93 Teles 2008. Increase in economic inequality, in turn, made it easier for the conservatives right to find deep-pocketed *patrons*, on whose essential role in the formation of an "alternative governing coalition" (alternative to the previous, equally hegemonic, "liberal legal network") see Teles 2008, 19–20.

94 Burgin 2012.

95 Bump 2017. That amount of money comes close to the total cost of those presidential elections, 5.7 billion dollars.

Not all political projects receive the same "kick for the buck" through the media system. Candidates and political parties may be more or less media savvy, and media reporting may be biased toward certain political projects, also depending on the independence of the media from corporate interests. According to an optimistic view, competition in the market for news serves as a vehicle for "the truth" to emerge: A plurality of heterogeneous media outlets complicates any attempt at capture.[96] Such "marketplace of ideas" has figured high in American thinking and Supreme Court's jurisprudence. More realistically, as Tim Wu puts it, it is "the structure of the information industries" [that] "determines who gets heard." The history of the media in the United States is marked by corporate actors repeatedly trying and often succeeding in "controlling the master switch."[97]

In recent decades, journalism has experienced a significant crisis, due to the shift to digital formats and the increasing importance of online advertising, which has severely impacted its revenue. The emphasis has shifted from hard news to soft news, and the role of Public Relations has grown.[98] Despite attempts to find new revenue models and forms of journalism, the overall impact on the industry has been severe. While it is possible that new forms of journalism that serve the needs of democracy will finally take hold, the ongoing transition is concerning, as the shortage of resources makes it easier for well-funded actors to exert political influence. This risk has been made palpable by the purchase of The Washington Post by Jeff Bezos in 2013, and Twitter (now named X) by Elon Musk in 2022.

CONCLUSIONS: LEGAL CORRUPTION IN THE UNITED STATES

A striking contrast emerges when examining corruption in the United States. On one hand, a circumscribed definition of the phenomenon would suggest that there is relatively little corruption, following a series of reforms that took place over a long historical period. Under these perspectives,

96 Besley and Prat 2006. Gentzkow and Shapiro 2008 offer an overall optimistic review of the question – or at any rate, a pessimistic view on possible alternatives to the "marketplace of ideas." However, they also recognize that such market is structurally thinner when it comes to local news, as compared to national ones, and increasingly so during the last decades. For a very critical view, see McChesney 2008.

97 Wu 2010, 13, who further cites Fred Friendly (onetime CBS News president): "Before any question of free speech comes the question of 'who controls the master switch'" (Wu 2010, 9).

98 McChesney 2008, 38–56.

the United States represents a success story, where reforms driven by anti-corruption motivations have made it a model of good governance. However, the United States has become a highly unequal and socially static society, contradicting the image and self-image of the country as a land of opportunities and a well-established prosperous democracy. This outcome suggests that the interests of the very wealthy have successfully infiltrated the political process through channels that I have described and that have become increasingly effective over time.

It could be argued that in the United States, one form of corruption (legal) has replaced another (illegal) because the former now fulfills the needs that previously necessitated the latter. These are questions that I explore in Chapter 9, which delves into legal corruption and other "geographies of corruption." Chapter 9 also marks the beginning of the third and last part of the book, which aims to extract relevant lessons from the countries we have considered, and to consolidate the themes that we have discussed thus far.

PART III

RETHINKING CORRUPTION

9

Legal Corruption and Other Societal Geographies

You don't have to break the law, when you make the law
Kyle Whitmire[1]

Part III of the book revisits the main themes that have been gradually developed, expanding on them in light of the three case studies discussed in Chapters 6–8, and drawing relevant lessons from them. Specifically, this chapter presents definitions of corruption that diverge from the prevailing ones, which tend to be narrow and focused on public office. These alternative definitions build upon the characterization of corruption offered in Chapter 5 and represent distinct interpretations of the "distance" between an ideal societal norm and the reality as observed.

Using a spatial metaphor, I first explore different societal geographies. One of these geographies is represented by the concept of legal corruption, which I define as actions that do not violate the law but have practical effects similar to those produced by bribes. To illustrate, consider a company successfully lobbying to remove an environmental regulation, thus avoiding the need to bribe the relevant inspectors. Referring back to the discussion in Chapter 5, the definition of legal corruption that I propose aligns with an ideal polity where the consequences of bribery do not occur. If we do observe these consequences, despite no law having been broken, then it can be considered a case of legal corruption.

The example above suggests that the legal and illegal alternatives have partially similar effects, as both allow the firm to increase its profits. However, there are significant differences between the two cases. When a firm successfully bribes an inspector, it only affects a specific inspection, while the future would likely require additional corrupt agreements. On

[1] Whitmire 2019, cited in Dincer and Johnston 2020b.

the other hand, the legal alternative, represented by successful lobbying to change the law and legalize pollution, promises to have a more lasting impact. Another consequential difference between the two cases is that one is a crime, while the other is not. In this regard, legal corruption appears to be preferable to its illegal counterpart, as implied by the quotation that opens this chapter. However, in Chapter 10, where corruption is discussed as a tool of government, we will also consider the practical advantages of breaking the law while influencing its enforcement. More broadly, once we distinguish between illegal and legal corruption, the question of their mutual relationships arises. This theme has already been touched upon in Chapter 8 with reference to the United States and will be further explored in the upcoming pages.

In exploring different societal geographies, I propose a specific approach to define an ideal normative state against which corrupt distances can be measured. I suggest that we could choose as the ideal state the aspirational definition that a polity offers of itself. Societies can be seen as having blueprints, which are inevitably subject to contestation, but may occasionally be expressed with relative precision, albeit conditionally to a set of premises. For instance, we can consider the ideal reference point to be a country's fundamental principles as expressed in its constitution or as inferred from a thoughtful public discourse. The United States is well suited for the application of such a concept due to the presence of the "American Dream," a pervasive and widely shared ideology that can reasonably serve as a reference point for how the polity perceives itself. Accordingly, a legitimate definition of corruption in the United States would be the discrepancy between what the American Dream implies and what is observed in reality.

Finally, in this chapter, I argue that legal corruption in the United States, and its deviation from its aspirational goal, can be understood as a vicious cycle resulting from the accumulation of economic and political power. This accumulation is driven by two types of struggles in which the wealthy are involved: one against the poor and the other within the elite itself.

THE IDEA OF LEGAL CORRUPTION

The prevailing narrow definition of corruption has not gone unchallenged. In particular, the thesis that corruption can also be legal has been a counterargument in the debate over the past few decades and is one of its "soft edges" that I am interested in. Daniel Kaufmann, a prominent figure in the promotion of an anti-corruption agenda at the World Bank, suggested in his farewell speech on December 9, 2008, that when discussing corruption, we should consider "how elites collude and purchase, or unduly influence the rules of the game, shape the institutions, the policies and regulations and the laws for their own private benefits." Kaufmann explicitly mentioned legal corruption as "getting particularly preferential treatment in terms of the regulatory environment through legal political contributions" and more generally proposed "redefining the notion of corruption," stating that it was "a bit obsolete to call it 'abuse of public office for private gain.' Instead, it is 'privatization of public policy,' a much higher-level political notion, and this crisp definition would encapsulate capture as well."[2]

The concept of "capture," as referred to by Kaufmann, has a long and interesting history. Capture can be defined as the process by which one societal actor successfully influences another actor to serve the interests of the former. The focus has mostly been on "state capture," where private interests influence and control the actions of the state and its institutions. In particular, the concept has been originally applied to the study of state regulation of corporations, within a significant debate on "regulatory capture" that emerged in the United States during the 1950s. This debate presented a critique of the regulatory state, which, as discussed in Chapter 8, was established in the course of the first part of the nineteenth century. The critique of regulatory capture was part of a resurgence of neoliberal ideas, as the New Deal Order gave way to the Neoliberal Order.[3]

The argument put forward, particularly during the 1960s and 1970s when "capture theory and social science investigations of regulatory agencies grew increasingly ideological,"[4] was that private interests would naturally and inevitably succeed in capturing their regulators. The implication was that since nothing could be done with the capturer, because to capture is in its nature, the problem was with the captured, to the point that regulations had to be dispensed with. William Novak notes that the critique witnessed the beginning of a "more general resurgence of interest in competition and private enterprise as countervailing forces to the rise of a bureaucratic state" and adds that "the political ramifications of that broad critique of government continue to be felt today both in the resilient influence of neoliberal policies such as deregulation and privatization as well as in the rise of more virulent and populist forms of anti-statism."

[2] Kaufmann 2008. On his speech, also see Rothstein 2011, 60.

[3] With reference to Gerstle 2022.

[4] Novak 2013, also for the citations that follow.

Similar conclusions were also reached from different ideological positions, as seen in the case of Gabriel Kolko, who viewed progressivism as a manifestation of the desires and needs of big business, including its regulatory aspects that were to outlast it.[5] William Novak notes that these different voices created "something like a cacophony of consensus" and shared a narrow historical view that overlooked the fact that the tradition of regulation in the United States is not solely a product of the Progressive Era. It dates back to the early days of the Republic and should be interpreted within the debate on the corrupting role of corporations. The significant growth of US corporations at the end of the nineteenth century certainly reignited public concerns about their corrupting influence. However, such concerns had been a prominent topic of discussion since the formative years of the Republic, following a historical development of ideas that I have outlined earlier in the book. William Novak concludes that, in this sense, the modern theory of regulatory capture although "frequently heralded as a new and distinctly contemporary economic theory, from the long perspective of history it looks more like old wine in new bottles." By disconnecting itself from the tradition of thought on corruption, modern regulatory theory had the effect, when not the intention, of circumscribing the debate and deflecting attention away from corporations.

The concept of capture, however, is quite adaptable. When it resurfaced in the early 2000s, interestingly, no meaningful reference was made to the previous debate on regulatory capture. Instead, corruption took center stage. The occasion was provided by the failed liberalization of the economies of former socialist countries during the previous decade. Joel Hellman, Geraint Jones, and Daniel Kaufmann observe that "after only a decade of transition, the fear of the *leviathan state* has been replaced by a new concern about powerful oligarchs who manipulate politicians, shape institutions, and control the media to advance and protect their own empires at the expense of the social interest." Capture and corruption are now intertwined, to the point that state capture is defined as a case of bribing: "the capacity of firms to shape and affect the formation of the basic rules of the game […] through private payments to politicians," while the activity of "influence" occurs if firms successfully intervene but bribing is absent.[6]

Daniel Kauffman and Pedro Vicente subsequently articulated a more comprehensive view of legal corruption.[7] They posited that legality in fact

[5] Kolko 1963.
[6] Hellman et al. 2000. See also David-Barrett 2021.
[7] Kaufmann and Vicente 2011.

should be seen as endogenous, since it is "defined at the political level" and it represents a "decision variable of the elite in power." Within this line of thought, they consider that an elite "may build a legal framework to protect her [sic] own conduct of corruption (e.g., legal lobbying)." This may only be done at a cost, so that when such investment is observed, it might be interpreted as a form of rent-seeking. The presence or absence of such a legal framework defines the distinction between forms of corruption that are legal or illegal. While these views align with my perspective on corruption as a tool of government, I will also clarify that elites may be content not to have such a "legal framework" in place if they have the opportunity to use justice as a cudgel. More generally, the interest and ability of elites to develop such a legal framework greatly depend on contextual factors.

Daniel Kaufmann's perspective becomes even more interesting when considering his role as the leader of the World Bank's anti-corruption initiatives during James Wolfensohn's presidency between 1995 and 2005, when the World Bank became a stronghold of the anti-corruption global regime.[8] However, the notion of legal corruption had been present in the corruption debate long before. For example, in 1993 Philip Jos noted that "insofar as the legal definition of corruption is subject to manipulation by powerful interests, it is an unreliable guide to 'corrupt' behavior."[9] As we also are about to do, Jos considered the distance that may be observed between the stated principles of a polity, and its reality, and argued that it may lead to public cynicism and demoralization. He mentioned the case of the Soviet Union, whose "political system [was] built on hypocrisy, where public trust and political legitimacy are destroyed and the public becomes cynical, jaded, and withdrawn." Jos also took on the United States, noting that "many worry that the post-Watergate era rise in public cynicism and distrust signals an increasingly corrupted, demoralized American polity." This line of reasoning allowed him to reconnect with views of corruption which I ascribed to Republican political thought, as it "was understood by normative theorists from the Greeks to Rousseau, who saw corruption as involving the 'decline in the ability and willingness of the citizens to act spontaneously or disinterestedly to support other citizens or communal institutions.'"[10]

8 See Kaufmann 2005.

9 Jos 1993, who interestingly provides the following example "In contemporary American politics [...] political action committees undermine open and fair access to the electoral and lawmaking processes."

10 Jos 1993, here citing Dobel 1978, 983.

More recently, Oguzhan Dincer and Michael Johnston have examined the concept of legal corruption, concluding that "grounds exist for arguing that legal corruption is a genuine analytical and political issue" and finding "widespread perceptions of legal corruption" in the United States.[11] Changes in campaign finance practices, on one hand, and the increase in economic inequality, on the other, have contributed to a surge in the interest in legal forms of corruption. Ray Fisman and Miriam Golden note that "the legal demarcation of corruption has become stricter and more standardized internationally with the passage of time," while proposing a nuanced interpretation of cases such as "U.S. Treasury Secretary Timothy Geithner becoming president of Warburg Pincus (a company he had been charged with regulating) in 2013, just over a year after leaving office," which was not illegal but could be perceived as corrupt.[12]

The debate on legal corruption can also be traced back to analyses of corruption that were framed within sociological functionalism. James Scott notes how "the routes by which wealth as a political resource influences government policies – and whether such routes are 'corrupt' or not – depend largely on the nature of the political system." In an example he provides, he implicitly acknowledges the endogenous nature of such outcomes, much like Kaufmann and Vicente would do more than forty years later: "In England, before civil service reforms eventually eliminated the practice, a tremendous number of sinecures ('offices without employment') and pensions were regularly distributed or sold by the crown with an eye to gaining allies and/or revenue. Although contemporary observers had begun to object to this custom, such patronage did not violate any existing law until the Whigs found it to their political advantage."[13]

Unlike for illegal corruption, there is no widely recognized measure of legal corruption (nor of "capture") that has gained significant public visibility. The under-theorization of the concept of legal corruption has hindered attempts at providing measures, and their absence has been an obstacle to research and public discourse, a question that I explored in

[11] Dincer and Johnston 2020a, with evidence on perceptions of legal corruption coming from Dincer and Johnston 2017, on which I will return.

[12] Fisman and Golden 2017, 25–29. They add that "influence peddling – the intrusion of big business's money into public life – is the leading candidate for expanding our definition to include acts by public officials that run counter to public interest or public opinion, even if they are legal," noting that "in the court of public opinion, influence peddling is deemed corrupt, despite being perfectly legal" (Fisman and Golden 2017, 44, and also 79, on the relevance of the concept of legal corruption).

[13] Scott 1969.

general terms in Chapter 3. However, some attempts have been made to quantifying legal corruption. Daniel Kaufmann and Pedro Vicente propose a measure based on answers to several survey questions on various types of political influence.[14] Oguzhan Dincer and Michael Johnston define legal corruption as "the political gains in the form of campaign contributions or endorsements by a government official in exchange for providing specific benefits to private individuals or groups, be it by explicit or implicit understanding." They measure this concept at the state level in the United States using a survey of local reporters.[15]

We are about to consider a further measure that develops the concept I introduced earlier, which is corruption as a distance between a polity's perceived identity and reality. In the case of the United States, the notion of the American Dream serves as a valuable benchmark for the nation's self-perception. The result will be a measure that is *not* of legal corruption, but that will however permit us to proceed in the exploration of those "geographies" where legal corruption also is located.

CORRUPTION AS AN "INTERNAL DISTANCE"

If it is true that every polity possesses a collective and disputed notion of its identity, the United States stands out in this regard due to the pervasive influence of the American Dream. This concept enjoys broad acceptance across the political spectrum, even during a time such as ours of heightened political polarization. Also for this reason, it provides fertile ground for applying a definition of corruption as the distance between a polity's self-presentation and the actual reality it faces.

Jennifer Hochschild contends that the American Dream is an "impressive ideology" that "promises that everyone, regardless of ascription or background, may reasonably seek success through actions and traits under their own control," "Not all Americans share it," she notes, and "at certain periods of our history its preeminence has waxed or waned; its definition has varied, as have its competitors. But since the era of Andrew Jackson (and perhaps before), the American dream has been a defining characteristic of American culture, aspirations, and — ostensibly, at least — institutions, against which all competitors must contend."[16] Jennifer Wolak

14 Kaufmann and Vicente 2011.

15 Dincer and Johnston 2020b. The same definition of legal corruption can be found in Dincer and Johnston 2017, and in Dincer and Johnston 2020a.

16 Hochschild 1995, 4 and 25.

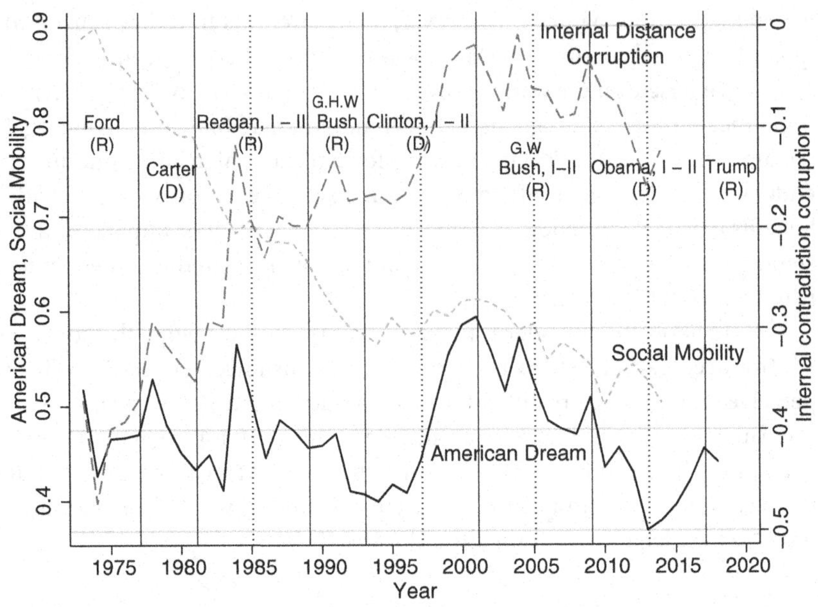

Figure 9.1 A measure of "internal distance corruption"
Source of the data. American dream index (left vertical axis): Wolak and Peterson 2020 (yearly averages). Social mobility index (left vertical axis): Chetty et al. 2017a (cohort mean, as in Wolak and Peterson 2020). Vertical lines indicate presidential inaugurations.

and David Peterson, who define the American Dream similarly, propose an interesting quantification of this concept, obtained by aggregating multiple surveys. This permits them to create a measure of the American Dream from 1973 to 2018.[17] When considering the possible determinants of this measure, they find that "declining social mobility and rising income inequality erode public belief in the American dream"; however, the effects that they detect, for example, of increases in inequality as it is measured by the Gini coefficients, are only temporary.

Over the long term, the American Dream appears to remain unaffected by the documented increase in economic inequality and decline in social mobility, regardless of any short-term effects. This is evident from Figure 9.1,

[17] Wolak and Peterson 2020. The measure considers "the pool of all survey questions that have been asked about components of the American Dream," using Stimson's 1999, 2018, "dyad ratios algorithm," to produce "a single series of the public's belief in the American Dream over time, built on the shared variance that exists between multiple measures across surveys" (Wolak and Peterson 2020). The proposed measure is quarterly, while I consider yearly averages.

which compares the measure of the American Dream with Chetty et al.'s indicator of social mobility discussed in Chapter 8. While belief in the American Dream has experienced significant fluctuations since the 1970s, there has been no enduring change in the overall trend. In fact, the most recent value of the index is comparable to the levels observed in the mid-1970s when economic inequality was significantly lower and social mobility was higher.[18]

I propose a definition of corruption as an "internal distance" within a society, which refers to the disparity between the society's self-representation and the observed reality. In the case of the United States, the American Dream serves as the societal representation, while one of its crucial aspects, social mobility as it is observed, represents reality. Purely for illustrative purposes, the concept of "internal distance corruption" can be quantified simply as the difference between the Wolak and Peterson's American Dream index and the measure of social mobility provided by Chetty et al. and discussed in Chapter 8. The measure (Figure 9.1) exhibits a significant increase between the mid-1970s and the end of the century, coinciding with a significant decrease in social mobility. Interestingly, the overall increase in this measure does not align with the relatively constant perceptions of corruption in the United States depicted in Figure 8.2 (page 144).

The term "internal distance corruption" encompasses a range of factors, including both legal and illegal actions, *as well as inaction*, that contribute to the disparity between societal representation and reality. For instance, the decline in income mobility in the United States has more than one cause, and, as discussed in Chapter 8, one of them is the concomitant long-term decline in economic growth.[19] Additionally, factors such as skill bias in technological change, and broader influences like globalization, may also have contributed to the decrease in mobility.[20] At least some of these causes, such as broadly defined globalization, may be considered to be exogenous to a given polity and independent from its actions.

[18] These data seem to disprove Hochschild 1995, 27, who predicted that the fantasies of success that are implied by the American Dream "are innocuous so long as resources roughly balance dreams for enough people enough of the time. But if they do not – worse yet, if they used to but do no longer – then the dream rapidly loses its appeal." However, almost in the same breath she defines the American Dream an "ideology of deception" (Hochschild 1995, 36).

[19] See page 155, with reference to Chetty et al. 2017a.

[20] For a critical appraisal of such view, see Atkinson 2015, 84–85.

It may seem unconventional to label inaction as corrupt, since corruption is typically associated with observable behaviors rather than lack thereof. However, this perspective on corruption is just one among many. For instance, Machiavelli would consider politically inactive citizens as corrupt due to their lack of virtue.[21] Acknowledging that the term "corrupt" can be applied to a condition caused by external forces beyond our control opens up the possibility for taking corrective actions to counteract those forces. In the United States, even those who believe that the increase in inequality and the decrease in social mobility have purely exogenous causes would likely agree that appropriate policies could have a countervailing effect. For example, higher taxes on the rich could finance a less classist education system. On the contrary, a view of corruption that is solely focused on behaviors, as is the prevailing view centered on public office, implies disregarding such corrective policies or making them less plausible on the political agenda. In conclusion, the value judgments upon which a particular concept of corruption is based also influence our understanding of the actions that can counter corruption. This is just as true for the "internal distance" measure of corruption of Figure 9.1, as it is for the view of corruption as an "abuse of entrusted power."

THE AMERICAN DREAM: PERCEPTIONS AND POLITICAL CHOICES

From the previous discussion, the important question arises of why Americans have kept their faith in their dream, despite a sharp decrease in social mobility and an increase in inequality. The resilience of the American Dream, despite its diminishing practical relevance, suggests the presence of a systematic shortsightedness among a significant portion of the population. To interpret this phenomenon, I turn to a metaphor introduced by Albert Hirschman half a century ago to illustrate tolerance (or lack thereof) for increasing inequality – the "tunnel effect":

> Suppose that I drive through a two-lane tunnel, both lanes going in the same direction, and run into a serious traffic jam. No car moves in either lane as far as I can see (which is not very far). I am in the left lane and feel dejected. After a while the cars in the right lane begin to move. Naturally, my spirits lift considerably, for I know that the jam has been broken and that my lane's turn to move will surely come any moment now. Even though I still sit still, I feel much better off than before because of the expectation that I shall soon be on the move. But suppose

[21] Viroli 1998, 131, describes corruption in Machiavelli as a "kind of laziness."

that the expectation is disappointed and only the right lane keeps moving: in that case I, along with my left lane co-sufferers, shall suspect foul play, and many of us will at some point become quite furious and ready to correct manifest injustice by taking direct action (such as illegally crossing the double line separating the two lanes).[22]

Witnessing someone getting ahead of us economically can either "lift spirits" or raise the suspicion of "foul play." In order to avoid resentment, those in the fast lane will want to convince the slower movers that they, too, will soon make progresses. In considering Wolak and Peterson's measure of the American Dream, we would conclude that most Americans, metaphorically driving inside Hirschman's tunnel, think that they are moving or that they are about to, when in fact they are not. It seems that most Americans suffer from a serious problem of perception regarding their economic predicaments. Larry Bartels addresses these broad questions and demonstrates the partisan slant of redistributive policies in the United States. Considering that the policies carried out by the Republican Party have led to a minority of rich becoming richer, we would expect well-informed and rational voters to vote them out of office and elect Democrats instead. Observing, to the contrary, that the Republican Party has often been victorious in the face of the continuously increasing levels of inequality that it has enabled may call into question one of the basic characteristics that a democracy should have: "Retrospective voting," where electors cast their ballot by considering how they have been served by incumbent politicians.[23]

Larry Bartels has documented how perception biases affect American voters and influence their electoral choices. For instance, many voters tend to exhibit a form of short-termism, focusing primarily on economic growth during the year prior to an election while ignoring growth during the earlier part of a presidential term.[24] This systematic bias favors Republican presidential candidates. In fact, Democrats often implement expansionary policies during their first year in the White House, at the expense of less growth or even recession toward the end of their term in office, whereas

22 Hirschman and Rothschild 1973 (Michael Rothschild authored only the mathematical appendix of the article).

23 Bartels 2016. Healy and Malhotra 2013 note that "the evaluation of incumbent performance at the ballot box plays a key role in democratic accountability."

24 See Bartels 2016, chapter 3, also for the rest of the paragraph. Ray Fair's model of presidential elections (Fair 2009) concurs with this conclusion and includes among his explanatory variables lagged economic growth of real per capita GDP of "the first three quarters of the election year" only. See, however, Ray Fair's exchange with Larry Bartels (Bartels and Fair 1997).

Republicans tend to do the opposite. These factors help explain why the vast majority of Americans who have seen their share of income and wealth decline over the past four decades have been unable or unwilling to reverse this trend at the ballot box.

True, electors consider various issues when making their decisions, and the distribution of economic resources is just one of them. Some argue that ideological considerations on sensitive issues like race, the right to bear arms, international politics, abortion, and nativism have influenced many poor voters who previously voted for the Democratic Party. For example, Thomas Frank claimed that "the Republican Party has forged a new 'dominant political coalition' by attracting working-class white voters on the basis of 'class animus' and 'cultural wedge issues like guns and abortion'."[25] Larry Bartels argues that economic issues remain highly important for Americans, with no indication of a declining role.[26] However, despite four decades of increasing economic inequality, Americans' perceived salience of economic issues has remained relatively unchanged. This is welcome news for the rich, who have benefited from the lack of consequential redistributive policies and an increasingly regressive tax system. The reasons for their political success, and overall Gramscian hegemony, are complex and raise an age-old question, to which I now turn: whether economic outcomes can be insulated from political ones and vice versa.

ECONOMIC INEQUALITY AND POLITICAL POWER: A PRIORI KNOWLEDGE AND DECIDING WHAT TO TEST

An informed reading of history suggests that those in positions of political power often utilize their influence to acquire additional economic resources. Likewise, when a small segment of society controls a significant share of economic resources, they tend to leverage that wealth to further enhance their political power. Under this light, substantial economic inequalities, as seen in the United States, seem to contradict a core prescription of democracy, requiring that citizens possess an equal level of political power, except for the disparities that arise from its democratically sanctioned delegation.

Indeed, there are institutions, broadly defined, that aim to separate politics from economic inequality, such as the regulations on political campaign

[25] Frank 2007.

[26] These considerations are in Bartels 2008, 83–90, and they do not appear in the 2016 edition of the book.

finance that we have discussed. Building a functioning democracy within capitalist and intrinsically unequal societies can be seen as an effort to establish such institutions. While it is not an inherent certainty that money cannot be insulated from politics in the presence of pronounced economic inequality, a well-informed reading of human history strongly suggests such a conclusion. Therefore, the burden of proof should rest on those who argue otherwise. When examining this question using statistical methods and traditional hypothesis testing, the null hypothesis should state that distributional considerations do influence political outcomes, rather than the opposite. Selecting the null hypothesis as the absence of such a relationship, as has been done repeatedly, may reflect an ideological stance that views our current times or country as exceptional. Seen from a different angle, if we choose as the alternative hypothesis of a statistical test a platitude (in the case at hand, that money matters in politics), what detecting that platitude (rejecting the null hypothesis) would prove is a rather uninteresting mixed bag which includes the informative content of the data and perhaps the dexterity of the researcher.

Extensive research has indeed been conducted on the relationship between campaign funding and electoral outcomes in the United States, and it has been argued that the relatively small amount of money involved in campaigns indicates that politics is effectively insulated from economic inequality. This view appears to be supported by data presented in Chapter 8, which demonstrates that although campaign funding has increased over time, it still represents only a small fraction of the value of policies at stake.[27] From a basic economic perspective, if money spent in politics is seen as a form of investment to advance one's interests, it would be expected to yield a rate of return similar to other types of assets. If we observe relatively modest investments, we could perhaps conclude that it is not possible to "buy policies" and that, potentially for the first time in human history, effective institutional safeguards have been established in the United States to separate the realms of the economy and politics.

Such a perspective was first put forth by Gordon Tullock in 1972. In a short comment significantly titled "The purchase of politicians," noting that "the role of large-scale contributions in politics is frequently emphasized in the press," he argued that contributors to candidates would reasonably "aim at a profitable return on their investment" and that "there is no reason why they should receive a return which is markedly higher than the return on any other investment." He concluded that "unless business and

27 See in particular Figure 8.5 at page 155, which however refers to federal elections only.

others are irrationally underinvesting in this area, the amount of influence that can be purchased by this method is small," while adding a corollary on which I will return shortly: "Efforts to restrict the size of political gifts can be thought of as a cartel restriction intended to maximize the profit for those people who would still be permitted to make campaign contributions under the new conditions."[28]

However, if Tullock's logic were correct, we would hardly observe "enough money" reflecting a reasonable rate of return on the investments made. Such investments would be very expensive, and it is likely that the privileged few would prioritize making the purchase of policies to capture the political process possible on more favorable terms. Additionally, let us consider again the data shown in Figure 8.6 on page 162, displaying the composition of the contributions received by political action committees (PACs). Labor's relative share has dramatically decreased (from 29% to 11%), while that of corporations has increased from 27% to 38%. The share of labor continues to fall also after 2010, when Citizens United v. Federal Election Commission removed any brakes on that type of expenditure, dispelling Tullock's fears of a "cartel restriction." If we were to adopt Tullock's logic, we would have to interpret such a reduction as stemming from a concomitant decrease in labor's rate of return on investments in politics, relative to that of other "investors." However, it would be an exotic interpretation if we consider that the trade unions of 2018 were the phantoms of those of 1972, and the relative decline in their share of PAC money reflects, quite simply, their very diminished role, power, and overall relevance in US politics. Considering that organized labor has lost ground across the board since the 1970s, its return on political investment today should be higher, and we would expect to observe more, not less, labor money going into PACs. Using the lenses of economic analysis, perhaps we could suggest that this isn't the case because of credit rationing that limits trade union from borrowing money to invest in politics on the hope for a high future return. But this would amount to byzantine reasoning. Instead, accounting for the structures and strictures of power suggests a more concise explanation: During the last decades, organized labor lost its battle and defeated armies did not shoot much, pace economic marginalism.

[28] Tullock 1972. Gordon Tullock, a member of the Mount Pelerin Society (on its historical role in the formation of neoliberalism, see Burgin 2012), was connected for many years with the Mercatus Center, a "libertarian free-market-oriented" think tank financed by the Koch's family. See Mercatus Center n.d., Bogardus 2004, and Dayen 2018.

Due to the increasing inequality discussed earlier, the idea that the rich are able to influence politics because of their wealth has gained traction. But Tullock's framing of the problem has maintained resonance over time. It broadly informs an influential article by Stephen Ansolabehere, John De Figueiredo, and James Snyder Jr., who two decades ago reviewed the available evidence on the question of "why there is the so little money in US politics."[29] In this academic literature, the null hypothesis is that money does not influence political outcomes, placing the burden of proof on the opposite proposition, which, as I argued, is a surprising choice. Additionally, money can be effective not only when spent but also when simply available to serve as a threat, for example, as retribution against political opponents in the form of negative ads, financing opposing candidates, or engaging in shadier smearing campaigns, as in what has become known as "swift-boating."[30] Increasing economic inequality, together with decreasing restrictions on independent political expenditures, has made the threat of political retribution very credible even when it is not observed in practice.

ECONOMIC INEQUALITY, POLITICAL POWER, AND THEIR MUTUAL RELATIONSHIP

High levels of economic inequality inevitably spill over into politics and may create a self-reinforcing cycle between economic and political inequality. Greed and ambition may explain the desire of the rich and powerful to accumulate more wealth and influence. Being very rich, to the extent that the position is not purely inherited, implicitly signals the presence of such qualities. Increasingly often in the United States, great fortunes are partly inherited, and inherited wealth comes with socialization that instills useful values in the offspring. Detailed accounts of inheritors like the Koch brothers (Mayer 2016) and the Sackler family (Radden Keefe 2021) illustrate the effectiveness of this value transmission. The rationalization of extreme wealth can be portrayed as a social role or personal mission, carrying the responsibility of funding worthy political causes.

In my description of the interaction between the accumulation of money and political power, greed and ambition take however a secondary

[29] Ansolabehere et al. 2003.

[30] With reference to a 2004 smear campaign against the then Democratic Party presidential candidate John Kerry, by an organization largely financed by billionaires with ties to the Republican Party. See Vogel 2010, and Open Secrets n.d.a.

role. I focus instead on a defensive preoccupation: the desire to safeguard one's economic and political resources against a perceived risk of expropriation. I use the term "expropriation" in a broad sense, to represent the fear of losing what may be perceived as one's own. In the realm of politics, expropriation is equated with a relative loss of power resulting from political competition, ranging from losing a democratic election to arbitrary imprisonment by a victorious opponent or worse.[31] Those who hold political power have a clear incentive to acquire more economic resources, for personal consumption and to finance their political careers. However, my main interest lies in the desire of economic elites to acquire even greater economic resources, which carries significant political implications.

In the economic domain, I use the term expropriation extensively to encompass taxation, industry regulation that decreases rents arising from market power, and partial or total loss following unsuccessful market activities. I also include expropriation *stricto sensu*, for example, as Russian capitalists and foreign investors experienced after the Revolution. The fear of economic expropriation and the difficulty that the wealthy encounter in accepting property concessions are partly explained by a binary nature of property rights. Even partial concessions may be perceived as dangerous since they imply that property rights are negotiable. Therefore, economic elites have an interest in presenting property rights as an absolute and an ahistorical category and in limiting any unavoidable concessions.[32]

When examining the potential for economic expropriation, the wealthy are engaged in two interconnected struggles. The first is a "social struggle" against the less privileged segments of society who seek a more equitable distribution of resources. The second is an "intra-elite struggle" among different factions and layers of the elite, driven by competition to increase market shares and profits. These struggles extend into the realm of politics, as elites endeavor to shape policies and decisions in their favor.

For example, prior to the introduction of general incorporation through state laws in the mid-nineteenth century, various wealthy interests competed in the United States to secure charters that granted monopoly rights

[31] My distinction between political and economic elites is merely a simplification, as it often becomes blurred in ways that are context-dependent. For instance, in Chapter 6, we examined the intertwining of business and political careers in Russia, and in the United States, tycoons have occasionally made forays into politics.

[32] Much of Piketty 2020 elaborates on this idea.

through incorporation. In the lead-up to the US Civil War, Southern agrarians advocated for free trade, while Northern industrialists favored protectionism. These struggles can give rise to coalitions that cut across class boundaries, as evidenced by the United States before the Civil War. Successfully warring states may bring about such coalitions, and Machiavelli comes to mind again, when in his "Discourses" he considers the delicate equilibrium between patricians and the plebeians in a rapidly expanding Republican Rome. In its crudeness, the distinction that I propose between a "social" and an "intra-elite" struggle aims to elucidate a mechanism that I find interesting, and we can learn something out of simplicity.

Recognizing the threat of expropriation, the wealthy have a vested interest in acquiring even more economic resources. This is because these resources can prove useful in both the social struggle and the intra-elite struggle. Within the social struggle, increased resources enable them to lobby more effectively for the protection of their specific assets and can serve as leverage to form coalitions that advance their interests. In the intra-elite struggle, greater economic resources give them an advantage over other elites in shaping policies and regulations. Moreover, extensive business activities are often considered "too big to fail," providing a form of insurance against adverse shocks. The cost structure of industries can naturally lead to expansion through economies of scale, and the presence of network externalities can create tipping points in certain markets. This is of particular relevance today, given the importance of network industries.[33] As the wealthy amass greater wealth, they are motivated to use it to wield political influence, thereby safeguarding themselves against the risk of future redistribution or expropriation. Consequently, economic elites are often compelled to persist in their struggle, not only to protect their existing holdings but also to increase their economic and political power, the more so, the more they have to lose.

The pursuit of greater wealth and political power by individual members of the wealthy class presents a dilemma. Certainly, individual success improves their standing in both struggles. However, in contributing to higher levels of inequality overall, it may provoke demands for redistribution or even revolutionary expropriation from the less privileged.[34]

[33] For a review of characteristics that might lead to "tipping over," in a contest of two-sided markets, see Rysman 2009.

[34] Such conclusion is not foregone, because increasing inequality could make the poor so destitute as to deprive them of a concrete possibility for political action, thus making them almost enslaved. Or it could tilt the balance of choice among the more entrepreneurial among them, who tend also to present a greater threat to the elites, from "voice," to emigration's "exit" (with reference to Hirschman 1970, 59–61, in particular).

While this dilemma would suggest self-restraint, elites face a collective action problem, as individual efforts to protect themselves against the risk of expropriation may ultimately harm the privileged group as a whole. Throughout history, recurring calls for restraint, in the form of reformist projects that are often part and parcel of divide-and-rule strategies, have been justified at least by the more discerning members of the elites as attempts to avoid future conflicts with the unprivileged.

The ruling elites face a difficult collective action problem when it comes to practicing self-restraint, since the individual incentives that we discussed above encourage aggrandizement instead. However, when it comes to safeguarding the status quo and a given distribution of wealth and power, their incentives are aligned. Their reduced number simplifies the collective action problem, and they possess abundant resources to defend their interests. The scarcity of historical episodes when elites have been expropriated by the poor (as opposed to intra-elite expropriations, and of expropriations of the lower classes by the elites) indicates that the odds are structurally stacked in their favor.

An objection to my grim analysis may be that institutions exist precisely to constrain behaviors. However, and turning our attention to the United States again, the past four decades have witnessed a rise in economic inequality and a relaxation of campaign finance regulations, suggesting that the powerful urges of economic and political elites described earlier have not been effectively checked. In fact, they have prevailed. There are indications that the mechanism that I have outlined, where the incentives to acquire more wealth and power reinforce each other, has led to what Luigi Zingales refers to as a "Medici vicious circle," drawing a parallel to the domination of medieval Florence by the Medici family. In that city and other *signorias* of the Italian Middle Ages, preexisting democratic institutions (the communes) were taken over "by rich and powerful families who ran the city-states with their own commercial interests as a main objective."[35] Florence, in particular, "one of the most industrialized and powerful cities in Europe," became "a marginal province of a foreign empire." Zingales strikes a note similar to mine when he notes that "in a winner-take-all economy, entrepreneurs

[35] Zingales 2017. Machiavelli was a direct observer of those tendencies in the Florence that had surrendered freedom (the Republic led by Pier Soderini, under whom Machiavelli had served) and restored the Medici *signoria* in 1513. Particularly in his Discourses on Livy, he recurrently reflects on the relationships between riches, power, and constitutional order. In his characteristically sharp tongue, on the corrupting effect of economic inequality, he quips: "well-ordered republics have to keep the public rich and their citizens poor" (Machiavelli 1996 [1531], 79).

lobby and corrupt, not only to seize a crucial first-mover advantage, but also to preserve their power over time. They fear political expropriation, which can stem from a populist revolt against the monopolist's abuses or from the rent-seeking of other politically influential parties."

Describing the potential vicious feedback between increasing economic and political inequality, Luigi Zingales squarely notes that the United States is at risk. There, the "Medici factor" is not a person or a family and its coterie, but the largest corporations that "facilitated a massive concentration of economic (and political) power in the hands of a few people, who are hardly accountable to anyone," in a situation where "the interaction of concentrated corporate power and politics is a threat to the functioning of the free-market economy and to the economic prosperity it can generate, and a threat to democracy as well." Chapter 8 explored the institutional context that allowed economic elites to capture the political process in the United States. This includes lax campaign finance rules, lobbying, and the presence of media-savvy think tanks. The collection of institutions that enables economic and political inequality to persist can be seen as a form of rent for those who benefit from it. This justifies rent-seeking investments to maintain the status quo.

The battle for ideas is a crucial front in this struggle.[36] Its ultimate prize is a shared view not only of the answers but also of the questions that are implicitly considered admissible, to the detriment of others that are invisible. An ideology draws a map even before it influences deliberation, a map whose geography includes places that are difficult to reach, others where metaphorically speaking there are lions, and many more places that fall outside of its boundaries. We see this mechanism at play in the debate on the insulation of the economic and political sphere, which originated with Gordon Tullock's marginalist sophistry. Within the debate on corruption, the use of a narrow definition of corruption and the emphasis on a particular version of quantification are but a part of an ideological map.

CONCLUSIONS: LEGAL AND ILLEGAL CORRUPTION

While the United States experiences relatively modest levels of corruption-related crimes, the political influence of moneyed interests has expanded in time. As economic inequality has grown, various factors have contributed

[36] Thomas Piketty 2020, 7, notes that "It is hardly surprising that the elites of many societies, in all periods and climes, have sought to 'naturalize' inequality. They argue that existing social disparities benefit not only the poor but also society as a whole and that any attempt to alter the existing order of things will cause great pain."

to the increased capture of the political process, including the relaxation of campaign finance rules, the influence of dark money, the shifting role of think tanks, the changing landscape of lobbying practices, and the prevalence of conflicts of interest, such as the revolving door phenomenon. Together, these factors have created a situation that can be accurately characterized as legal corruption.

The relationship between illegal and legal forms of corruption has not been researched enough. Bård Harstad and Jakob Svensson have proposed a model that accounts for "the common perception that bribery is relatively more common in poor countries, whereas lobbying is relatively more common in rich ones."[37] However, Omer Gokcekus and Sertac Sonan suggest that political contributions and federal corruption convictions are substitutes in the United States,[38] and Oguzhan Dincer and Michael Johnston find that in US states there is "complementary relationship between illegal and legal corruption which is bidirectional."[39]

In Chapter 8, I hypothesized that illegal corruption in the United States may have diminished historically due to the emergence of legal mechanisms that fulfilled the same purpose within a broader transformation of American society and politics. This transformation occurred over several decades, starting at the end of the nineteenth century, and took place at the level of the "higher subsystem" as discussed in Chapter 5. However, it should be noted that this remains a conjecture, and further research is needed to understand the relationship between illegal and legal forms of corruption, in the United States and elsewhere. It is also important to note that the specific relationship found at a particular point in time may differ from what is observed in historical development. For example, relative differences in US states institutional quality may be persistent over the long term, leading to a positive correlation between legal and illegal corruption at a given point in time if weaker institutions lead to more of both varieties. This scenario can coexist with the presence of a common shift, such as the Age of Reform, which may have led all states to partially substitute illegal corruption with its legal variety. As a result, a positive correlation at a specific point in time could coexist with negative correlation in historical development.

The cases of Russia and Brazil also provide valuable insights into the interplay between legal and illegal corruption. While the analysis of these

37 Harstad and Svensson 2011.

38 Gokcekus and Sonan 2017.

39 Dincer and Jonston 2020b.

countries has primarily focused on illegal corruption, it is important to acknowledge the presence of legal corruption as well. In Russia, the "loans for share" scheme (see page 100) may be seen as one of the most egregious cases of legal corruption of the last century. In Brazil, Bolsonaro's alliance with economic groups favorable to extreme forms of exploitation of the Amazon is a case of legal corruption. In those two countries, both types of corruption have coexisted, and our understanding of their interconnectedness remains limited.

Turning our gaze toward the future, history may be a valuable teacher. The US Constitution was drafted during a time when American society was significantly more egalitarian than it is today, and the country has experienced two major periods of increased inequality: the Gilded Age and the one that began in the late 1970s. The debate on inequality in the United States continues, and just a few years after Donald Trump's very inegalitarian tax reform, his successor in the Presidency, Joe Biden, marked his first 100 days in office by condemning trickle-down economics,[40] which is one of the ideological underpinnings of low taxes for the rich. There is a possibility that the majority of Americans, who collectively own no assets and who still largely believe in the American Dream, may eventually find reasons and ways to act to further their interests. However, any changes in this regard will eventually come from popular demands for greater equality or perhaps for less legal corruption, and will not be aided by the narrow definition of corruption that still prevails today. In their narrowness, the prevailing ideas on corruption would only deprive the struggle for greater equality – and, as Louis Brandeis would have observed, for more democracy – of the possibility to label the privileged elite as corrupt.

[40] Biden 2021.

10

A Problem of Control

Corruption Is a Tool of Government

> In framing a government which is to be administered by men over men, the great difficulty lies in this: you must first enable the government to control the governed; and in the next place oblige it to control itself.
>
> James Madison[1]

In my discussion of corruption in Russia and Brazil, I argued that corruption is often utilized as a tool of government. In this chapter, I explore why this is so. One reason is quite straightforward: A bribe serves as a powerful incentive for the recipient to fulfill the wishes of the giver. Another reason arises from consideration of corruption as a social construct, emerging from the incessant struggle among different definitions of corruption as a phenomenon. Chapter 5 outlined a set of characteristics shared by all definitions of corruption, which are rooted in normative judgments concerning the desired state of the polity, the extent to which reality deviates from a normative point of reference, and the negativity or even repugnance that is attributed to the observed deviation. These normative choices carry significant implications. Certain societal actors may possess the power to propose and even to impose a specific definition of corruption, ideally branding political enemies with the scarlet "C" letter. When this occurs, they gain a means to influence others to act in accordance to their own desires.

Consequently, one can argue that corruption serves as a tool of government – an instrument that aids in addressing the problem of control. Not only does it "enable the government to control the governed," as Madison

[1] Hamilton et al. 2008 [1788], 257 (Federalist No. 51).

believed is necessary, but it also serves a broader purpose to control the execution of policies and to guarantee political order. While these policies may benefit the people to some extent, the widely shared negative opinion of corruption should not be altered. As a tool of government, corruption complicates the other task that James Madison wrote of: obliging the government to control itself. Corruption is inherently flawed as a tool of government.

This chapter delves into the reasons why corruption serves as a tool of government. The starting point will be the principal–agent model, as it has been applied to the study of corruption. Building upon these insights, we revisit the cases of Russia and Brazil to further interpret them. Consideration of additional cases will add generality to the conclusion that corruption is a tool of government.

A PROBLEM OF CONTROL IN THE ANTECHAMBER OF POWER

The obverse of my claim that corruption cannot be unambiguously defined is that any competing definition of corruption must be deemed legitimate as long as it receives some attention in society and is not blatantly absurd. This certainly applies to the definition of corruption as "the abuse of entrusted power for private gain," which is currently the most popular definition and a suitable starting point for discussing how corruption can function as a tool of government. We have observed that this definition has been interpreted through the lens of the principal–agent model, where the principal is identified with the citizenry, that entrusts power to various types of public officials who may exploit it for personal gain. The power is entrusted to act, and the principal (the people) expects tangible outcomes from their agent (the ruler), irrespective of the political regime where the entrusting occurs. This holds true in democracies, but the fate of dictators also hinges on the effectiveness of their policies, whether aimed at providing solace to their subjects or, if necessary, at oppressing those whom they have not satisfied otherwise.

Analyzing corruption through the lens of the principal–agent model rises in fact two problems of entrusting: the translation of entrusted power into political will and the execution of that political will. However, applications of the principal–agent model to the study of corruption have largely focused on the former problem and ignored the latter. The execution of policies is not simply a binary choice between corruption and honesty, as if it were a box-ticking exercise, but it involves various decisions and actions by agents responsible for implementing his decisions.[2] The reality is indeed much more complex, as the ruler, to whom power is entrusted, assumes the role of the principal in a broader relationship with agents responsible for implementing her decisions. These agents have a range of options when determining whether and how to comply with the ruler's bidding and may engage in behaviors that are not to her liking. For instance, they themselves may accept or solicit bribes, provide misleading information, embezzle resources, or neglect their duties. Such pitfalls in the execution of policies create a highly problematic situation for the ruler, whose will is separated from its execution by an obfuscating screen. Furthermore, not only does the ruler have agents to deal with, but many of these agents also have agents of their own, each of whom may have multiple principals.[3] Last, the figure of the ruler is but an abstraction, and overall, there are so many real-life complexities in the execution of policies that I can hardly attempt to enumerate them all.

However, simplicity has its value, and to depict the complexity of the situation, let us linger further over the image of the ruler who would like to get things done. Carl Schmitt's concept of the "antechamber of power" provides a vivid image of such a situation. Schmitt notes that "the human individual, in whose hand the great political decisions lie for an instant, can only form his will under given presuppositions and with given means," and underlines the complexity of the execution of the political will: "Even the most absolute prince is reliant on reports and information and dependent on his counsellors." Schmitt concludes that "every direct power is promptly subordinated to indirect influences," which inevitably result in an "antechamber" of power, "a path of access to the ear, a corridor to the soul of the holder of power. There is no human power without this antechamber and without this corridor." It is an antechamber populated by "ministers and ambassadors in grand uniform, but also father-confessors and bodily physicians, adjutants and secretaries, chamber servants and mistresses,"[4] who threaten to undermine the actual power chamber and

[2] The more restrictive view permeates Rose-Ackerman's original path-breaking analyses (Rose-Ackerman 1975 and 1978). Occasionally, the execution of policies has been further problematized. Della Porta and Vannucci 1999, 17, declare that "The principal is the state, or, better, the citizenry," while recognizing in the same breath that "the functioning of a democratic government can in fact be conceived as a system of principal-agent relationships between electorate, elected officials, and bureaucrats."

[3] The presence of multiple principals notoriously complicates applications of the principal–agent model (see the discussion in Miller 2005).

[4] Schmitt 2015, 34–36.

to "fill it with intrigue and lies."[5] The challenges in executing the ruler's will extend well beyond his immediate antechamber where his more proximate agents are, because collaboration is also required of a long sequence of actors at a greater distance. The abuse of his entrusted power can come from the minister, his counselor or secretary, all the way along to the humblest executor, all of them democratically united in sharing the power to corrupt the execution of the ruler's will.

Schmitt's concept of the "antechamber of power" only partially captures the wider political and administrative spaces where the political will of the ruler is at risk of being muddled by his agents. Additionally, Schmitt's vague characterization of the ruler "in whose hand the great political decisions lie for an instant" leaves room for interpretation. Schmitt's ruler could be a dictator or a democratically elected official, and in most contemporary situations, the exercise of power is divided among distinct branches and levels of government. Nevertheless, the vagueness of Schmitt's concept encourages us to focus on the fact that the execution of a will to act is constantly at risk of being corrupted, regardless of the concrete genesis, conditions, and legitimacy of power. This corruption corresponds to the "indirect influences" that Schmitt saw as subordinating "every direct power" and can be described as a problem in the antechamber of power.

Corruption can be a powerful tool of government because rulers have the resources to bribe and can exploit their influence in determining what is corrupt and what is not. To analyze the practical relevance of these effects, we return to Brazil and to Russia.

A TOOL OF GOVERNMENT IN BRAZIL AND IN RUSSIA

In Brazil, the *Mensalão* scandal of 2005 serves as a clear example of the direct effect of corruption, involving payments made to deputies in exchange for passing legislation. The case demonstrates that bribes can be employed not only by private individuals and companies to buy the decisions of public officials but also by those in power to fulfill their promises. However, delivering on promises has been challenging in post-dictatorship Brazil due to the characteristics of the 1988 Constitution, the result of a political compact that restored democracy while maintaining an elitist social structure. Corruption has aided presidents and their political parties in enacting legislation and gaining the necessary super-majority to amend an overly detailed constitution. Some of these policies have contributed to Brazil's

[5] Han 2018, 63.

success story, as the country has made progress in the decades following the end of the military dictatorship in 1985, particularly in improving conditions for the poor.

Were there alternatives to corruption in democratic Brazil? Certainly, alternatives of the "can opener" type were available.[6] We could simply assume that the various presidents of Brazil, from José Sarney in 1985 up until Jair Bolsonaro and Lula and the relevant elites around them, all embroiled in various corruption scandals, would have behaved themselves. However, such presumption would be both unrealistic and disingenuous for multiple reasons. First, the elites in a highly unequal society are served quite well by the status quo. It is expected that they will continue to pursue self-interest and seek more economic and political power, as discussed in Chapter 9. These elites face a serious collective action problem, particularly when they number in the thousands and are divided along various lines. Effecting changes in this regard would necessitate the establishment of new institutions that provide alternatives to corruption as a tool of government.

The case of Russia indicates that the positive incentives of bribes are particularly potent when the justice system can be manipulated to threaten bribe recipients. Their vulnerability serves as the second important lever that amplifies the power of corruption as a tool of government. In such cases, corruption provides both rewards and threats, enticing and coercing individuals. The coexistence of these incentives in Russia has made corruption an effective tool in helping the state to survive after the collapse of the Soviet Union. Among the observers who have highlighted the make-or-break character of that historical juncture is Eugene Huskey, who in considering Russia perhaps comes closest to my point of view when he notes that "besides assessing the capacity of society to hold its leaders accountable – the democracy test – one must also measure the capacity of the state to 'control the governed,' to use Madison's phrase."[7]

We have observed that in Russia, in the words of Alena Ledeneva, all "disregard at least some laws," while "the actual punishment is 'suspended' as it is not feasible to prosecute everyone."[8] Ledeneva sees this as a case of "legal nihilism," which, in 2008, then presidential candidate Medvedev famously pledged to overcome.[9] Kathryn Hendley affirms that legal nihilism is, "at

[6] With reference to the joke in which an economist proposes to his fellow castaways in a deserted island, who discover a much-needed can containing food, to open it simply by "assuming" the presence of a can opener.

[7] Huskey 2009, with reference to the quotation opening this chapter.

[8] Ledeneva 2013, 14.

[9] See Barber et al. 2008.

its core, a lack of respect for law"[10] In fact, the same phenomenon could paradoxically be considered a case of "legal maximalism": To the extent that lack of respect for the law is an important ingredient of corruption as a tool of government, laws are in fact omnipresent and highly relevant, as they express their perverse influence through the regularity with which they are broken. Widespread violation of the law has significant implications for the ruling elites, as evidenced by the data on crimes of corruption presented in Figure 6.7 (page 107). The approximately 5,000 cases that are brought to court for the crime of bribe-taking each year certainly represent a small fraction of the total number of such crimes that are committed. However, they are numerous enough to make the threat of serious punishment credible, thanks to the joint effect of selective and instrumental prosecution and the strong accusatorial bias of the penal justice system.

To a considerable extent, bribes in Russia have been made possible by the presence of vast natural resources that have supplied a vital flow of funds to the state, particularly since the late 1990s (Figure 6.2 at page 91). Bribes have been particularly enticing due to high levels of economic inequality, suggesting that there is no economic salvation in Russia away from the centers of redistribution. The prospect of conviction represents a double threat because of the concrete risk of jail and expulsion from the circles benefiting from corrupt rents, thus favoring the cohesion of elites. Insiders find it difficult to exit such relationships where mutual advantages are interlaced with threats, and generalized corruption provides a lever and a powerful instrument to obtain compliance and carry out the business of government.[11] Insecure factions in Russia may engage in furious intra-elite quarrels, in a situation where, as Richard Sakwa notes, "intra-elite cartel pluralism [...] compensates for the weakness of formal institutions," within "a system where the winner does *not* take all, every faction has enough of a stake to ensure its loyalty, and none is allowed to gain predominance to threaten the existence of the others."[12] However, the shared vulnerabilities that I have described place a limit to these struggles, even under conditions of extreme stress, as the ongoing Russian invasion of Ukraine tragically demonstrates.

Corruption ensures a minimum standard for the execution of public policies by fostering a certain level of cohesiveness. From a historical

[10] Hendley 2012.

[11] Diego Gambetta has researched the working of similar mechanisms in organized crime. See, for example, Gambetta 2009, chapter 3, and Gambetta 2018, citing Schelling 1960, 43–44, as applied to an analysis of corruption in Italy, a theme on which I will return soon.

[12] Sakwa 2010.

perspective, corruption played a significant role in saving the Russian state from collapse during the 1990s, providing the state with the means to defend itself against geopolitical and economic failures. Corruption functioned as an institution, influencing and constraining behaviors: In this sense, *corruption is an institution*. Therefore, it would be unrealistic to imagine a fundamentally different and more virtuous governance model in Russia during that time. Such an imagination would be a fantasy or, as discussed in Chapter 5, a metaphysically unsound counterfactual.

The notion that widespread corruption serves as a means to govern Russia has been proposed before. Alena Ledeneva argues that establishing the rule of law as an alternative to the prevailing "informal governance" would "incur a certain loss of manageability of the formal institutions required to control powerful clans," which supports the view that corruption is a tool of government. Ledeneva's ethnographic analysis centers on the concept of "*sistema*," which is based on the mutual vulnerability of its actors: "To be appointed, one must 'hang' on a hook (*na krychke ili v kompromisse*)." The result is "a powerful grip over the society," and a "common, yet not articulated, perceptions of power and the system of governance." The *sistema* includes a range of informal practices, of which outright bribing is just one. Ledeneva explicitly takes a functionalist perspective on this mechanism when she asserts that "there is no obvious way of tackling sistema without weakening the various kinds of social cohesion that enable Russian society to function," while also noting that "the key question, therefore, is how to modernize the informal networks behind sistema without losing their functional potential while limiting their dysfunctional implications."[13] Finally, Ledeneva links the current sistema to older practices, such as informal networks in Soviet times based on *blat*, which subverted the socialist system but at the same time also supported its existence.

Blat, "a colloquial term to denote ways of getting things done through personal contacts, associated with using connections, pulling strings and exchanging favours,"[14] is distinct from bribing, but its consideration raises the question of how current practices relate to those observed in Soviet and older times. A long view of the historical continuity in the practice of corruption in Russia is present in the analysis by Günther Schulze and Nikita Zakharov. They trace corruption in Russia back to the Golden Horde's

13 Ledeneva 2013, 14, 37, 1–2, and 7.

14 Ledeneva 2018. There are different terms in Russian to indicate corruption or bribing, which are understood to be sharply different from *blat*.

domination (1240–1480). Its extractive practices later "became an institution known as *kormlenie* ('feeding' or 'nourishment' in Russian): a vicegerent received a province to supply ("feed") him and his servants as a reward for service and tax collection."[15] Such practices have persisted in various forms over time and to these days, when "appointment to the region as a governor comes with an opportunity to engage in illegal but financially rewarding activities, which are often tolerated by the federal center if coupled with loyalty and electoral support." Schulze and Zakharov strike a note that is analogous to mine: "as corruption is illegal, corrupt officials can be exposed any time, which enforces loyalty towards the powers that be; thus, corruption is a method of governance," and conclude that their view "is opposed to the popular perception of corruption as a sign of a malfunctioning state. In fact, it is creating stability in autocratic regimes." As I will clarify shortly, this may be true not only of autocratic regimes.

These authors belong to a tradition of thought that has considered corruption in Russia to be "indissolubly interlaced with the whole system and political life," as Isaac Berlin, a perceptive publicist, noted in 1910.[16] He cites Mikhail Saltykov-Shchedrin's "The Pompadours," where a bribe-taker, "for the sake of the opportunity to steal an extra penny, [...] is ready to get along with any kind of internal politics, to believe in any God you like." In conclusion, "corruption exists so that, having received privileges of an economic or political nature, the recipient may as a consequence 'be thankful' towards the giver." Overall, bribes ensure "docility and an accommodating nature," and, in the words of Berlin, no *Revizor* (the government inspectors in charge of stamping out corruption) could change that fundamental fact. As we observe in Gogol's *Revizor*, where a traveler to a provincial city, mistakenly believed to be one such inspector, is quickly taken in a flurry of corrupting entreaties by the predictably corrupt local leaders.

GENERALIZATIONS: THE UNITED STATES AND STATE CORRUPTION ABROAD

Since the demise of functionalist interpretations of corruption, views with a functionalist slant have not disappeared, as we have seen in the case of Russia. In particular, as I mentioned in Chapter 1 as an example of the soft

15 Schulze and Zacharov 2018, also for the citations that follow. They refer to Hedlund 2005, for his "account of path-dependence in institutional development from the early times of Kiev Rus through the collapse of the Soviet Union." See also Pavroz 2017, who notes that corruption has supported state institutions.

16 Berlin 1910.

edges in the current debate on corruption, corruption is occasionally considered to be "systemic," meaning that it is pervasive and deeply ingrained. When this occurs, some commentators have recognized that corruption represents an important characteristic of the way the business of government gets done, and that under the observed circumstances, it is difficult to contemplate counterfactual alternatives. For example, Larry Diamond affirms that in "many new democracies," corruption is "not some flaw that can be corrected with a technical fix or a political push. It is the way that the system works, and it is deeply embedded in the norms and expectations of political and social life."[17]

However, the use of bribery as a tool to solve a problem of control has been mostly ignored in the context of advanced democracies. A vast literature on political control was initiated by a series of works in the late 1980s by Matthew D. McCubbins, Roger G. Noll, and Barry R. Weingast (sometimes collectively referred to as "McNollgast"). They introduced a valuable political approach to the analysis of the business of government in the United States,[18] while assuming away the possibility of bribes. For example, they explored "the principals of political control of bureaucratic decisions" using a principal–agent model, where the agents are self-serving but otherwise honest.[19] They considered how Congress may dominate its relationships with the agencies that are to carry out its policies, thanks to administrative procedures that they saw as rather effective in solving the principal–agent problem. The large literature that followed also did not consider the possibility of bribes, a choice which may be justified in a country like the United States where levels of illegal corruption are believed to be relatively modest.

However, a type of corruption that has often been overlooked, perhaps because under some circumstances it is considered unavoidable and taken for granted, occurs in the realm of international relations when the government of a country, directly or through its agents or proxies, uses bribery to influence developments in a foreign country. The US involvement in the Afghan war is a blatant case in point, beginning in 2001 with the ousting of the Taliban from power and ending in 2021 with their return to power.

17 In Carothers et al. 2017.

18 See Moe 2013, 1148, who as an aside notes that "during the early decades of the twentieth century, reactions against political corruption and party machines led scholars to see bureaucracy as the savior of good government and as properly nonpolitical."

19 McCubbins et al. 1987. The same applies to another McNollgast landmark article published two years later (McCubbins et al. 1989).

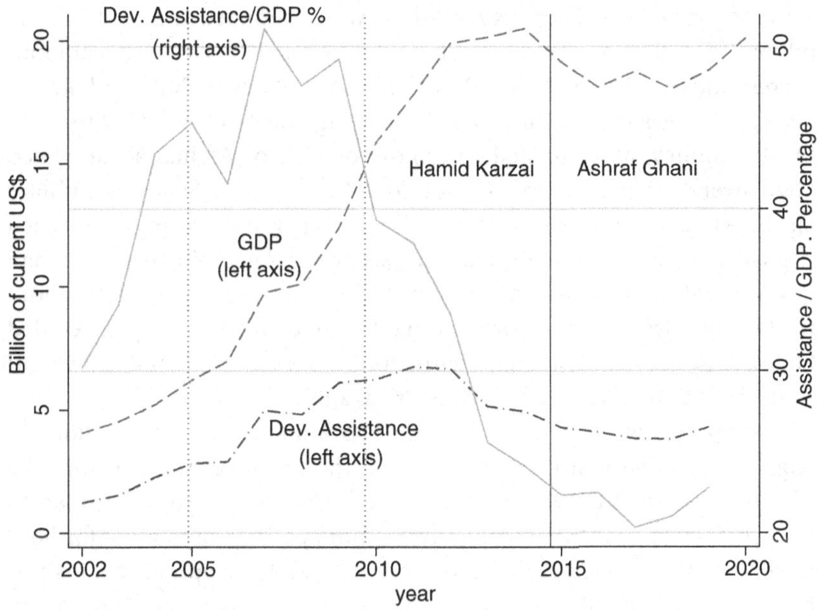

Figure 10.1 GDP and net official development assistance received, current US dollars (Afghanistan)
Source of the data. The World Bank. Gross Domestic Product and Net official development assistance received (left axis: Current US$ in billions; right axis: As percentage of GDP of Afghanistan). Vertical dotted lines: Presidential elections of October 9, 2004, and of August 20, 2009, both won by Karzai. Prior to becoming President, Karzai had served as the Head of the Afghan Transitional Authority. Vertical continuous line: Accession to the presidency of Asraf Ghani, substituting Hamid Karzai.

Foreign resources flowing into Afghanistan were astonishingly large compared to the country's income. As a percentage of GDP, development assistance peaked in 2007 at over 50% of Afghanistan's GDP (Figure 10.1). Between 2002 and 2014, the GDP of Afghanistan more than quadrupled to reach approximately 20 billion that however correspond to a meager one-thousandth of the GDP of the United States. The economic disparity between the two countries was so significant that one could reasonably believe that it could buy the other. Afghanistan's population increased rapidly since 2002, by around 70%, resulting in only a modest increase in per capita income during that time. Per capita income has not increased since 2012, fueling dissatisfaction with the Ghani's government and contributing to the Taliban's return to power in 2021.

Besides development assistance, there were military expenditures by the participating allied forces in Afghanistan, with the United States bearing most of the burden. These expenditures were estimated at a total of 2,313 billion US dollars over a period of approximately 10 years.[20] This amount corresponds to 11% of the GDP of the United States in 2019, and a staggering 8.7 times the accumulated GDP of Afghanistan from 2002 to 2020. Of this money, an estimated 73 billion, or 27% of Afghan accumulated GDP over that period, was disbursed by the United States as military aid to Afghanistan. While not all military expenditures directly reached Afghanistan, except for military and security-related aid to the Afghan government, a substantial portion of it did, in various ways. Throughout the two decades of occupation by a coalition of countries led by the United States, Afghanistan was deluged with money to such an extent that it would be difficult to find a comparable historical antecedent.

Corruption was inherent to the US and allied intervention in Afghanistan. The vast disparity between the resources injected into the country, and what the country could realistically have produced if left to its own devices, made the temptation of money too great to resist for both the taker and the giver. It was unrealistic to expect corruption-free institutions to emerge and be strong enough to resist such enormous temptation. Corruption was practiced systematically because it was both possible and necessary. The United States and its allies faced a difficult problem of control that I consider while referring to the reporting of Craig Withlock, a journalist with *The Washington Post* who researched documents from the Special Inspector General for Afghan Reconstruction related to the US war in Afghanistan.[21] One critical logistical challenge for the United States was supplying troops in a large, mountainous, and land-locked country that was never fully secured. Corruption was considered an indispensable tool to achieve this crucial goal. According to Withlock, "The single biggest generator of corruption was the U.S. military's sprawling supply chain," and to ensure deliveries, "trucking companies paid fat bribes to warlords, police chiefs, and Taliban commanders to guarantee safe passage through their turf."[22] The situation had escalated to the point where "a 2010 congressional report called the system 'a vast protection racket' that was underwritten

[20] Estimates of cost of the war for the United States are from the Stockholm International Peace Research Institute and are reported in Tian 2021. These figures do not include the costs incurred by the other coalition countries. The estimated cost to the three main contributors after the United States has been estimated to equal 30, 19, and 7 billion US$, respectively, for Great Britain, Germany, and Italy. See BBC 2021 and MilEx 2021.

[21] Whitlock 2021. The documents referred as the "Afghanistan papers" were obtained by The Washington Post through the Freedom of Information Act. See Withlock 2019.

[22] Whitlock 2021, 187, also for the citation that follows.

by U.S. taxpayers." Moreover, there were allegations of buying votes from Afghan-elected representatives: "from the beginning, their experience with democracy was one in which money was deeply embedded."[23]

Frequent expressions of concern by high-ranking officials indicate that the United States acknowledged the detrimental impact of corruption on its mission in Afghanistan. Despite significant resources allocated to anti-corruption initiatives of various kinds, often accompanied by exaggerated reports of progress, it remains uncertain whether these efforts were driven by opportunism or a genuine desire for change. In Afghanistan, corruption was not the problem, but rather the solution, in the context of a fundamentally misguided mission. While it can be argued that armies have historically used bribes to secure intelligence, alliances, and ultimately achieve victory, this recognition also suggests that in a complex world, when push comes to shove and delivering on actions is imperative, corruption is there to provide assistance.

GENERALIZATIONS: CAMBODIA, CHINA, AND ITALY

Push did come to shove in Cambodia, where corruption was used to build consensus among the relevant factions vying for power, so as to bring peace in the aftermath of Civil War and the horrors of Khmer Rouge rule.[24] Cambodia is but an example of a broader tendency to end civil wars by buying the good will of the players involved. As Dominik Zaum and Christine Cheng state, "to bring an end to the fighting, peace agreements and power-sharing arrangements that implicitly allow for corruption may be a necessary, if unpalatable feature of peacebuilding."[25] To determine the extent to which selective justice is used in addition to direct incentives of corruption, as seen in Russia, would require a wider analysis. However, weak institutions are often present in countries emerging from periods of internal strife and sometimes need to be developed from scratch. The practical difficulties of establishing a well-working judiciary suggest that the use of selective justice may be common.

Other cases where justice may be used instrumentally include China, which is part of a group of countries that have attracted attention due to the perceived challenge of reconciling high levels of corruption with remarkable (present or past) economic successes, such as Japan, South Korea,

[23] Withlock 2021, 185.
[24] Biddulph 2014.
[25] Zaum and Cheng 2011.

and Italy.[26] In 2013, Xi Jinping initiated an anti-corruption campaign that, unlike previous crackdowns, has become a long-term effort. Andrew Wedeman suggests that the campaign has been motivated by genuine concerns about corruption as well as political goals. Selective justice has also been employed, evident in "the removal of figures such as Bo Xilai, Zhou Yongkang, Ling Jihua, General Guo Boxiong, and General Xu Caihou," which "has certainly enabled Xi to consolidate his grip on the Chinese political system."[27] The anti-corruption campaign in China is ongoing and has become the new normal, indicating that it is now an integral part of exercising an increasingly autocratic power.

The presence of punitive mechanisms may seem to depend on the degree to which justice can be instrumentally steered. However, the case of Italy, to which I turn, suggests prudence in drawing such a conclusion. Diego Gambetta proposes a "bold conjecture" that a carrot-and-stick system of incentives linked to corruption is also at play in Italy.[28] Gambetta contends that "Italy has a largely independent and incorruptible law and order system," but there is a twist to the story because, as he quips, Italy has "the worst judiciary that money cannot buy." The system is overburdened and characterized by a "near-automaticity of the investigative process," which arises from a "duty to open an investigation whenever it receives information of a crime (*notitia criminis*)." Even evidence received anonymously or from an undisclosed police informant, while not admissible in court, can trigger an investigation. Overall, "the probability of being caught and convicted for any one violation in an overburdened system comes to depend almost entirely on whether someone will inform the authorities and induce them to act rather than on the latter's independently initiated investigations. The fear of sanctions becomes ancillary to the fear of someone informing on one."

Adding to this, Gambetta notes that "most people have some 'dirt' on some other people without even looking for it—they know of their landlords' tax evasion, of their neighbors' illegal building extensions, of their colleagues' shirking and of friends' cheating in exams, drink-driving, dope-smoking or patronizing prostitutes." Such a situation creates ample opportunities for sharing compromising information, which, however, in

[26] On China, see Wedeman 2012 and 2018, and Ang 2020. On South Korea, Wedeman 2012, chapter 2.

[27] Wedeman 2019, 219 and 202. See also the considerations of Fisman and Golden 2017, 77–78, both on China and, more generally, on how anti-corruption campaigns may be "smoke screens for political vendettas."

[28] Gambetta 2018.

equilibrium does not happen often because if A rats out B, B can retaliate on A, because they all have something to hide. The result is a "culture of tacit complicity."

Diego Gambetta's conjecture may seem plausible and interestingly indicates a case where the "stick" part of the system of incentives that makes corruption a tool of government may take more subtle forms. Its presence in Italy also emerges from nonacademic analyses, such as that proposed by Giuliano Ferrara, a well-known abrasive journalist (and former minister in the first government presided by Silvio Berlusconi) when he affirmed that "you must be blackmailable. To be in politics, you have to belong to a system which accepts you because [...] you are willing to do your share and be part in an associative mechanism through which the elites [*classi dirigenti*] are selected."[29] In Italy, it would not be a corruptible or otherwise subservient justice that delivers selective punishment, but a largely honest one that, almost unwittingly, lends itself to be used in a decentralized fashion as a credible threat against those contemplating the violation of pacts of corruption.[30]

CONCLUSIONS: THE GENERALITY OF CORRUPTION AS A TOOL OF GOVERNMENT

The idea that corruption is a tool of government has been largely absent from the current debate on corruption, with some notable exceptions. These exceptions arise in accounts that deal with systemic corruption, meaning that it is perceived to be widespread and deeply ingrained in the ways of government. In such accounts, a line is often drawn between countries where systemic corruption may occur, such as "many new democracies" as mentioned by Larry Diamond, and those where corruption is considered an aberration from the normal mode of functioning of politics and administration.

I have disagreed with this view. The enticement of bribes is an obviously powerful tool for the ruler to solve a problem of control "in the

[29] Cited in Beccaria and Marcucci 2015.

[30] Or of other more honorable pacts: Gambetta 2018 surmises that "the same web of complicity that sustains corruption might have a sunnier side and be a substitute to the slow justice system. While mafias exact a heavy cost on development, [sharing compromising information] is cheap, non-violent, manageable without third-party interference, and requires minimal organization. Nothing prevents people from exploiting [the sharing of compromising information] as a mutual insurance to cooperate in legal ventures (or play on both the legal and illegal table at the same time)."

antechamber of power" – in Brazil, in Russia, in the United States fighting in Afghanistan, and elsewhere. Whereas corruption always presents a positive incentive to act according to the desires of the briber, the degree to which the threat of selective justice may be present is highly context-dependent. There is at least indirect evidence that the question has general relevance, if we consider the very widespread tendency of politicians accused of corruption to accuse judges of political partiality. It is true that the accused has an obvious interest in instilling doubts among the public by pointing the finger at the accuser, regardless of merit. However, the prevalence of such discourse indicates that it is considered plausible.

In the end, corruption serves as a tool of government because it involves contested value judgments about what is right and wrong, with results that may imply punishment by the law or the negative effects of stigma. While corruption is perhaps the strongest such contested value judgment in the sphere of politics, both in terms of potential punishments and enticements, it is certainly not the only one. Any set of behaviors that the public tends to dislike, even when not criminal, can serve similar purposes. Regarding corruption in Italy, Diego Gambetta mentions "patronizing prostitutes," which is not a crime in Italy but may carry a stigma. Mark Granovetter considers workplaces where it is known that "some pilferage" will occur, and employers have an interest in framing such behaviors as "perks" rather than unauthorized appropriation. This gives them "leeway to discipline or fire employees not to their liking for violating a formal if typically unenforced rule."[31] Such widespread violations create bonds of trust among participants. Even gossip may serve similar purposes, and it "might facilitate human interactions also because it is perceived to be ethically wrong."[32]

All these "normative spaces" share a common characteristic: They all facilitate forms of group cohesion. They exist not only as systems that promote normative views but also as mechanisms that, through varying degrees of violation of these norms, contribute to social cohesion. Within these systems, an act of rebellion is not found in breaking the rules, but in meticulously adhering to them. These considerations are particularly pertinent to corruption, which distinguishes itself because of the occasional lavishness of the perks it offers and the severity of the possible punishment, of which social stigma is but one aspect.

[31] Granovetter 2007, 156.
[32] Picci 2019, 503.

11

Fighting Corruption, Fighting for Corruption

We also need to address transparency, accountability, and institutional capacity. And let's not mince words: we need to deal with the cancer of corruption.

Jim Wolfensohn[1]

Italy's President Giovanni Leone, that in Chapter 2 we saw involved in the Lockheed scandal, resigned in 1978 due to a combination of facts and unproven allegations. It is certain that the Lockheed corporation had paid bribes to sell its airplanes to the Italian Air Force. A US Senate Select Committee, chaired by Senator Frank Church, presented substantial damning evidence in this respect, and even the ruling Christian Democrats, of which Leone was a prominent figure, could not ignore it. In March 1977, for eight full days the Italian Chamber of Deputies and the Senate met in joint session dedicated to the case, which ended with a majority vote on the prosecution of two former defense ministers. In a distinct ruling, the general and former chief of staff of the Italian Air Force, who had also been involved in a previous corruption incident regarding the procurement of French airplanes, was demoted to Airman.[2]

The opposition Communist Party was eager to score political points. Its widely read official mouthpiece, *L'Unità*, dedicated its opening to the parliamentary debate that took place in March for as long as it lasted.[3] However,

[1] From Jim Wolfensohn's World Bank/IMF Annual Meetings' Address, October 1, 1996. Cited in Kaufmann 2005.

[2] Shuster 1977. See also Caprara 2001, 1154.

[3] With the exception of March 12, the day after the closing of the joint session, when the opening of "l'Unità" was dedicated to the killing of a student by the police force during student riots at the University of Bologna. On March 7, the Lockheed scandal shared the opening with news of a major earthquake in Romania. See l'Unità n.d. On the political stance of the Communist Party regarding the Lockheed affair, see Caprara 2001, 1148.

the Communist Party was also walking a fine line, since it was hoping for a political deal with the Christian Democrats. Perhaps for this reason, its Secretary-General, Enrico Berlinguer, did not personally participate in the parliamentary debate.

The final blow to President Leone's political fate came in the form of a book written by Camilla Cederna, a reputed investigative journalist. The book, published by a well-known left-leaning publisher, quickly became a bestseller. Its allegations went well beyond corruption in the Lockheed case and represented a classic case of character assassination. In the meantime, the small and combative Radical Party was waging a vicious campaign against Leone, whose own party, the Christian Democrats, mostly left him undefended. Divided as it was into powerful factions, the misfortune of one of their notables had become part of an intricate internal power game.

Those years were particularly complicated for Italy, with much political violence, the shady involvement of the secret services in political life and criminal activities, and a planned *coup d'etat* by neo-fascist forces. A clandestine organization which originated as a Masonic lodge, known as "P2," operated as a shadow government of sort.[4] This context provides the backdrop for Camilla Cederna's likely errors. While it is impossible to identify with any certainty "Antelope Cobbler," the main recipient of bribes, it is unlikely that it was Giovanni Leone. He was likely framed, possibly with the unwitting help of Camilla Cederna, who had a source commonly associated with a sector of the secret services.[5] Anti-corruption had served as a tool of politics, which is the theme of this chapter.

There is a simple sense in which anti-corruption is a tool of politics. Whenever corruption is a tool of government, it also becomes a tool of politics because the business of government *is* politics. However, the case of Giovanni Leone indicates different uses of corruption. Various actors, including opposition political forces, factions within Leone's own party, and shady political fixers, used allegations of corruption to gain political advantages. Corruption served as a political resource, and this chapter aims to clarify in what sense we can consider this resource a tool.

4 Sergi and Vannucci 2023, chapter 2.

5 Cederna's source was Mino (Carmine) Pecorelli, who ran a news agency and was also a member of the P2 secret organization. He was assassinated in 1979. Giulio Andreotti, a prominent Christian Democrat, was eventually acquitted of accusations of being the instigator of the crime. Another Christian Democrat suspected of being "Antelope Cobbler," Aldo Moro, was kidnapped and killed by the Red Brigades in 1978. Those were the times, to be remembered as "*anni di piombo*" (years of lead), referring both to the material from which bullets are made and their oppressive atmosphere.

For a resource to be a tool, there needs to be systematic utilization according to a discernible pattern of uses and purposes, leading to the emergence of a well-defined and purposeful agency. This chapter delves into one aspect of this issue, which holds particular significance when analyzing global anti-corruption movements: the incentives to promote an anti-corruption political platform. By studying these incentives through models of political spatial competition, we can observe that there is a greater inclination toward anti-corruption when political parties face challenges to distinguish themselves along different dimensions. The waning relevance of ideological differences, particularly after the collapse of the Soviet Union and the radical alternative it presented to liberal democracies, has contributed to the rise of the anti-corruption movement in recent decades.

In the following pages, anti-corruption emerges as a tool of politics, providing a dimension along which political forces may compete and a way to bring individuals together for a common political goal. In this context, I reconsider the anti-corruption movements in Russia and Brazil also to highlight intrinsic weaknesses of anti-corruption policies: the uncertainty of their outcomes, the possibility of backfiring, and their potential to crowd out alternative political projects.

THE DEMAND FOR VALENCE ISSUES

Luigi Curini observes that political "campaigns are also about positioning and highlighting issues on the political agenda" and that "political corruption […] is one of the issues that parties can put forward during such electoral events."[6] That is, anti-corruption is a tool of politics, as it may be instrumentally used to fight political battles. Curini notes in particular that corruption belongs to the category of "valence issues," which are those issues that "merely involve the linking of the parties with some condition that is positively or negatively valued by the electorate."[7] For valence issues, "there is (virtually) no disagreement," so that parties "are differentiated not by what they advocate but by the degree to which they are linked in the public's mind with conditions or goals or symbols of which almost everyone approves or disapproves."[8] Honesty and competence are typical positive valence issues, while corruption is the quintessential negative one. I note in passing that valence issues may also be used one against the other,

[6] Curini 2017, xiii.
[7] Stokes 1963.
[8] Stokes 1992.

as exemplified in Russia, where organizations such as Navalny's used corruption as a valence issue, only to be attacked by a countervailing one of "extremism."[9] Such accusations became particularly appealing to states after the terrorist attack of September 11, 2001, which provided an opportunity, in the United States and elsewhere, to justify policies of invasive state control or outright repression. Navalny's organization was outlawed on such grounds, demonstrating the unrivaled powers of the state to influence the terms of the discussion, on corruption and on valence issues more generally.

Returning to what concerns us more directly, Curini considers the incentives of political parties to highlight corruption as a valence issue, which "increase when the spatial distance separating a party from its ideological adjacent decreases."[10] Beyond the formalization that such a question admits using models of spatial political competition, the intuition is simple: Party competition mostly takes place in the dimension where it may be more fruitful to its participants. If there is little opportunity for ideological battles, parties will attempt to distinguish themselves along different dimensions, valence issues representing an option. Curini then tests the "hypothesis of an inverse relationship between the distance of a party from its ideological competitor and its incentive to campaign on political corruption," for which he finds support in different settings. For the United States, in particular, he uses a measure of spatial pressure and one on the emphasis on corruption which derives from a textual analysis of political parties' manifestos.[11] Curini also considers multi-party systems,[12] where "new political parties tend to politicize corruption more than mainstream ones". On this count, he notes that "there are three [parties] that have run their European campaigns almost only on non-policy valence issues: *Podemos* in Spain, Five Stars Movement in Italy, and the Left Front in France".

Mention of these cases leads us to consider the phenomenon of populism, whose single most important defining trait is perhaps an "us vs. them"

[9] Navalny's organization was outlawed "on the grounds it is 'extremist'" (Roth 2021).

[10] Curini 2017, xiv. Valence and nonvalence issues interact in different ways. For example, "parties/candidates must balance the incentive to announce policies reflective of their sincere and possibly noncentrist preferences against the incentive to moderate in order to win the election" (Curini 2017, 31).

[11] See in particular Figure 2.2 in Curini 2017, 47.

[12] Curini 2017, 130. Multi-party systems differentiate themselves with respect to two-party systems in the way that incentives to adopt salience issues play out. In particular, in multi-party systems, "parties' incentive for negative campaigning can be considered less important than that for positive campaigning, since in the former case, a party cannot completely internalize the electoral benefits of such a move" (Curini 2017, 91, and 93).

rhetoric, where a series of stigmatizing attitudes, including corruption, are attributed to political adversaries. More generally, the rise in the use of valence issues in political campaigns should be considered together with the decrease in ideological distance, which followed the loss of attractiveness of the socialist alternative represented by the Soviet Union. Under this light, we may appreciate the presence and increased fortunes of a populist strategy, one of whose traits is the emphasis on valence issues. These considerations shed light on the demand side of anti-corruption policies, to the extent that they form a global regime. Its "principles, norms, rules, and decision-making procedures"[13] supply symbolic material and assets of various types that local actors may draw upon to serve their needs, depending on the possibilities offered by the local context. We consider this theme with reference to the cases of Russia and Brazil.

NATIONAL ADOPTION OF THE ANTI-CORRUPTION GLOBAL REGIME

In December 2008, during the first year of Medvedev's presidency, an anti-corruption law was passed in Russia, accompanied by subsequent reforms aimed at addressing what was termed "legal nihilism." Russia has been actively engaged in global discussions on combating corruption since the early 1990s,[14] and it has made nominal commitments to the global anti-corruption regime. Notably, Russia became a party to the United Nations Convention against Corruption in 2003 and ratified the OECD Anti-Bribery Convention in 2012.[15] Additional reforms mentioned in Chapter 6 sought to align Russia with liberal democracies in the aftermath of the Soviet Union's collapse. These reforms were part of a broader global regime that extends beyond the scope of my analysis.

During the protests that began in late 2011 and continued until the significant events at Bolotnaya Square on May 6, 2012, corruption emerged as a prominent theme. The newly appointed Putin administration responded with a combination of repression and political actions, aimed at demonstrating efforts in addressing the issue and avoiding the risk of losing

[13] Once more, with reference to the definition of global regimes provided by Krasner 1982, considered in Chapter 2.

[14] Russia started being covered by Transparency International's Corruption Perception Index in 1996, and the Russian chapter of Transparency International was founded in December 1999 (it has been forced to close in 2022; see Novaya Gazeta Europe 2023).

[15] In 2019, the OECD Working Group on Bribery noted that Russia has not investigated nor prosecuted any case since ratifying the Anti-Bribery Convention (OECD 2019).

legitimacy. I have extensively argued that Russia currently relies on corruption and cannot do without it. The regime carefully crafted its response to the protests to avoid questioning this fundamental condition and even appropriated the global anti-corruption regime to score domestic political points.[16] While the actions primarily targeted corruption at lower levels of the administration, they also selectively pursued elite members as a form of political retribution. This approach allowed the regime to reframe the issue of corruption in the public eye "as a problem of street-level organizations and a few rogue elites," while presenting itself as responsive to the problem. The regime also promoted "systemic" anti-corruption activities, thus contesting that political space as well.[17] The struggle between Navalny and the regime was also for the appropriation of a political space centered on corruption as a valence issue. Navalny squarely indicated that corruption was right at the top, while the regime attempted to deny him the use of such an issue, also by staging accusations to neutralize him through personal disqualification and imprisonment.[18] In summary, the Kremlin successfully manipulated the global anti-corruption regime, occasionally paying lip service to its principles but ultimately using them to serve its own interests while rejecting them.

Adoption of the anti-corruption global regime in Brazil differed significantly from Russia. Similar to Russia, Brazilian presidents also felt the need to demonstrate an interest in addressing corruption to maintain their legitimacy with an attentive citizenry. Within the Worker's Party leadership, this concern may have also been driven by the belief that fighting corruption was necessary due to its association with a historically elitist social system that contradicted the party's interests. However, unlike Russia, the influence of the global anti-corruption regime in Brazil was substantial and had significant consequences. In contrast to the subservient judiciary in Russia, the judiciary in Brazil played a leading role in a major push against

[16] The motives that I consider also emerge from 20 interviews with local anti-corruption practitioners (10 from governmental and 10 from nongovernmental organizations) carried out by Marina Zaloznaya and William M. Reisinger in the Summer and Fall of 2015 (Zaloznaya and Reisinger 2020, also for the citation that follows).

[17] Zaloznaya and Reisinger 2020, who add that "most 'non-governmental' anti-corruption action in present-day Russia originates from the *Obschestvennie palaty* (Public Chambers), the official goal of which is to oversee the activity of various governmental institutions. Ironically, members of these chambers are selected by governmental officials, while most of their organizational funding comes from the state." On Russia's "'parastatal' anti-corruption movement," see also Aburamoto, 2019, considering the state-sponsored All-Russia People's Front.

[18] See Dolbaum et al. 2021, and in particular, chapter 2.

corruption, spearheading reforms that occasionally went beyond the confines of their constitutional prerogatives.[19]

The legal specialists involved in the *Lava Jato* operation represented a new generation compared to those who had participated "in the constitutional debates and corporate battles of the first decade after the military regime" and who had striven "to build independent power bases anchored in the courts, public ministries, and the expansion of state bureaucracy that were permeated by models of respect for legal rules."[20] The new generation, recruited in the 2000s and sometimes educated abroad, advocated for a punitive criminal law model[21] and introduced a novel form of judicial protagonism. The Italian antecedent of *Mani pulite* was widely cited, and its lessons, particularly on the importance of a favorable public opinion to sustain a major anti-corruption effort, informed a savvy and unscrupulous relationship with the media that characterized *Lava Jato* and relied on well-timed (and illegal) leaks.

Important institutions, particularly the Public Prosecutor's Office, played an increasingly central role in the years leading to *Lava Jato* and developed strong connections with international actors involved in shaping the anti-corruption global regime, such as Transparency International, think tanks, and academic institutions.[22] These connections provided domestic legitimacy to the judges and prosecutors involved in *Lava Jato*, as they came to be seen as representatives of an anti-corruption global regime that was perceived as "appropriate and legitimate."[23] The perceived legitimacy, and in some cases even international public fame, brought personal advantages to those involved.[24] The relationship between the legal

[19] See Da Ros and Taylor 2022, 137, also on the so-called *10 Medidas contra a Corrupção* (ten measures against corruption), "a package of legislative changes drafted predominantly by task force prosecutors." Of Sérgio Moro becoming Minister of Justice under the presidency of Jair Bolsonaro, see Chapter 7.

[20] Engelmann and de Moura Menuzzi 2020.

[21] Engelmann 2020, who considers that such punitive model at the core represents a reactivation of "the authoritarian traditions that have characterized the trajectory of the state in Brazil," and more generally, that "the anti-corruption political doctrine was simply a new variant of an authoritarian pattern that has recurred in different forms throughout Brazilian political history."

[22] Engelmann and de Moura Menuzzi 2020.

[23] With reference to Meyer and Rowan 1977, and to the discussion of these themes in Chapter 2.

[24] At least some of them later landed well-paid jobs in the private sector. See Engelmann and de Moura Menuzzi 2020, who also provide evidence of the intense participation of prosecutors to meetings abroad that, being hosted by prestigious institutions, conferred symbolic capital.

professionals in *Lava Jato* and the international organizations representing the global anti-corruption order was mutually beneficial. While the former gained legitimization from the latter, the apparent successes of *Lava Jato*, coupled with its significant popularity, served as a positive example for the international actors supporting the anti-corruption global regime. Until, with the election of Jair Bolsonaro as President of Brazil, it wasn't.[25]

THE UNINTENDED CONSEQUENCES OF ANTI-CORRUPTION CAMPAIGNS

The cases of Russia and Brazil serve as examples of how the global anti-corruption regime may be adapted to local contexts. Adaptation implies a degree of deviation from the original plan and contributes to unpredictability of its effects, which are usefully considered with reference to the two distinct subsystems of historical change presented in Chapter 5. Within the lower subsystem, an anti-corruption drive may or may not be successful in punishing corrupt individuals. In Brazil, the anti-corruption campaign achieved this goal, as it also happened in Italy in the early 1990s. In both cases, there followed significant political changes.

In Italy, *Mani pulite* resulted in the end of the so-called First Republic, with the disappearance of most political parties and the emergence of transformed or new ones, such as Silvio Berlusconi's *Forza Italia* and the *Lega Nord* ("Northern League"), which in 1994 formed a winning coalition with the former neo-fascist *Alleanza Nazionale* ("National Alliance"). Both in the Italian and Brazilian cases, apparently momentous positive changes resulted to be much ado about little or worse. In Brazil, important anti-corruption reforms laboriously made during three decades were partly undone during Bolsonaro's presidency. In Italy, there was intermittent progress after the judicial "big push" of the early 1990s,[26] with setbacks occurring mainly during Berlusconi's tenures as Prime Minister.

[25] A perceptive observer, writing after Bolsonaro's very good showing in the first round of the 2018 presidential elections, noted that "those Brazilians who believe that electing a figure like Bolsonaro will help address the country's serious corruption problems are fooling themselves" and that "even if one were convinced that Bolsonaro was a cleaner option, his electoral success should serve as a reminder of something that should be obvious but that those of us who focus on corruption for a living sometimes seem to forget: There are indeed more important issues than corruption, sometimes voters are right to prioritize those other issues, and indeed sometimes it's a bit terrifying if they don't" (Stephenson 2018).

[26] Including the passing of the comprehensive anti-corruption law in 2012 that included the establishment of an independent anti-corruption authority (see Chapter 2), as well as the implementation of transparency-enhancing measures such as a timid freedom of

The case of Brazil and the earlier case of Italy illustrate how efforts to combat corruption are constantly at risk of failing, even when they appear to be successful. They can be co-opted by societal interests that may be no better, and sometimes are worse, than those they seek to oppose. The outcome of anti-corruption efforts in Russia is a distinct example of this pitfall. The Russian anti-corruption movement was not even apparently successful, and in fact it triggered a repressive response from the state that resulted in an overall decline in civil liberties, as discussed in Chapter 6. The uncertainties that are inherent in changes that occur in the lower subsystem are not amenable to a linear or incremental model of historical development. While a limited increase in transparency can promote vertical accountability, when a certain threshold is reached, the fear of system-wide empowerment may lead to a system-wide reaction, as seen in Russia. The Russian case lends support to the general considerations proposed in Chapter 4, according to which the question of which policies work is more complicated than what regression coefficients, or even the results of randomized controlled trials, might suggest.

The uncertainties we observe within the lower subsystem are compounded by ignorance about the degree to which the history of events influences the higher subsystem. To the extent that corruption serves as a tool of government, even spectacular changes occurring within the lower subsystem – such as those we described in Brazil following *Lava Jato* – may not amount to much, if new ways to govern do not emerge. The case of Italy after the *Mani pulite* operation is also illustrative of this point. In the years following the crackdown on corruption, public investments decreased significantly, which also led to a temporary reduction in corrupt transactions.[27] The nature of bribery in Italy has changed since *Mani pulite*.[28] Until the early 1990s, political parties, particularly the Christian Democrats and the Socialist Party, were the main organizers of the corrupt exchanges. Today, political parties are distant shadows of what they used to be, and bribes are managed in a more decentralized and local manner by a broader range of agents.

information act in 2016 (Picci and Vannucci 2018, 161). The *Mani pulite* operation also prompted reforms of public procurement laws (Golden and Picci 2006), but not of a chronically inefficient judiciary.

[27] Golden and Picci 2006, and in particular Figure 16.1. On the relationship between levels of public investments and of corruption, see the considerations on Spain in Chapter 3, also with reference to the important distinction between levels of corruption and propensity to corruption.

[28] Picci and Vannucci 2018, 81.

One further consideration on the Italian case brings us back to the complex and little researched question of the relationship between illegal bribes and what in Chapter 10 I defined as legal corruption. The way politics is financed has changed after *Mani pulite*. Until the early 1990s, corruption took place in a context of intra-party competition, where a proportional, open-list electoral system encouraged the collection of vast sums of political money.[29] *Mani pulite* determined the end of that system and ushered in new forms of money influence in politics. In particular, it enabled the political rise of media tycoon Silvio Berlusconi, who represented an example of state capture by economic interests, via organizational capital (his business organization turned political machine) and financial resources (of dubious origins), that to a certain degree compensated for the end of the flow of bribes. Today, the Italian political system continues to face strong pressure to finance political parties and campaigns, possibly resulting in legal corruption replacing bribes. For instance, a prime minister who inaugurates a new cigarette factory and promotes its benefits in public does not commit a crime, even if the multinational corporation involved had contributed to that politician's political organization.[30] The Italian case hints at a further possible unintended consequence of anti-corruption campaigns: When they are successful, they may encourage legal forms of corruption.

ANTI-CORRUPTION CROWDS OUT ALTERNATIVE STRATEGIES

The anti-corruption flag waves on a contested field, and it is fought over in the competition for power and for a more favorable share of the available resources. It is often used as a tool to build a collective action project, as was the case in Brazil, where a dissatisfied middle class rallied behind it. In some situations, as in Russia before the attempted assassination of Navalny, choosing to fight corruption may have been the only viable option to fight for change. This is especially true given that the allegations of corruption against the Russian ruling elite are well founded, whereas alternative rallying cries, such as environmental issues, are more difficult to articulate and tend to be localized.[31] In all cases, choosing anti-corruption as a tool of

[29] Golden and Picci 2008 and 2015.

[30] Portici 2016, and Pipitone 2019.

[31] A series of protests have taken place in Russia on broadly defined environmental issues. See BBC 2017. Other vociferous protests have taken place on local issues, as it happened in Yekaterinburg, in 2019, when the construction of a new church was planned in a public park. See BBC 2019a. These initiatives have been narrowly focused: "The only issues that

politics implies, at least to some extent, shelving other potential strategies. By focusing on anti-corruption, other politically charged issues, such as clamoring for more equality, increased social mobility, or decisive action against climate change, are crowded out. Moreover, when a particular definition of corruption is proposed, such as Navalny's implied definition of corruption as the stealing of public goods, alternative ideas on corruption are neglected.

It is important to consider that the political space is not determined once and for all, but rather it is shaped by the moves of political actors. When a political actor decides on which dimension to compete, it also projects a vision of where competition should occur and what matters in politics. For instance, when it is claimed that corruption is the main problem in Russia and that without corruption ordinary Russians would prosper, the choice of that particular valence issue doubles as a particular view of the world. It is a world where narrowly defined corruption is the primary issue to address and where a counterfactual of significantly less corruption is plausible. A set of interlaced ideas forms an ideology: In an apparent paradox, the choice of a valence issue, whose political mileage derives from appearing nonideological, has revealed itself to be quite the opposite.

CONCLUSIONS: THE COMPLIANCE TRAP OF ANTI-CORRUPTION

We return to the theme of compliance, considered in Chapter 2, to reassess it under the light of the present discussion.

We have observed that the anti-corruption global regime creates a set of political material that can be adopted and adapted according to local conditions and needs. This material can be used as a pretext to further political projects, as it is "taken for granted as legitimate," and as such it helps decouple elements of structure from activities and from each other.[32] The result is a ceremonialization of anti-corruption efforts, and a possible compliance trap, "emphasizing rule-following rather than the aspects of justice that might be essential to building vigorous and sustainable demands for better government."[33] The emphasis on rule-following is a significant facet of the anti-corruption global order, because it provides a rationale for

have brought crowds into the streets are trash removal and occasional opposition to projects that involve cutting through forests and protected areas" (Gustafson 2021, 43).

32 Meyer and Rowan 1977.

33 Dincer and Johnston 2020a.

the presence of suppliers of services aimed at helping with the adoption of those rules. These suppliers include branches of international organizations and national governments, international NGOs such as Transparency International, and various consultants specializing in different aspects of compliance. They also include lawyers in various aspects of corporate compliance law that I alluded to in my discussion on compliance in Chapter 2.

The theory of political republicanism provides a key to interpret the current emphasis on compliance. Within this tradition of thought, there is a dialectic relationship between republican individual virtues and a type of virtue that pertains to a polity because of its design. Such virtue-by-design does not require a particular individual inclination, because appropriately crafted rules lead to a "mechanization of virtue" – that is, to collective virtue, possibly in the absence of an individual inclination to virtue. The types of rules that may bring about such results are various. They could represent the detailed working of a specific institution, as are those describing the voting procedures of Venice's ancient "*sala del consiglio grande*," "an enormous physical device for eliminating extraneous pressures and ensuring—almost enforcing—rationality in choosing for the public good."[34] Or they may refer to constitutional arrangements, like those that were at the center of the preoccupations of the American Federalists in the 1780s, well summarized in James Madison's consideration that "ambition must be made to counteract ambition."[35]

The distinction between the two poles – individual republican virtue on one hand and virtue-by-design on the other – is certainly nuanced. For example, in his Discourses, Machiavelli considers the importance of *virtù* among the Romans, while couching its effects within constitutional considerations on the beneficial effects of the contrast between the patricians and the tribunate. A later influential American thinker, John Calhoun, interpreted such institutional devices in Machiavelli's reading of republican Rome as a case of "mechanized virtue."[36] Also, the Federalists were skeptical about whether the new Constitution could achieve such "mechanization," or whether any constitution could do so. Like Machiavelli before them,[37] they emphasized the necessity of individual virtues to prevent corruption and ensure the survival of the Republic.

[34] James Pocock 1975, 285, referring to Donato Giannotti's description.

[35] Hamilton et al. 2008 [1788], 257 (Federalist No. 51).

[36] See Vajda 2001.

[37] See in particular Machiavelli 1996 [1531], 49: "I shall presuppose a very corrupt city, by which I shall the more increase such a difficulty, for neither laws nor orders can be found that are enough to check a universal corruption. For as good customs have need of laws to maintain themselves, so laws have need of good customs so as to be observed." I am grateful to Maurizio Viroli for a discussion of these and other aspects of Machiavelli's thought.

While emphasis may be placed in one or the other of these two poles, the anti-corruption global regime has leaned in favor of the *mechanization of virtue*, at least in part because of the cultural tradition which produced it and that we have discussed. I surmise that in this, too, the choice has not been neutral, and that it has come with a cost. With the ritualization of compliance, decoupling may occur not only at the organizational level, but in a sense also within the individual, where the ritual of virtuosity may appear to be a good enough substitute for its substance.

12

Conclusions

Whither Corruption?

From the Central Plateau, from this solitude that will soon become the mind where the most important national decisions will be made, I look once more to the future of my country and foresee the sunrise with unbreakable faith and unlimited trust in its great destiny.

Juscelino Kubitschek, President of Brazil, October 2, 1956

In this book, I have placed the elusive and contested context of corruption at the center stage. I have argued that the never-ending debate on corruption and the impossibility of conclusively pinning down what it really is, is what corruption is about. As a social construction, corruption is a struggle to propose and, when possible, impose one's views of the polity and of politics. It is a high-stakes game where the players promote and, when possible, inflict their judgment on what and who is corrupt. At stake are forms of control of the loser by the winner and the political dividend that comes with it. This dividend may be in the form of control by the ruler of the execution of policies, obtained through bribing and possibly through the threat of selective punishment. It may be in the damage inflicted to such ruler, whenever his opposers successfully label him as corrupt.

To interpret the stubborn persistence of corruption, we have observed its *longue durée* with a detached eye. We have considered a "higher subsystem" where the ways in which the business of government is carried out are stubbornly persistent. Focusing on the social construction of corruption has also allowed us to maintain a distance from the usual object of inquiry in corruption studies, which is corruption as a phenomenon. However, while such observational distance should be maintained, we cannot escape the debate on corruption as a phenomenon and on attempts to fight it. This is because we cannot avoid discussing ideals of the polity, how what we observe may differ from those ideals, and how, from our current position, we can get closer to them. Within this debate, we cannot help but take sides. In this book, I have done so repeatedly, particularly when arguing that instead of the narrow view of corruption that prevails today, we should pay more attention to forms of legal corruption.

Such a thesis, along with any position on corruption as a phenomenon, necessarily depends on the political values and normative views of the observer. We, as researchers, should be more forthcoming on these values. We are immersed in the present of history, and it is understandable to consider the current incarnation of the concepts we toil with as all that matters. However, we must also recognize that a form of self-interest is at play. Specialization in research encourages narrow views on complex problems, both in scope and in historical depth. We tend to present our views as different from those that came before us, as a necessary condition to communicate their higher value compared to older and perhaps dispensable stocks of knowledge. We also have an interest in presenting our findings as providing useful policy implications, which implies a bias in favor of affirming the possibility of human agency. Use of certain tools of analysis, such as the regression model, fortifies that bias. Policymakers, on their side, like to claim that they know new ways to solve old problems. As long as someone is willing to give them the benefit of the doubt, this choice is preferable to candidly admitting that the problem at hand is complicated and that all we may do is to muddle through it. Wrapping proposed fixes to political problems using scientific papers provides legitimacy. This, in turn, raises the incentives of researchers to be pliant to the policymakers' needs, also to improve their chances to eventually double as paid consultants, policy advisors, etc.

While these incentives might also be framed as forms of conflicts of interest, a concept ambiguously related to current definitions of corruption, I do not imply that the prevailing thinking on corruption should be given a taste of its own medicine and be defined, itself, "corrupt."[1] However, we should be more mindful of the existence of personal motivations and incentives, and how they may affect our thinking on corruption. Simply checking the "no conflict of interest to report" box before publication does

[1] Such stern sentence moreover would also inculpate myself, considering that over the years I have collaborated as an expert to various anti-corruption projects.

not guarantee that all is well, as it may reflect one more case of how compliance may be a substitute for substance.

SHOULD WE CONTINUE THE FIGHT AGAINST CORRUPTION?

We also cannot dismiss the debate on the current narrow definition of corruption, as much as we may criticize it. People worldwide confront dishonest politicians, government officials, and businesses that, by offering or accepting bribes, rob them of vital services, distort the selection and implementation of public policies, and deny legitimate aspirations for social inclusion and upward mobility.

On this note, I emphasize again my position on the challenge of achieving change without addressing the root problem of control in government. Obtaining change requires new ways to obtain control, that is, new institutions. Broad reform projects should not be framed solely in terms of fighting corruption. Narrowly defined "anti-corruption campaigns" may certainly play a role – they are a "tool of politics" after all – but only if they are part of a broader policy package, whose emphasis should be elsewhere.[2]

The contents of these broad packages, I believe, should depend on the specific context. The cases discussed in this book suggest that local conditions play a significant role, and I described historical change as nonlinear and not obediently responding to the common average effects that the linear regression model implies. To the extent that corruption helps in solving a problem of control in government, reforms should think of democratic ways to solve the same problems differently. To the extent that it serves to keep elite cohesive, an important question regards the motives why such "trust booster" is needed, and what other strategy may be available, in a given context, to obtain a necessary cohesion.

How to frame these considerations into an appealing political project represents a difficult question. However, I do not see any shortcut available in this respect, and difficult questions must be asked even when they lead to confront answers that one may not like. In Brazil, as I suggested, we would perhaps conclude that corruption is linked to a political compact, which has guaranteed an economic and political elite to continue enjoying the vast privileges implied by a very pronounced and culturally entrenched

[2] Together with Alberto Vannucci, I proposed similar ideas, when arguing in favor of a "Zen approach" to anti-corruption. Picci and Vannucci 2018.

inequality. In Russia, I underlined the presence of a statist ideology that has been inimical to the development of checks and balances, which in turn would seem to be a prerequisite for moving forward. Probing that ideology would likely involve broader questions on national identity and would lead to tackle themes that apparently have little to do with bribes paid to voracious public officials. In considering the United States, we were confronted with stubborn popular beliefs in the American Dream, regardless of the mounting evidence that contradicts its tenets. Increased inequality should be interpreted within a broader outlook, perhaps also as a factor that permits the United States to maintain vast armed forces at a sustainable cost.[3] Machiavelli's interpretation of the political compact between patricians and plebeians in republican Rome comes to mind once again. A debate on legal corruption in the United States should consider also its place in the world, and what it implies for the construction of a domestic consensus, as fraught as it is today.

A theme that in the book I only have sketched regards the relationship between bribes and forms of legal corruption. In the case of the United States, I conjectured that historically, and within profound transformations that took place starting in the late nineteenth century and which spanned decades, illegal corruption could diminish also because new and legal forms of political influence emerged. Possibilities of this type should give us pause. For example, observing fewer bribes in public procurement would certainly be a reason for joy. But if political parties are not financed by those bribes any longer (as, e.g., it used to be in Italy before *Mani pulite*), but party leaders find solace in more or less "dark money" provided by business, it is not clear whether what we observe is progress.

As for the measures that currently are enumerated in anti-corruption packages, I believe that they may in fact be useful, but only under certain circumstances. For instance, more transparency is commendable in itself, unless it triggers countervailing reactions, as it happened in Russia. And returning once more to the concept of compliance, setting standards aimed at models of "good governance" may have positive effects that go beyond a narrow preoccupation with corruption, to the extent that they encourage sound organizational practices. Unless they are ritualized or, worse, unless the new rules become one of those "normative spaces" discussed in Chapter 10, whose coercive value reflects not their apparent normative intentions but, at the opposite, their being systematically violated.

3 In fact, pays in the military have increased compared to the civilian counterpart, and "military service [is] one of the last bastions of middle class social mobility" (Stickles 2018).

CORRUPTION AND MODERNITY

A different angle from which to consider the fight against corruption takes us back to the point of departure of this book.

On October 28, 2018, Jair Bolsonaro's supporters celebrated his historical victory, in front of the National Congress in Brasília. On its opposite side, the National Congress flanks the symbolically named "Square of the Three Powers" along with two more of Niemeyer's masterpieces – the Presidential Palace and the Supreme Federal Court. This vast esplanade is where the visionary sentence that opens this chapter is written on a huge slab of concrete. The newly founded city of Brasília was meant to represent the sunrise of a radiant future of modernity for the country, to be observed with "unbreakable faith and unlimited trust in its great destiny." Inscribed into the political heart of its new modernist capital, this optimistic vision of the future was but a facet of Brazil's contradictory relationship with modernity.[4] Juscelino Kubitschek's optimism was to give way to the somber years of the dictatorship. The return of democracy brought new hopes, ambitious institutions, and many consequential transformations, but a series of scandals, culminating in *Lava Jato*, revealed massive amounts of one of the least modern manifestations of human society, corruption.

I have explored the motives that contributed to the emergence of the current consensus view on corruption and the emphasis on anti-corruption policies, and I suggest that these motives also found a fertile ground in the ideological substratum of modernity. Modernity sees social order not as an abstract form but as the result of human agency, which acts in a purely profane, secularized history where events are casually related to one another. To contemplate agency and intervene in the causality relationships among events in such a history requires a disputation of the authority of the ancients. This outlook often implies an idea of progress, where continuous improvements of the social order are possible through human agency. Furthermore, this idea of modernity reflects the affirmation of the modern scientific method, which presupposes the accumulation and improvement of knowledge.[5]

Consequently, in modern times each generation may consider itself at the cusp of knowledge also with respect to the problem of corruption. A certain shortsightedness with respect to the past, and to the recurrent

[4] See Mota and Delanty 2015, who frame their analysis in terms of Eisenstadt "multiple modernities" framework (Eisenstadt 2000).

[5] Taylor 2004, 182, and Eisenstadt 2000, also with reference to Max Weber. On modernity and progress, see Mouzakitis 2017.

failures in the fight against corruption, might then also be seen as an expression of a modernist ideology and perhaps of modernist hubris. In this light, we may be justified in ignoring the historical *longue durée* of corruption, assuming that we are observing it with new and more discerning eyes. Eyes that restrict the phenomenon of corruption to well-defined forms that are anchored in a modern concept of public service, thereby discarding older and imprecise notions. Eyes that are also scientific, because they employ quantitative information and statistical methods, whose conclusions are wrong only in a comfortably small portion of possible cases, as quantified by the "p-value" of statistical tests. In this particular aspect at least, we observe a type of modernity with a veneer of high modernism, to the extent that it inherits the tradition of "high econometrics."[6] If this is the case, if the prevailing view of corruption is also an expression of modernism and perhaps also of modernist hubris, then the stubborn persistence of corruption represents a challenge to modernity.

Another way to view the failure to combat corruption is by examining a fundamental characteristic of modernity – the separation of the private and public spheres. This division emerged gradually, but accelerated during the late eighteenth and early nineteenth centuries, driven by a desire to eliminate ambiguities and create order through distinctions and classifications, of which that between private and public is the most crucial.[7] Corruption as a thorn in the side of modernity is also a warning that the great division of spheres that it presupposes, public and private, is not possible if not as an approximation. Any attempt to force such separation, any attempt at fighting corruption in the current sense of the term, may at best be muddled through. This book has provided a further reason for such difficulties, or perhaps has looked at them from a different angle, in focusing on the perverse aptness of corruption to serve both as a tool of government and of politics, which makes it difficult to dispense with.

Yet again, we observe corruption, along with the legitimate and commendable desires of large swathes of the world's population to root it out. In considering how to address the problem of corruption, I have not abandoned that belief in human agency that is a cornerstone of modernity, but hopefully I have highlighted the practical difficulties that it encounters.

6 With reference to the discussion in Chapter 4.

7 Ivo Engels notes that the desire (which occasionally he sees as an obsession) to separate the private from the public is a chimera, also because "both sides [have] good reasons for cooperation," which in turn "requires social proximity, or better yet, interrelations" (Engels 2017 and references therein). See also Bratsis 2003 on the "fetishistic nature of the public/private split."

References

Abbott, Kenneth W., and Duncan Snidal. 2002. "Values and interests: International legalization in the fight against corruption." *The Journal of Legal Studies* 31 (S1): S141–S177.

Aburamoto, Mari. 2019. "The politics of anti-corruption campaigns in Putin's Russia: Power, opposition, and the All-Russia People's Front." *Europe-Asia Studies* 71 (3): 408–425.

Adam, Isabelle, and Mihály Fazekas. 2021. "Are emerging technologies helping win the fight against corruption? A review of the state of evidence." *Information Economics and Policy* 57: 100950.

Ades, Alberto, and Rafael Di Tella. 1996. "The causes and consequences of corruption: A review of recent empirical contributions." *IDs Bulletin* 27 (2): 6–11.

Alacevich, Michele. 2021. *Albert O. Hirschman: An Intellectual Biography.* New York: Columbia University Press.

Alstadsæter, Annette, Niels Johannesen, and Gabriel Zucman. 2018. "Who owns the wealth in tax havens? Macro evidence and implications for global inequality." *Journal of Public Economics* 162: 89–100.

Alvaredo, Facundo, Thomas Piketty, Lucas Chancel, Emmanuel Saez, and G. Gabriel Zucman (editors). 2018. *World Inequality Report 2018.* Cambridge: Belknap Press.

Amnesty International. 2014. "Russia: Guilty verdict in Bolotnaya case – Injustice at its most obvious." February 21, 2014. www.amnesty.org/en/latest/news/2014/02/russia-guilty-verdict-bolotnaya-case-injustice-its-most-obvious/

Amorim Neto, Octavio. 2019. "Cabinets and coalitional presidentialism." In *Routledge Handbook of Brazilian Politics*, edited by Barry Ames, 293–312. Abingdon: Routledge.

Amorim Neto, Octavio, and Gabriel Alves Pimenta. 2020. "The first year of Bolsonaro in office: Same old story, same old song?" *Revista de Ciencia Política* 40 (2): 187–213.

Amos, Howard. 2017 "Cultural twists: Literary references in Ulyukayev's last words explained." *The Calvert Journal*, December 8. www.calvertjournal.com/articles/show/9332/cultural-twists-ulyukayevs-last-words-in-russian-corruption-trial

Ananyev, Maxim. 2018. "Inside the Cremlin." In *The New Autocracy: Information, Politics, and Policy in Putin's Russia*, edited by Daniel Treisman, 29–48. Washington, DC: Brookings Institution Press.

Anders, Gerhard, and Monique Nuijten. 2007. "An introduction." In *Corruption and the Secret of Law: A Legal Anthropological Perspective*, edited by Monique Nuijten and Gerhard Anders, 1–26. Farnham: Ashgate Publishing.

Ang, Yuen. 2020. *China's Gilded Age: The Paradox of Economic Boom and Vast Corruption.* Cambridge: Cambridge University Press.

Ansell, Aaron, and Ken Mitchell. 2011. "Models of clientelism and policy change: The case of conditional cash transfer programmes in Mexico and Brazil." *Bulletin of Latin American Research* 30 (3): 298–312.

Ansolabehere, Stephen, James M. Snyder Jr, and Micky Tripathi. 2002. "Are PAC contributions and lobbying linked? New evidence from the 1995 Lobby Disclosure Act." *Business and Politics* 4 (2): 131–155.

Ansolabehere, Stephen, John M. De Figueiredo, and James M. Snyder Jr. 2003. "Why is there so little money in US politics?" *Journal of Economic Perspectives* 17 (1): 105–130.

Anti-corruption Foundation. 2020. "Коррупция севодня – главная проблема россии." Archive.org, May 12, 2020. Accessed June 15, 2023. https://web.archive.org/web/20200511214203/https://fbk.info/about/

Aranha, Ana Luiza. 2020. "Lava Jato and Brazil's web of accountability institutions. A turning point for corruption control?" In *Corruption and the Lava Jato Scandal in Latin America*, edited by Paul Lagunes and Jan Svejnar, 94–112. Abingdon: Routledge.

Arantes, Rogerio B. 2005. "Constitutionalism, the expansion of justice and the judicialization of politics in Brazil." In *The Judicialization of Politics in Latin America*, edited by Rachel Sieder, Line Schjolden and Alan Angell, 231–262. London: Palgrave Macmillan.

Arcidiacono, Peter, Josh Kinsler, and Tyler Ransom. 2022. "Legacy and athlete preferences at Harvard." *Journal of Labor Economics* 40 (1): 133–156.

Atkinson, Anthony B. 2015. *Inequality*. Cambridge: Harvard University Press.

Autorità Nazionale Anticorruzione. 2016. *Relazione Annuale 2015.* Rome: Autorità Nazionale Anticorruzione.

Avelar, Idelber. 2021. *Eles em nós: retórica e antagonismo político no Brasil do século xxi.* Rio de Janeiro: Editora Record.

Avritzer, Leonardo, and Lucio Rennó. 2021. "The pandemic and the crisis of democracy in Brazil." *Journal of Politics in Latin America* 13 (3): 442–457.

Azfar, Omar, Young Lee, and Anand Swamy. 2001. "The causes and consequences of corruption." *The Annals of the American Academy of Political and Social Science* 573 (1): 42–56.

Baker, Paula, Daniel Czitrom, Mary Berry, James Kloppenberg, Barbara Hahn, Naomi Lamoreaux, and David Witwer. 2019. "Interchange: Corruption has a history." *Journal of American History* 105 (4): 912–938.

Barber, Lionel, Neil Buckley, and Catherine Belton. 2008. "Laying down the law: Medvedev vows war on Russia's 'legal nihilism'." *The Financial Times*, December 24, 2008. www.ft.com/content/e46ea1d8-c6c8-11dd-97a5-000077b07658

Barnes, Robert. 2022. "Supreme Court suggests higher bar may be needed for corruption cases." *The Washington Post*, November 28, 2022. www.washingtonpost.com/politics/2022/11/28/public-corruption-supreme-court-new-york/

Barro, Robert J. 1991. "Economic growth in a cross section of countries." *The Quarterly Journal of Economics* 106 (2): 407–443.

Barroso Vargas, Fernando. 2012. "Subvenciones, drogas, y «rock and roll»." In *Aquellos maravillosos años*, edited by Rafael Aníbal, 69–86. Madrid: Continta me tienes.

Barros de Mello, Fernando. 2009. "Família de Jânio tenta repatriar '20 milhões'." *Folha de S.Paulo*, April 1, 2009. www1.folha.uol.com.br/fsp/brasil/fc0104200903.htm

Bartels, Larry M. 2008. *Unequal Democracy: The Political Economy of the New Gilded Age*. 1st ed. Princeton: Princeton University Press.

Bartels, Larry M. 2016. *Unequal Democracy: The Political Economy of the New Gilded Age*. 2nd ed. Princeton: Princeton University Press.

Bartels, Larry M., and Ray Fair. 1997. "Correspondence." *Journal of Economic Perspectives* 11 (3): 195–199.

Baumann, Hannes. 2020. "The corruption perception index and the political economy of governing at a distance." *International Relations* 34 (4): 504–523.

BBC. 2017. "Goodbye Russia: A generation packs its bags." December 23, 2017. www.bbc.com/news/stories-42431009; https://meduza.io/en/feature/2021/12/08/the-past-is-a-foreign-country

BBC. 2019a. "Activists storm Yekaterinburg Russia park in protest against new church." May 15, 2019. www.bbc.com/news/world-europe-48276170

BBC. 2019b. "Joaquín "El Chapo" Guzmán: lo que dijo el narcotraficante mexicano al ser condenado a cadena perpetua en Estados Unidos." July 17, 2019. www.bbc.com/mundo/noticias-america-latina-49022667

BBC. 2021. "Afghanistan: What has the conflict cost the US and its allies?" September 3, 2021. www.bbc.com/news/world-47391821

BBC-Russian Service. 2011. "Главным по борьбе с коррупцией в РФ назначен Сугробов." June 28, 2011. www.bbc.com/russian/rolling_news/2011/06/110628_rn_russia_sugrobov

BBC-Russian Service. 2017a. "Как вам спится по ночам?Генерал Феоктистов на процессе Улюкаева." September 20, 2017. www.bbc.com/russian/av/media-41326253

BBC-Russian Service. 2017b. "Приговор бывшему генералу Сугробову сократили на 10 лет." December 19, 2017. www.bbc.com/russian/news-42413394

BBC-Russian Service. 2022. "Бывший российский министр Алексей Улюкаев вышел из колонии." May 12, 2022. www.bbc.com/russian/news-61406512

Beccaria, Antonella, and Gigi Marcucci. 2015. *I segreti di Tangentopoli*. Rome: Newton and Compton.

Beebee, Helen, Christopher Hitchcock, and Peter Menzies. 2009. "Introduction." In *The Oxford Handbook of Causation*, edited by Helen Beebee, Christopher Hitchcock, and Peter Menzies, 1–18. Oxford: Oxford University Press.

Benson, Todd, and Asher Levine. 2013. "Biggest protests in 20 years sweep Brazil." *Reuters*, June 18, 2013. www.reuters.com/article/us-brazil-protests-idUSBRE95G15S20130618

Berlin, Pavel Abramovich. 1910. "Русское взяточничество, как социально-историческое явление." *Современный мир* 8, 48–56.

Berman, Yonatan, and Branko Milanovic. 2020. "Homoploutia: Top labor and capital incomes in the United States, 1950–2020." World Inequality Lab, Working Paper 2020/27.

Besley, Timothy, and Andrea Prat. 2006. "Handcuffs for the grabbing hand? Media capture and government accountability." *American Economic Review* 96 (3): 720–736.

Biden, Joe. 2021. "Address to a joint session of Congress U.S. capitol." April 28, 2021. Accessed May 25, 2023. www.whitehouse.gov/briefing-room/speeches-remarks/2021/04/29/remarks-by-president-biden-in-address-to-a-joint-session-of-congress/

Biddulph, Robin. 2014. "Can elite corruption be a legitimate Machiavellian tool in an unruly world? The case of post-conflict Cambodia." *Third World Quarterly* 35 (5): 872–887.

Blundo, Giorgio. 2007. "Hidden acts, open talks. How anthropology can 'observe' and describe corruption." In *Corruption and the Secret of Law: A Legal Anthropological Perspective*, edited by Monique Nuijten and Gerhard Anders, 27–52. Farnham: Ashgate Publishing.

Bogardus, Kevin. 2004. "Koch's low profile belies political power." *The Center for Public Integrity*, July 15, 2004. https://publicintegrity.org/environment/kochs-low-profile-belies-political-power/

Boldrini, Laura. 2013. "La corruzione avvelena il nostro Paese sottraendo ai cittadini onesti 60 miliardi l'anno." *Facebook*, June 13, 2013. www.facebook.com/permalink.php?story_fbid=399630830147121&id=325228170920721

Bonica, Adam, and Maya Sen. 2021. "Estimating judicial ideology." *Journal of Economic Perspectives* 35 (1): 97–118.

Bourdieu, Pierre. 1998. *The State Nobility: Elite Schools in the Field of Power*. Stanford: Stanford University Press.

Bowman, Karlyn. 2020. "The ACA at year 10." *Forbes*, March 9, 2020. www.forbes.com/sites/bowmanmarsico/2020/03/09/public-opinion-the-aca-at-year-10/?sh=546c9b6f745b

Bratsis, Peter. 2003. "The construction of corruption, or rules of separation and illusions of purity in bourgeois societies." *Social Text* 21 (4): 9–33.

Brewster, Rachel. 2017. "Enforcing the FCPA: International resonance and domestic strategy." *Virginia Law Review* 103: 1611–1682.

Brinkley, Alan. 1985. "Richard Hofstadter's the age of reform: A reconsideration." *Reviews in American History* 13 (3): 462–480.

Bruder, Jessica. 2017. *Nomadland: Surviving America in the Twenty-First Century*. New York: W. W. Norton & Company.

Buchan, Bruce, and Lisa Hill. 2014. *An Intellectual History of Political Corruption*. New York: Springer.

Bump, Philip. 2017. "Assessing a Clinton argument that the media helped to elect Trump." *The Washington Post*, September 12, 2017. www.washingtonpost.com/news/politics/wp/2017/09/12/assessing-a-clinton-argument-that-the-media-helped-to-elect-trump/

Bunzl, Martin. 2004. "Counterfactual history: A user's guide." *The American Historical Review* 109 (3): 845–858.

Burgin, Angus. 2012. *The Great Persuasion*. Cambridge: Harvard University Press.

Camera dei Deputati. 2013. "Proposta di legge, presentata il 15 marzo 2013." www.camera.it/leg17/995?sezione=documenti&tipoDoc=lavori_testo_pdl&idLegislatura=17&codice=17PDL0003330

Campbell, Peter Scott. 2013. "Democracy v. concentrated wealth: In search of a Louis D. Brandeis quote." *Green Bag* 16 (3): 251–256.

Campello, Daniela. 2015. *The Politics of Market Discipline in Latin America: Globalization and Democracy*. Cambridge: Cambridge University Press.

Capoccia, Giovanni, and R. Daniel Kelemen. 2007. "The study of critical junctures: Theory, narrative, and counterfactuals in historical institutionalism." *World Politics* 59 (3): 341–369.

Caprara, Maurizio. 2001. "Il caso Lockheed in Parlamento." In *Storia d'Italia, Annali 17, Il Parlamento*, edited by Luciano Violante, 1127–1154. Torino: Einaudi.

Cardoso, Adalberto. 2020. *Classes médias e políticas no Brasil. 1922–2016*. Rio de Janeiro: FGV Editora.

Carothers, Thomas, Jean Bethke Elshtain, Larry Jay Diamond, Anwar Ibrahim, and Zainab Hawa Bangura. 2017. "A quarter-century of promoting democracy." *Journal of Democracy* 18 (4): 112–126.

Cartwright, Nancy. 1999. *The Dappled World: A Study of the Boundaries of Science.* Cambridge: Cambridge University Press.

Carvalho, Laura. 2018. *Valsa brasileira: do boom ao caos econômico.* São Paulo: Editora Todavia.

Case, Anne, and Angus Deaton. 2017. "Mortality and morbidity in the 21st century." *Brookings Papers on Economic Activity* 2017: 397–444.

Case, Anne, and Angus Deaton. 2020. *Deaths of Despair and the Future of Capitalism.* Princeton: Princeton University Press.

Cederna, Camilla. 1978. *Giovanni Leone. La carriera di un presidente.* Milano: Feltrinelli.

Centers for Medicare & Medicaid Services. n.d. "Historical N.H. Tables." www.cms.gov/Research-Statistics-Data-and-Systems/Statistics-Trends-and-Reports/NationalHealthExpendData/NationalHealthAccountsHistorical

Chang, Eric C. C. 2005. "Electoral incentives for political corruption under open-list proportional representation." *The Journal of Politics* 67 (3): 716–730.

Chang, Eric CC, and Miriam A. Golden. 2007. "Electoral systems, district magnitude and corruption." *British Journal of Political Science* 37 (1): 115–137.

Chayes, Sarah. 2020. "This is how kleptocracies work." *The Atlantic,* February 23, 2020. www.theatlantic.com/ideas/archive/2020/02/how-kleptocracies-work/606958/

Chetty, Raj, David Grusky, Maximilian Hell, Nathaniel Hendren, Robert Manduca, and Jimmy Narang. 2017a. "The fading American dream: Trends in absolute income mobility since 1940." *Science* 356 (6336): 398–406.

Chetty, Raj, John N. Friedman, Emmanuel Saez, Nicholas Turner, and Danny Yagan. 2017b. "Mobility report cards: The role of colleges in intergenerational mobility." National Bureau of Economic Research, No. w23618.

Clausing, Kimberly A. 2019. "Fixing five flaws of the tax cuts and jobs act." *Columbia Journal of Tax Law* 11: 31–75.

Cobain, Ian. 2014. "Boris Berezovsky inquest returns open verdict on death." *The Guardian,* March 27, 2014. www.theguardian.com/world/2014/mar/27/boris-berezovsky-inquest-open-verdict-death

Coffee Jr, John C. 1991. "Does unlawful mean criminal: Reflections on the disappearing tort/crime distinction in American law." *Boston University Law Review* 71: 193–246.

Cohen, Robin A., Emily P. Terlizzi, Amy E. Cha, and Michael E. Martinez. 2021. *Health Insurance Coverage: Early Release of Estimates From the National Health Interview Survey, January–June 2021.* Division of Health Interview Statistics, National Center for Health Statistics. www.cdc.gov/nchs/data/nhis/earlyrelease/insur202102-508.pdf

Collier, David, Fernando Daniel Hidalgo, and Andra Olivia Maciuceanu. 2006. "Essentially contested concepts: Debates and applications." *Journal of Political Ideologies* 11 (3): 211–246.

Corriere della Sera. 2012. "Bruxelles all'Italia: 'Norme anticorruzione insufficienti, e basta leggi ad personam.'" February 3, 2012. www.corriere.it/politica/14_febbraio_03/bruxelles-all-italia-norme-anticorruzione-insufficienti-basta-leggi-ad-personam-eef7a66a-8cc3-11e3-b3eb-24c163fe5e21.shtml

Cravo, Alice, and Daniel Gullino. 2022. "Orçamento secreto: Bolsonaro afirma que pagamento de emendas 'ajuda a acalmar' o Congresso." *O Globo,* April 11, 2022.

https://oglobo.globo.com/politica/orcamento-secreto-bolsonaro-afirma-que-pagamento-de-emendas-ajuda-acalmar-congresso-25470933

Cuéllar, Mariano-Florentino, and Matthew Stephenson. 2020. "Taming systemic corruption: The American experience and its implications for contemporary debates." *QoG Working Paper Series 2020*, no. 6.

Curini, Luigi. 2017. *Corruption, Ideology, and Populism: The Rise of Valence Political Campaigning*. New York: Springer.

Cutler, David M., and Edward L. Glaeser. 2021. "When innovation goes wrong: Technological regress and the opioid epidemic." *Journal of Economic Perspectives* 35 (4): 171–196

Da Ros, Luciano, and Matthew T. Taylor. 2017. "Opening the black box: Three decades of reforms to Brazil's judicial system." *School of International Service Research Paper* 2017 (3).

Da Ros, Luciano, and Matthew C. Ingram. 2018. "Law, courts, and judicial politics." In *Routledge Handbook of Brazilian Politics*, edited by Barry Ames, 339–357. Abingdon: Routledge.

Da Ros, Luciano, and Matthew T. Taylor. 2022. *Brazilian Politics on Trial: Corruption and Reform Under Democracy*. Boulder: Lynne Rienner Publishers.

Datafolha. 2005. "Em simulações para 2006, Serra empata com Lula no primeiro turno e supera presidente no segundo." August 12, 2005. http://datafolha.folha.uol.com.br/opiniaopublica/2005/08/1222265-aprovacao-cai-reprovacao-continua-subindo-e-lula-atinge-pior-avaliacao-de-seu-mandato.shtml

David-Barrett, Elizabeth. 2021. "State capture and inequality." *Pathfinder Research Paper*, New York University.

David-Barrett, Elizabeth, and Mark Philp. 2022. "Political corruption." In *Political Ethics: A Handbook*, edited by Edward Hall and Andrew Sable, 170–192. Princeton: Princeton University Press.

Davis, Jonathan, and Bhashkar Mazumder. 2017. [revised in 2020]. "The decline in intergenerational mobility after 1980." *Federal Reserve Bank of Chicago. Working Paper* 2017(5).

Dawisha, Karen. 2015. *Putin's Kleptocracy: Who Owns Russia?* New York: Simon & Schuster.

Dayen, David. 2018. "Koch-funded think-tank linked to George Mason University is now pretending it's not part of George Mason University." *The Intercept*, September 19, 2018. https://theintercept.com/2018/09/19/the-mercatus-center-is-a-part-of-george-mason-university-until-its-not/

Deaton, Angus, 2020. "Introduction. Randomization in the tropics revisited: A theme and eleven variations." In *Randomized Controlled Trials in the Field of Development: A Critical Perspective*, edited by Florent, Bédécarrats, Isabelle Guérin and François Roubaud, 29–46. Oxford: Oxford University Press.

Deaton, Angus, and Nancy Cartwright. 2018. "Understanding and misunderstanding randomized controlled trials." *Social Science & Medicine* 210: 2–21.

De Figueiredo, John M., and Brian Kelleher Richter. 2014. "Advancing the empirical research on lobbying." *Annual Review of Political Science* 17: 163–185.

De Luca, Davide. "La bufala dei 60 miliardi di euro di corruzione in Italia." *Il Post*, February 3, 2014. www.ilpost.it/davidedeluca/2014/02/03/la-bufala-dei-60-miliardi-euro-corruzione/

della Porta, Donatella. 2001. "A judges' revolution? Political corruption and the judiciary in Italy." *European Journal of Political Research* 39 (1): 1–21.

della Porta, Donatella e Alberto Vannucci. 1999. *Corrupt Exchanges: Actors, Resources, and Mechanisms of Political Corruption.* Abingdon: Routledge.

della Porta, Donatella, and Alberto Vannucci. 2007. "Corruption and anti-corruption: The political defeat of 'Clean Hands' in Italy." *West European Politics* 30 (4): 830–853.

della Porta, Donatella, and Alberto Vannucci. 2012. *The Hidden Order of Corruption: An Institutional Approach.* Abingdon: Routledge.

Desposato, Scott W. 2006. "Parties for rent? Ambition, ideology, and party switching in Brazil's chamber of deputies." *American Journal of Political Science* 50 (1): 62–80.

Desrosières, Alain. 1998. *The Politics of Large Numbers: A History of Statistical Reasoning.* Cambridge: Harvard University Press.

Dincer, Oguzhan, and Michael Johnston. 2017. "Political culture and corruption issues in state politics: A new measure of corruption issues and a test of relationships to political culture." *Publius* 47: 131–148.

Dincer, Oguzhan, and Michael Johnston. 2020a. "Legal corruption?" *Public Choice* 184 (3): 219–233.

Dincer, Oguzhan, and Michael Johnston. 2020b. "Pas de Deux of illegal and legal corruption in America." *Institute for Corruption Studies Working Paper* No. 2.

Dobel, J. Patrick. 1978. "The corruption of a state." *American Political Science Review* 78 (3): 958–973.

Dollbaum, Jan Matti, Morvan Lallouet, and Ben Noble. 2021. *Navalny: Putin's Nemesis, Russia's Future?* London: C. Hurst & Company.

Doshi, Rush, Judith G. Kelley, and Beth A. Simmons. 2019. "The power of ranking: The ease of doing business indicator and global regulatory behavior." *International Organization* 73 (3): 611–643.

Durlauf, Steven N. 2009. "The rise and fall of cross-country growth regressions." *History of Political Economy* 41 (S1): 315–333.

Durlauf, Steven N., Paul A. Johnson, and Jonathan R. W. Temple. 2005. "Growth econometrics." In *Handbook of Economic Growth,* edited by Philippe Aghion and Steven Durlauf, 555–678. Amsterdam: Elsevier Science, North-Holland.

Easterly, William. 2013. *The Tyranny of Experts: Economists, Dictators, and the Forgotten Rights of the Poor.* New York: Basic Books.

Eika, Lasse, Magne Mogstad, and Basit Zafar. 2019. "Educational assortative mating and household income inequality." *Journal of Political Economy* 127 (6): 2795–2835.

Eisenstadt, Schmuel N. 2000. "Multiple modernities," *Daedalus* 129: 1–29.

Eliason, Randall D. 2023. "Why the Supreme Court is blind to its own corruption." *The New York Times,* May 18, 2023. www.nytimes.com/2023/05/18/opinion/supreme-court-clarence-thomas-corruption.html

Elster, Jon. 1978. *Logic and Society: Contradictions and Possible Worlds.* New York: Wiley.

Engelmann, Fabiano. 2020. "The 'Fight against Corruption' in Brazil from the 2000s: A political crusade through judicial activism." *Journal of Law and Society* 47 (S1): S74–S89.

Engelmann, Fabiano, and Eduardo de Moura Menuzzi. 2020. "The internationalization of the Brazilian public prosecutor's office: Anti-corruption and corporate investments in the 2000s." *Brazilian Political Science Review* 14: 1–35.

Engels, Jens Ivo. 2017. "Corruption and anticorruption in the era of modernity and beyond." In *Anti-corruption in History: From Antiquity to the Modern Era,* edited by Ronald Kroeze, André Vitória, and Guy Geltner, 167–180. Oxford: Oxford University Press.

Escresa, Laarni, and Lucio Picci. 2016. "Trends in corruptions around the world." *European Journal on Criminal Policy and Research* 22 (3): 543–564.

Escresa, Laarni, and Lucio Picci. 2017. "A new cross-national measure of corruption." *The World Bank Economic Review* 31 (1): 196–219.

Escresa, Laarni, and Lucio Picci. 2020. "The determinants of cross-border corruption." *Public Choice* 184 (3–4): 351–378.

Fair, Ray C. 1984. *Specification, Estimation, and Analysis of Macroeconometric Models.* Cambridge: Harvard University Press.

Fair, Ray C. 2009. "Presidential and congressional vote-share equations." *American Journal of Political Science* 53 (1): 55–72.

Faure, Michael, and Laarni Escresa. 2011. "Social stigma." In *Encyclopedia of Law and Economics,* edited by Baudewijn Bouckaert and Gerrit De Geest, 205–227. Cheltenham: Edward Elgar.

Fazekas, Mihály, and Gábor Kocsis. 2020. "Uncovering high-level corruption: Cross-national objective corruption risk indicators using public procurement data." *British Journal of Political Science* 50(1): 155–164.

Fearon, James D. 1991. "Counterfactuals and hypothesis testing in political science." *World Politics* 43(2): 169–195.

Federal Procurator of the Russian Federation. n.d. "Federal portal of judicial statistics." Accessed June 30, 2023. http://crimestat.ru/

Federal Reserve Bank of New York. 2020. *Quarterly Report on Household Debt and Credit. Fourth Quarter.* New York: Federal Reserve Bank of New York.

Fernández-Villaverde, Jesús. 2008. "Horizons of understanding: A review of Ray Fair's *Estimating How the Macroeconomy Works.*" *Journal of Economic Literature* 46 (3): 685–703

Ferrari Filho, Fernando, and Fábio Henrique Bittes Terra. 2023. "The political economy of Bolsonaro's government (2019–2022) and Lula da Silva's third term (2023–2026)." *Investigación económica* 82 (324): 27–50.

Fisman, Raymond, and Miriam A. Golden. 2017. *Corruption: What Everyone Needs to Know.* Oxford: Oxford University Press.

Fleischer, David. 1997. "Political corruption in Brazil: The delicate connection with campaign finance." *Crime, Law and Social Change* 25: 297–321.

Fogel, Benjamin. 2019. "Brazil: Corruption as a mode of rule: Tracing the roots of corruption in Brazil from Vargas to Bolsonaro reveals a political strategy that has long been woven into the fabric of Brazilian politics." *NACLA Report on the Americas* 51 (2): 153–158.

Folha de São Paulo. 2005. "Para 78%, há corrupção no governo Lula." July 24, 2015. www1.folha.uol.com.br/fsp/brasil/fc2407200504.htm

Frank, Thomas. 2007. *What's the Matter with Kansas?: How Conservatives Won the Heart of America.* London: Picador.

French, John D. 2020. *Lula and His Politics of Cunning: From Metalworker to President of Brazil.* Chapel Hill: University of North Carolina Press.

Gallie, Walter Bryce. 1956. "Essentially contested concepts." *Proceedings of the Aristotelian Society* 56: 167–198.

Gambetta, Diego. 2009. *Codes of the Underworld. How Criminals Communicate.* Princeton, NJ: Princeton University Press.

Gambetta, Diego. 2018. "Why is Italy disproportionally corrupt?: A conjecture." In *Institutions, Governance and the Control of Corruption*, edited by Kaushik Basu and Tito Cordella, 133–164. London: Palgrave Macmillan.

Garavini, Giuliano. 2012. *After Empires: European Integration, Decolonization, and the Challenge from the Global South 1957–1986.* Oxford: Oxford University Press.

Garcia Quesada, Mónica, Fernando Jiménez-Sánchez, and Manuel Villoria. 2013. "Building local integrity systems in Southern Europe: The case of urban local corruption in Spain." *International Review of Administrative Sciences* 79 (4): 618–637.

Garrett, Brandon L. 2014. *Too Big to Jail: How Prosecutors Compromise with Corporations.* Cambridge: Cambridge University Press.

Garrett, Brandon L. 2018. "Individual and corporate criminals." In *Research Handbook on Corporate Crime and Financial Misdealing*, edited by Jennifer Arlen, 40–58. Cheltenham: Edward Elgar.

Garrett, Brandon L. 2020. "Declining corporate prosecutions." *American Criminal Law Review* 57: 109.

Gaspar, Malu. 2020. *A organização: A Odebrecht e o esquema de corrupção que chocou o mundo.* São Paulo: Companhia das Letras.

Gaughan, Anthony G. 2016. 'The forty-year war on money in politics: Watergate, FECA, and the future of campaign finance reform." *Ohio State Law Journal* 77: 791–838.

Gawthorpe, Andrew J. 2018. "'Mad Dog?' Samuel Huntington and the Vietnam War." *Journal of Strategic Studies* 41 (1–2): 301–325.

Geddes, Barbara, and Artur Ribeiro Neto. 1992. "Institutional sources of corruption in Brazil." *Third World Quarterly* 13 (4): 641–661.

Gentzkow, Matthew, Edward L. Glaeser, and Claudia Goldin. 2006. "The rise of the fourth estate: How newspapers became informative and why it mattered." In *Corruption and Reform: Lessons from America's Economic History*, edited by Edward L. Glaeser and Claudia Goldin, 187–230. Chicago: University of Chicago Press.

Gentzkow, Matthew, and Jesse M. Shapiro. 2008. "Competition and truth in the market for news." *Journal of Economic Perspectives* 22 (2): 133–154.

Gerken, Heather K., 2014. "Boden lecture: The real problem with citizens united: Campaign finance, dark money, and shadow parties." *Marquette Law Review* 97 (4): 903–923.

Gerstle, Gary, 2022. *The Rise and Fall of the Neoliberal Order: America and the World in the Free Market Era.* Oxford: Oxford University Press.

Gethin, Amory, and Marc Morgan. 2021. "Democracy and the politicization of inequality in Brazil, 1989–2018." *World Inequality Lab – Working Paper* N° 2021/07.

Giannakopoulou, Melina. 2020. "Olympic gigantism and the multifaceted concept of sports venues." In *Cultural and Tourism Innovation in the Digital Era*, edited by Vicky Katsoni, Thanasis Spyriadis, 111–121. New York: Springer.

Glezer, Rubens. 2020. "A ilusão da Lava Jato." *piauí* 162: 28–31.

Gokcekus, Omer, and Sertac Sonan. 2017. "Political contributions and corruption in the United States." *Journal of Economic Policy Reform* 20 (4): 360–372.

Golden, Miriam A., and Lucio Picci. 2006. "Corruption and the management of public works in Italy." In *International Handbook on the Economics of Corruption*, edited by Susan Rose-Ackerman, 457–483. Cheltenham: Edward Elgar.

Golden, Miriam A., and Picci, Lucio. 2008. "Pork barrel politics in postwar Italy, 1953–1994." *American Journal of Political Science* 52 (2): 268–289.

Golden, Miriam A., and Picci, Lucio. 2015. "Incumbency effects under proportional representation: Leaders and backbenchers in the postwar Italian chamber of deputies." *Legislative Studies Quarterly* 40 (4): 509–538.

Gorman, Steve. 2021. "NASA scores Wright Brothers moment with first helicopter flight on Mars." *Reuters*, April 20, 2021. www.reuters.com/lifestyle/science/nasas-mars-helicopter-makes-history-with-successful-flight-red-planet-2021-04-19/

Gustafson, Thane. 2021. *Klimat: Russia in the Age of Climate Change*. Cambridge: Harvard University Press.

Granovetter, Mark. 2007. "The social construction of corruption." In *On Capitalism*, edited by Victor Nee and Richard Swedberg, 152–173. Stanford: Stanford University Press.

Guriev, Sergei, and Andrei Rachinsky. 2005. "The role of oligarchs in Russian capitalism." *Journal of Economic Perspectives* 19 (1): 131–150.

Haberman, Maggie, and Michael S. Schmidt. 2020. "Trump gives Clemency to more allies, including Manafort, Stone and Charles Kushner." *The New York Times*, December 23, 2020. Updated January 17, 2021. www.nytimes.com/2020/12/23/us/politics/trump-pardon-manafort-stone.html

Hamilton, Alexander, James Madison, and John Jay. 2008 [1788]. *The Federalist Papers*. Oxford: Oxford University Press.

Han, Byung-Chul. 2018. *What Is Power?* Hoboken: John Wiley & Sons.

Harstad, Bård, and Jakob Svensson. 2011. "Bribes, lobbying, and development." *American Political Science Review* 105 (1): 46–63.

Hartocollis, Anemona. 2023. "Rick Singer, mastermind of Varsity Blues scandal, is sentenced to 3½ years in prison." *The New York Times*, January 4, 2023. www.nytimes.com/2023/01/04/us/rick-singer-sentenced-college-admissions-scandal.html

Healy, Andrew, and Neil Malhotra. 2013. "Retrospective voting reconsidered." *Annual Review of Political Science* 16: 285–306.

Heckman, James J., and Rodrigo Pinto. 2022. "The econometric model for causal policy analysis." *Annual Review of Economics* 14: 893–923.

Hedlund, Stefan. 2005. *Russian Path Dependence: A People with a Troubled History*. Abingdon: Routledge.

Hellman, Joel S., Geraint Jones, and Daniel Kaufmann. 2000. "Seize the state, seize the day." *Policy Research WP 2444*. The World Bank.

Hendley, Kathryn. 2012. "Who are the legal nihilists in Russia?" *Post-Soviet Affairs* 28 (2): 149–186.

Hendley, Kathryn. 2017. *Everyday Law in Russia*. Ithaca: Cornell University Press.

Hennessey, Jessica L., and John Joseph Wallis. 2017. "Corporations and organizations in the United States after 1840." In *Corporations and American Democracy*, edited by Naomi R. Lamoreaux, and William J. Novak, 74–105. Cambridge: Harvard University Press.

Hertel-Fernandez, Alexander, Theda Skocpol, and Jason Sclar. 2018. "When political mega-donors join forces: How the Koch network and the Democracy Alliance influence organized US politics on the right and left." *Studies in American Political Development* 32 (2): 127–165.

Hicks, John R. 1937. "Mr. Keynes and the 'classics' a suggested interpretation." *Econometrica* 5 (2): 147–159.

Hirsch, Francine. 2005. *Empire of Nations: Ethnographic Knowledge and the Making of the Soviet Union*. Ithaca: Cornell University Press.

Hirschfeld Davis, Julie, Sheryl Gay Stolberg, and Thomas Kaplan. 2018. "Trump alarms lawmakers with disparaging words for Haiti and Africa." *The New York Times*, January 11, 2018. www.nytimes.com/2018/01/11/us/politics/trump-shithole-countries.html.

Hirschman, Albert O. 1970. *Exit, Voice, and Loyalty: Responses to Decline in Firms, Organizations, and States*. Cambridge: Harvard University Press.

Hirschman, Albert O. 1977. *The Passions and the Interests. Political Arguments for Capitalism before Its Triumph*. Princeton: Princeton University Press.

Hirschman, Albert O. 1982. *Shifting Involvements*. Princeton: Princeton University Press.

Hirschman, Albert O., and Michael Rothschild. 1973. "The changing tolerance for income inequality in the course of economic development: With a mathematical appendix." *The Quarterly Journal of Economics* 87 (4): 544–566.

Hitchcock, Christopher, 2021. "Probabilistic causation." In *The Stanford Encyclopedia of Philosophy* (Spring 2021 Edition), edited by Edward N. Zalta. https://plato.stanford.edu/archives/spr2021/entries/causation-probabilistic/

Hochschild, Jennifer L. 1995. *Facing Up to the American Dream: Race, Class, and the Soul of the Nation*. Princeton: Princeton University Press.

Hofstadter, Douglas R. 1979. *Gödel, Escher, Bach: An Eternal Golden Braid*. New York: Basic Books.

Hofstadter, Richard. 1955. *The Age of Reform: From Bryan to FDR*. New York: Random House.

Huntington, Samuel P. 1968a. *Political Order in Changing Societies*. New Haven: Yale University Press.

Huntington, Samuel P. 1968b. "The bases of accommodation." *Foreign Affairs* 46 (4): 642–656.

Huskey, Eugene. 2009. "An introduction to post-communist officialdom." In *Russian Bureaucracy and the State. Officialdom From Alexander III to Vladimir Putin*, edited by Dan K. Rowney and Eugene Huskey, 215–230. London: Palgrave Macmillan.

Huskey, Eugene. 2010. "Pantouflage à la russe: The recruitment of Russian political and business elites." In *Russian Politics from Lenin to Putin*, edited by Stephen Fortescue, 185–204. London: Palgrave Macmillan.

IBGE. 2017. "Sistema de Contas Regionais: Brasil 2017. Contas Nacionais n. 68." https://biblioteca.ibge.gov.br/visualizacao/livros/liv101679_informativo.pdf

Institute for the Rule of Law. n.d. "Criminal case trajectory." https://enforce.spb.ru/images/infographics/CRIMINAL_CASE_TRAJECTORY.pdf

Interfax. 2021. "ФБК официально прекратил существование." September 1, 2021. www.interfax.ru/russia/787974

Issacharoff, Samuel, and Pamela S. Karlan. 1998. "Hydraulics of campaign finance reform." *Texas Law Review* 77: 1705–1738.

Ivanova, Anna, Michael Keen, and Alexander Klemm. 2005. "The Russian 'flat tax' reform." *Economic Policy* 20 (43): 398–444.

Jacobs, Lawrence, and Theda Skocpol. 2016. *Health Care Reform and American Politics: What Everyone Needs to Know. Third Edition*. Oxford: Oxford University Press.

Jiménez-Sánchez, Fernando. 2008. "Boom urbanístico y corrupción política en España." *Mediterráneo económico* 14: 263–285.

Jos, Philip H. "Empirical corruption research: Beside the (moral) point?" *Journal of Public Administration Research and Theory* 3 (3): 359–375.

Jungblut, Cristiane. 2005. "Não vamos acobertar ninguém', diz Lula." *O Globo*, June 8, 2005. www2.senado.leg.br/bdsf/bitstream/handle/id/390775/noticia.htm

Jupille, Joseph, and James A. Caporaso. 2022. *Theories of Institutions*. Cambridge: Cambridge University Press.

Justiça Federal da 1ª Região. 2021. "N. 1070239-94.2021.4.01.3400. Ação penal." https://static.poder360.com.br/2022/01/triplex-arquivado-27jan2022.pdf

Kang, Michael S. 2010. "After citizens united." *Indiana Law Review* 44: 243–254.

Kaufmann, Daniel. 2005. "Corruption matters at the World Bank – Selective history and Jim Wolfensohn's legacy The World Bank." *Mimeo*.

Kaufmann, Daniel. 2008. "Governance, crisis, and the longer view: Unorthodox reflections on the new reality. Farewell event for Daniel Kaufmann." December 8, 2008. *Mimeo*.

Kaufmann, Daniel, Aart Kraay, and Zoido-Lobatón. 1999a. "Aggregating governance indicators." *World Bank Policy Research Working Paper 2195*.

Kaufmann, Daniel, Aart Kraay, and Pablo Zoido. 1999b. "Governance matters." *World Bank Policy Research Working Paper 2196*.

Kaufmann, Daniel, and Pedro C. Vicente. 2011. "Legal corruption." *Economics & Politics* 23 (2): 195–219.

Kaczmarek, Sarah C., and Abraham L. Newman. 2011. "The long arm of the law: Extraterritoriality and the national implementation of foreign bribery legislation." *International Organization* 65 (4): 745–770.

Katzarova, Elitza. 2019. *The Social Construction of Global Corruption. From Utopia to Neoliberalism*. New York: Springer.

Kelley, Judith G., and Beth A. Simmons. 2019. "Introduction: The power of global performance indicators." *International Organization* 73 (3): 491–510.

Kelley, Judith G., and Beth A. Simmons. 2021. "Governance by other means: Rankings as regulatory systems." *International Theory* 13 (1): 169–178.

Keynes, John Maynard. 2017 [1919]. *The Economic Consequences of the Peace*. Abingdon: Routledge, 2017.

Keynes, John Maynard, 1936. *The General Theory of Employment, Interest and Money*. London: Palgrave Macmillan.

King, Gary, Robert O. Keohane, and Sidney Verba. 1994. *Designing Social Inquiry: Scientific Inference in Qualitative Research*. Princeton: Princeton University Press.

Klein, Lawrence R. 1985. "New developments in project LINK." *The American Economic Review* 75 (2): 223–227.

Knigths, Mark. 2017. "Anticorruption in seventeenth and eighteenth-century Britain." In *Anti-corruption in History: From Antiquity to the Modern Era*, edited by Ronald Kroeze, André Vitória, and Guy Geltner, 181–196. Oxford: Oxford University Press.

Knights, Mark. 2022. *Trust and Distrust: Corruption in Office in Britain and Its Empire, 1600–1850*. Oxford: Oxford University Press.

Koehler, Mike. 2012. "The story of the foreign corrupt practices act." *Ohio State Law Journal* 73: 929–1014.

Kolko, Gabriel. 1963. *The Triumph of Conservatism: A Reinterpretation of American History, 1900–1916*. Chicago: Quadrangle Books.

Krasner, Stephen D. 1982. "Structural causes and regime consequences: Regimes as intervening variables." *International Organization* 36 (2): 185–205.

Krastev, Ivan. 2004. *Shifting Obsessions. Three Essays on the Politics of Anticorruption.* Budapest: Central European University Press.

Kroeze, Ronald, André Vitória, and Guy Geltner. 2017. "Introduction." In *Anti-corruption in History: From Antiquity to the Modern Era*, edited by Ronald Kroeze, André Vitória, and Guy Geltner, 1–20. Oxford, Oxford University Press.

Kubitschek, Juscelino. 2000 [1976]. *Por que construí Brasília?* Brasília: Senado Federal, Conselho Editorial, 2000.

Kunicova, Jana E., and Susan Rose-Ackerman, 2005. "Electoral rules and constitutional structures as constraints on corruption." *British Journal of Political Science* 35 (4): 573–606.

l'Unità. n.d. "Archivio storico digitale." Accessed June 15, 2023. https://archivio.unita.news/

La Repubblica. 2012. "Rapporto Ue sulla corruzione: legge italiana insufficiente, un costo da 60 miliardi annui. La metà dell'intera Europa." February 3, 2012. www.repubblica.it/politica/2014/02/03/news/ue_legge_anticorruzione_italiana_insufficiente-77586035/

Lagunes, Paul, 2020a. "An interview with Deltan Dellagnol." In *Corruption and the Lava Jato Scandal in Latin America*, edited by Paul Lagunes and Jan Svejnar, 113–128. Abingdon: Routledge.

Lagunes, Paul, 2020b. "An interview with Sérgio Moro." In *Corruption and the Lava Jato Scandal in Latin America*, edited by Paul Lagunes and Jan Svejnar, 129–140. Abingdon: Routledge.

Lagunes, Paul, and Jan Svejnar. 2020. *Corruption and the Lava Jato Scandal in Latin America.* Abingdon: Routledge.

Lagunes, Paul, Gregory Michener, Fernanda Odilla, and Breno Pires. 2021. President Bolsonaro's promises and actions on corruption control. *Revista Direito GV* 17 (2): 1–55

Lamberova, Natalia, and Sonin Konstantin 2018. "The role of business in shaping economic policy." In *The New Autocracy: Information, Politics, and Policy in Putin's Russia*, edited by Daniel Treisman, 137–158. Washington, DC: Brookings Institution Press.

Lambsdorff, Johann Graf, 2006. "Consequences and causes of corruption – what do we know from a cross-section of countries?" In *International Handbook on the Economics of Corruption*, edited by Susan Rose-Ackerman, 3–52. Cheltenham: Edward Elgar.

Lamoreaux, Naomi R. 1985. *The Great Merger Movement in American Business, 1895–1904.* Cambridge: Cambridge University Press.

Lamoreaux, Naomi R., and Jean-Laurent Rosenthal. 2006. "Corporate governance and the plight of minority shareholders in the United States before the Great Depression." In *Corruption and Reform: Lessons from America's Economic History*, edited by Edward L. Glaeser and Claudia Goldin, 125–152. Chicago: University of Chicago Press.

Lascoumes, Paul. 1999. *Corruptions.* Paris: Presses de Sciences Po.

Latin American Public Opinion Project. n.d. "Americas Barometer." Accessed June 15, 2023. www.vanderbilt.edu/lapop/

Ledeneva, Alena V. 2013. *Can Russia Modernise?: Sistema, Power Networks and Informal Governance.* Cambridge: Cambridge University Press.

Ledeneva, Alena. 2018. "Blat." In *The Global Encyclopaedia of Informality, Volume 1: Towards Understanding of Social and Cultural Complexity*, edited by Alena Ledeneva with Anna Bailey, Sheelagh Barron, Costanza Curro and Elizabeth Teague, 40–42. London: UCL Press.

Leff, Nathaniel H. 1964. "Economic development through bureaucratic corruption." *American Behavioral Scientist* 8 (2): 8–14.

Lenta.ru. 2014. "Володин отождествил Россию и Путина." October 22, 2014. https://lenta.ru/news/2014/10/22/waldai/

Levada Center. 2017. "Corruption." www.levada.ru/en/2017/04/21/corruption/

Levada Center. 2020. "Тревожащие Проблемы." September 10, 2020, www.levada.ru/2020/09/10/trevozhashhie-problemy-3/

Levada Center. n.d. "Putin's approval rating." www.levada.ru/en/ratings/

Lindblom, Charles E. 1959. "The science of muddling through." *Public Administration Review* 19 (2): 79–88.

Lipman, Maria, Anna Kachkaeva, and Michael Poyker. 2018. "Media in Russia: Between modernization and monopoly." In *The New Autocracy: Information, Politics, and Policy in Putin's Russia*, edited by Daniel Treisman, 159–190. Washington, DC: Brookings Institution Press.

Lo Prete, Renata. 2005. "Contei a Lula do "mensalão," diz deputado." *Folha de S.Paulo*, June 6, 2005. www1.folha.uol.com.br/fsp/brasil/fc0606200504.htm

Londoño, Ernesto. 2017. "A judge's bid to clean up Brazil from the bench." *The New York Times*, August 25, 2017. www.nytimes.com/2017/08/25/world/americas/judge-sergio-moro-brazil-anti-corruption.html

Louçã, Francisco. 2007. *The Years of High Econometrics: A Short History of the Generation that Reinvented Economics*. Abingdon: Routledge.

Loveman, Brian. 1997. "Protected democracies: Antipolitics and political transitions in Latin America, 1978–1994." In *The Politics of Antipolitics: The Military in Latin America*, edited by Brian Loveman and Thomas Davies, 366–397. Washington, DC: Rowman & Littlefield.

Loveman, Brian, and Davies, Thomas. 1997. "The politics of antipolitics." In *The Politics of Antipolitics: The Military in Latin America*, edited by Brian Loveman and Thomas Davies, 3–14. Washington, DC: Rowman & Littlefield.

Luna, Francisco Vidal, and Herbert S. Klein. 2014. "Transformações econômicas no período militar (1964–1985)." In *A ditadura que mudou o Brasil*, edited by Daniel Aarão Reis, 92–111. São Paulo: Companhia das Letras.

MacFarquhar, Neil. 2018. "Yevgeny Prigozhin, Russian Oligarch indicted by U.S., is known as 'Putin's Cook'." *The New York Times*, February 16, 2018. www.nytimes.com/2018/02/16/world/europe/prigozhin-russia-indictment-mueller.html

MacLeod, W. Bentley, and Miguel Urquiola. 2021. "Why does the United States have the best research universities? Incentives, resources, and virtuous circles." *Journal of Economic Perspectives* 35 (1): 185–206.

Machiavelli, Niccolò. 1996 [1531]. *Discourses on Livy*. Chicago: University of Chicago Press.

Mahoney, James. 2001. *The Legacies of Liberalism: Path Dependence and Political Regimes in Central America*. Baltimore: JHU Press.

Mainwaring, Scott. 1999. *Rethinking Party Systems in the Third Wave of Democratization: The Case of Brazil*. Stanford: Stanford University Press.

Malbin, Michael J., and Brendan Glavin. 2020. "CFI's guide to money in federal elections. Essays and tables covering the elections of 1974–2018." http://cfinst.org/pdf/federal/2018Report/CFIGuide_MoneyinFederalElections_2018upd.pdf

Mankiw, N. Gregory. 2006. "The macroeconomist as scientist and engineer." *Journal of Economic Perspectives* 20 (4): 29–46.

Markley, Stephen. 2018. *Ohio.* New York: Simon & Schuster.

Martin, Andrew D., and Kevin M. Quinn. 2002. "Dynamic ideal point estimation via Markov chain Monte Carlo for the U.S. Supreme Court, 1953–1999." *Political Analysis* 10 (2): 134–53.

Maslow, Abraham. 1966. *The Psychology of Science: A Reconnaissance.* New York: Harper Collins.

Mauro, Paolo. 1995. "Corruption and growth." *The Quarterly Journal of Economics* 110 (3): 681–712.

Mayer, Jane. 2016. *Dark Money: The Hidden History of the Billionaires behind the Rise of the Radical Right.* London: Penguin.

McChesney, Robert W. 2008. *The Political Economy of Media.* New York: Monthly Review Press.

McCubbins, Mathew D., Roger G. Noll, and Barry R. Weingast. 1987. "Administrative procedures as instruments of political control." *The Journal of Law, Economics, and Organization* 3(2): 243–277.

McCubbins, Matthew D., Roger G. Noll, and Barry R. Weingast. 1989. "Structure and process, politics and policy: Administrative arrangements and the political control of agencies." *Virginia Law Review* 75: 431.

Medvetz, Thomas. 2012. *Think Tanks in America.* Chicago: University of Chicago Press.

Men, Tamara, Paul Brennan, Paolo Boffetta, and David Zaridzeet. 2003. "Russian mortality trends for 1991–2001: Analysis by cause and region." *British Medical Journal* 327 (7421): 964–966.

Mercatus Center. n.d. "Gordon Tullock." Accessed May 25, 2023. www.mercatus.org/people/gordon-tullock

Merica, Dan, Gloria Borger, Jim Acosta, and Betsy Klein. 2017. "Ivanka Trump is making her White House job official." *CNN*, March 30, 2017. https://edition.cnn.com/2017/03/29/politics/ivanka-trump-white-house-job/index.html

Merton, Robert K. 1972 [1957]. "The latent functions of the machine." Reprinted in *Urban Bosses, Machines, and Progressive Reformers*, edited by Bruce M. Stave and Sondra Astor Stave, 27–37. Malabar: Krieger Publishing Company.

Merton, Robert K. 1968 [1949]. *Social Theory and Social Structure.* New York: The Free Press.

Meyer, John W., and Brian Rowan. 1977. "Institutionalized organizations: Formal structure as myth and ceremony." *American Journal of Sociology* 83 (2): 340–363.

Michener, Gregory, and Carlos Pereira. 2016. "A great leap forward for democracy and the rule of law? Brazil's Mensalão trial." *Journal of Latin American Studies* 48 (3): 477–507.

Migration Policy Institute. n.d. "U.S. immigrant population and share over time, 1850–present." www.migrationpolicy.org/programs/data-hub/charts/immigrant-population-over-time

Milanovic, Branko. 2019. *Capitalism, Alone: The Future of the System that Rules the World.* Cambridge: Harvard University Press.

MilEx. 2021. "Osservatorio sulle spese militari. 2021. Afghanistan: un conflitto costato all'Italia 8,4 miliardi." April 2021. https://milex.org/wp-content/uploads/2021/04/Scheda-costi-Afghanistan-Mil%E2%82%ACx-aprile-2021.pdf

Miller, Gary. 2005. "The political evolution of the principal-agent model." *Annual Review of Political Science* 8: 203–225.

Mittelhammer, Ron C. 2013. *Mathematical Statistics for Economics and Business.* New York: Springer. 2nd edition.

Mitrova, Tatiana. "Energy and the economy in Russia." In *The Palgrave Handbook of International Energy Economics*, edited by Manfred Hafner and Giacomo Luciani, 649–666. London: Palgrave Macmillan.

Moe, Terry M. 2013. "Delegation, control, and the study of public bureaucracy." In *The Handbook of Organizational Economics*, edited by Robert Gibbons and John Roberts, 1148–1182. Princeton: Princeton University Press.

Mota, Aurea, and Gerard Delanty. 2015. "Eisenstadt, Brazil and the multiple modernities framework: Revisions and reconsiderations." *Journal of Classical Sociology* 15 (1): 39–57.

Mouzakitis, Angelos. 2017. "Modernity and the idea of progress." *Frontiers in Sociology* 2 (3).

Müller, Martin. 2014. "After Sochi 2014: Costs and impacts of Russia's Olympic games." *Eurasian Geography and Economics* 55 (6): 628–655.

Mungiu-Pippidi, Alina 2015. *The Quest for Good Governance: How Societies Develop Control of Corruption.* Cambridge: Cambridge University Press.

Mungiu-Pippidi, Alina. 2020. *Europe's Burden: Promoting Good Governance across Borders.* Cambridge: Cambridge University Press.

Mungiu-Pippidi, Alina, and Michael Johnston. 2017. "Conclusions and lessons learned." In *Transitions to Good Governance: Creating Virtuous Circles of Anti-corruption*, edited by Alina Mungiu-Pippidi and Michael Johnston, 234–266. Cheltenham: Edward Elgar.

Murphy, Kevin M., Andrei Shleifer, and Robert W. Vishny. 1991. "The allocation of talent: Implications for growth." *Quarterly Journal of Economics* 106 (2): 503–530.

Mutch, Robert E. 2014. *Buying the Vote. A History of Campaign Reform.* Oxford: Oxford University Press.

Mutch, Robert E. 2016. *Campaign Finance: What Everyone Needs to Know.* Oxford: Oxford University Press.

National Institute on Drug Abuse. n.d. "Drug overdose death rates." https://nida.nih.gov/research-topics/trends-statistics/overdose-death-rates

Nicholson, Amy. 2021. "'Operation Varsity Blues' review: Failing the ethics test." *The New York Times*, March 17, 2021. www.nytimes.com/2021/03/17/movies/operation-varsity-blues-review.html

Nobre, Marcos. 2013. *Imobilismo em movimento: da abertura democrática ao governo Dilma.* São Paulo: Companhia das Letras.

Noonan, John T. 1984. *Bribes.* New York: Macmillan Publishing House.

Novak, William J. 2013. "A revisionist history of regulatory capture." In *Preventing Regulatory Capture: Special Interest Influence and How to Limit It*, edited by Daniel Carpenter and David A. Moss, 25–48. Cambridge: Cambridge University Press.

Novaya Gazeta Europe. 2023. "Russia bans Transparency International," March 6, 2023. https://novayagazeta.eu/articles/2023/03/06/russia-bans-transparency-international-en-news

Novokmet, Filip, Thomas Piketty, and Gabriel Zucman. 2017. "From Soviets to Oligarchs: Inequality and Property in Russia 1905–2016." *WID.world Working Paper* N° 2017/09.

Novokmet, Filip, Thomas Piketty, and Gabriel Zucman. 2018. "From communism to capitalism: Private versus public property and inequality in China and Russia." *WID.world Working Paper* N° 2018/02.

Nye, Joseph S. 1967. "Corruption and political development. A cost-benefit analysis." *American Political Science Review* 61 (2): 417–427.

OECD. 1997. "Convention on combating bribery of foreign public officials in international business transactions, and related documents." Accessed June 8, 2023. www.oecd.org/daf/anti-bribery/ConvCombatBribery_ENG.pdf

OECD. 2004. "Italy: Phase 2. Report on the application of the convention on combating bribery of foreign public officials in international business transactions and the 1997 recommendation on combating bribery in international business transactions." Accessed June 8, 2023. www.oecd.org/daf/anti-bribery/anti-briberyconvention/33995536.pdf

OECD. 2019. "Russia must urgently step up fight against foreign bribery." April 4, 2019. Accessed May 25, 2023. www.oecd.org/corruption/russia-must-urgently-step-up-fight-against-foreign-bribery.htm

Olken, Benjamin A. 2007. "Monitoring corruption: Evidence from a field experiment in Indonesia." *Journal of Political Economy* 115 (2): 200–249.

Open Secrets. n.d.a. "Top contributors, 2004." Accessed May 25, 2023. www.opensecrets.org/527s/527cmtedetail_contribs.php?ein=201041228&cycle=2004

Open Secrets. n.d.b. "Cost of election." Accessed June 14, 2023. www.opensecrets.org/elections-overview/cost-of-election. Bottom line (total cost, F.E.C.).

Open Secrets. n.d.c. "Elections overview." Accessed June 14, 2023. www.opensecrets.org/elections-overview?cycle=1990&display=T&type=A

Open Secrets. n.d.d. "Lobbying data summary." Accessed June 14, 2023. www.opensecrets.org/federal-lobbying/

Osrecki, Fran. 2017. "A short history of the sociology of corruption: The demise of counter-intuitivity and the rise of numerical comparisons." *The American Sociologist* 48 (1): 103–125.

Paneyakh, Ella, and Dina Rosenberg. 2018. "The courts, law enforcement, and politics." In *The New Autocracy: Information, Politics, and Policy in Putin's Russia*, edited by Daniel Treisman, 217–247. Washington, DC: Brookings Institution Press.

Pavroz, Alexander. 2017. "Corruption-oriented model of governance in contemporary Russia." *Communist and Post-Communist Studies* 50 (2): 145–155.

Pedlowski, Marcos. 2016. "*Governo Dilma: um caso clássico de boi de piranha.*" March 13, 2016. https://blogdopedlowski.com/2016/03/13/governo-dilma-um-caso-classico-de-boi-de-piranha/

Pellegrini, Lorenzo. 2011. "Causes of corruption: A survey of cross-country analyses and extended results." In *Corruption, Development and the Environment*, edited by Lorenzo in Pellegrini, 29–51. New York: Springer.

Pereira, Anthony W. 2005. *Political (in)Justice: Authoritarianism and the Rule of Law in Brazil, Chile, and Argentina.* Pittsburgh: University of Pittsburgh Press.

Pereira, Anthony W. 2010. *Ditadura e repressão: O autoritarismo e o estado de direito no Brasil, no Chile e na Argentina.* Rio de Janeiro: Paz e Terra.

Pereira, Carlos, and Frederico Bertholini. 2019. "Coalition management in multiparty presidential regimes." In *Routledge Handbook of Brazilian Politics*, edited by Barry Ames, 313–330. Abingdon: Routledge.

Persson, Torsten, Guido Tabellini, and Francesco Trebbi. 2003. "Electoral rules and corruption." *Journal of the European Economic Association* 1 (4): 958–989.

Petrov, Nikolay, and Eugenia Nazrullaeva. 2018. "Regional elites and Moscow." In *The New Autocracy: Information, Politics, and Policy in Putin's Russia*, edited by Daniel Treisman, 109–136. Washington, DC: Brookings Institution Press.

Philp, Mark. 1997. "Defining political corruption." *Political Studies* 45 (3): 436–462.

Philp, Mark. 2002. "Conceptualizing political corruption." In *Political Corruption: Concepts and Contexts*, edited by Arnold J. Heidenheimer, and Michael Johnston, 41–57. New Brunswick, NJ: Transaction Publishers.

Philp, Mark. 2014. "The definition of political corruption." In *Routledge Handbook of Political Corruption*, edited by Paul M. Heywood, 17–29. Abingdon: Routledge.

Philp, Mark. 2017. "Conceptualizing political corruption." In *Political Corruption*, edited by Arnold I. Heidenheimer, and Michael Johnston, 41–58. Abingdon: Routledge.

Picci, Lucio. 2011. *Reputation-based Governance*. Stanford: Stanford University Press.

Picci, Lucio. 2018. "The supply-side of international corruption: A new measure and a critique." *Journal on Criminal Policy and Research* 24 (3): 289–313.

Picci, Lucio. 2019. "Gossip, internet-based reputation systems, and governance." In *The Oxford Handbook of Gossip and Reputation*, edited by Francesca Giardini, and Rafael Wittek, 496–511. Oxford: Oxford University Press.

Picci, Lucio. 2024. "Narratives of historical change." *Mimeo.*

Picci, Lucio, and Alberto Vannucci. 2018. *Lo Zen e l'arte della lotta alla corruzione*. Milano: Altraeconomia.

Piketty, Thomas. 2014. *Capital in the Twenty-First Century*. Cambridge: Harvard University Press.

Piketty, Thomas. 2020. *Capital and Ideology*. Cambridge: Harvard University Press.

Pineda Sleinan, Juliet. 2021. "Brazil dismantles anti-corruption task force behind Lava Jato." *OCCRP*, February 8, 2021. www.occrp.org/en/daily/13817-brazil-dismantles-anti-corruption-task-force-behind-lava-jato

Pinheiro da Fonseca, Joel. 2022. "Hora de admitir: talvez Bolsonaro seja um pouquinho corrupto ... Carreira do presidente é marcada por enriquecimento suspeito de mulheres e filhos." www1.folha.uol.com.br/colunas/joel-pinheiro-da-fonseca/2022/04/hora-de-admitir-talvez-bolsonaro-seja-um-pouquinho-corrupto.shtml

Pipitone, Giuseppe. 2019. "Open, i finanziatori della fondazione che hanno beneficiato di scelte del governo Renzi: dal gruppo Gavio alla lobby del tabacco." *Il Fatto Quotidiano*, November 27, 2019. www.ilfattoquotidiano.it/2019/11/27/open-i-finanziatori-della-fondazione-che-hanno-beneficiato-di-scelte-del-governo-renzi-dal-gruppo-gavio-alla-lobby-del-tabacco/5582478/

Pistor, Katharina. 2019. *The Code of Capital: How the Law Creates Wealth and Inequality*. Princeton: Princeton University Press.

Pocock, John C. A. 1975. *The Machiavellian Moment: Florentine Political Thought and the Atlantic Republican Tradition*. Princeton: Princeton University Press.

Pomeranz, William E. 2019. *Law and the Russian State: Russia's Legal Evolution from Peter the Great to Vladimir Putin*. New York: Bloomsbury Academic.

Portici, Laura. 2016. "Una tassa sulle sigarette. Anzi no. E Renzi inaugura lo stabilimento della Philip Morris." *La Repubblica*, September 23, 2016. www.repubblica.it/economia/rubriche/affari-in-piazza/2016/09/23/news/una_tassa_sulle_sigarette_anzi_no_e_renzi_inaugura_lo_stabilimento_della_philip_morris-148390204/

Power, Timothy J., and Matthew Taylor. 2011. "Introduction." In *Corruption and Democracy in Brazil*, edited by Timothy J. Power and Matthew Taylor, 1–30. Notre Dame: University of Notre Dame Press.

Radden Keefe, Patrick. 2021. *Empire of Pain: The Secret History of the Sackler Dynasty*. New York: Doubleday.

Radio Free Europe. 2020. "Putin gives 'Hero Of Labor' award to close associate for Crimean Bridge." *Radio Free Europe*, March 17, 2020 www.rferl.org/a/putin-gives-hero-of-labor-award-to-close-associate-for-crimean-bridge/30492367.html

Ramsey, Frank. P. 1928. "A mathematical theory of saving." *Economic Journal* 38: 543–559.

Rankin, Jennifer. 2014. "Russia ordered to pay $50bn in damages to Yukos shareholders." *The Guardian*, July 28, 2014. www.theguardian.com/business/2014/jul/28/russia-order-pay-50bn-yukos-shareholders-khodorkovsky-court

Ratcliffe, Rebecca. 2022. "Aung San Suu Kyi faces total of 26 years in prison after latest corruption sentencing." *The Guardian*, October 12, 2022. www.theguardian.com/world/2022/oct/12/aung-san-suu-kyi-faces-total-of-26-years-in-prison-after-latest-corruption-sentencing

Rennó, Lucio R. 2020. "The Bolsonaro voter: Issue positions and vote choice in the 2018 Brazilian presidential elections." *Latin American Politics and Society* 62 (4): 1–23.

Rocha de Barros, Celso. 2020. "How Lava Jato died – And what comes next." *Americas Quarterly*, October 15, 2020. www.americasquarterly.org/article/how-lava-jato-died-and-what-comes-next/

Rogov, Kirill, and Maxim Ananyev. 2018. "Public opinion and Russian politics." In *The New Autocracy: Information, Politics, and Policy in Putin's Russia*, edited by Daniel Treisman, 195–200. Washington, DC: Brookings Institution Press.

Roland, Gérard. 2004. "Understanding institutional change: Fast-moving and slow-moving institutions." *Studies in Comparative International Development* 38 (4): 109–131.

Rose-Ackerman, Susan. 1975. "The economics of corruption." *Journal of Public Economics* 4 (2): 187–203.

Rose-Ackerman, Susan. 1978. *Corruption: A Study in Political Economy*. New York: Academic Press.

Rosenn, Keith S. 2014. "Recent important decisions by the Brazilian Supreme Court." *The University of Miami Inter-American Law Review* 45 (2): 297.

Roth, Andrew. 2021. "Russian court outlaws Alexei Navalny's organisation." *The Guardian*, June 9, 2021. www.theguardian.com/world/2021/jun/09/russian-court-expected-to-outlaw-alexei-navalnys-organisation

Rothstein, Bo. 2011. *The Quality of Government. Corruption, Social Trust and Inequality in International Perspective*. Chicago: Chicago University Press.

Rothstein, Bo. 2021. *Controlling Corruption: The Social Contract Approach*. Oxford: Oxford University Press.

Rysman, Marc. 2009. "The economics of two-sided markets." *Journal of Economic Perspectives* 23 (3): 125–143.

Saez, Emmanuel, and Gabriel Zucman. 2019. *The Triumph of Injustice: How the Rich Dodge Taxes and How to Make them Pay*. New York: WW Norton & Company.

Saez, Emmanuel, and Gabriel Zucman. 2020. "The rise of income and wealth inequality in America: Evidence from distributional macroeconomic accounts." *Journal of Economic Perspectives* 34 (4): 3–26.

Sakwa, Richard. 2010. "The dual state in Russia." *Post-Soviet Affairs* 26 (3): 185–206.

Saisana, Michaela, and Andrea Saltelli. 2012. "Corruption Perceptions Index 2012 Statistical Assessment." *JRC Scientific and Policy Reports*.

Sampson, Steven. 2013. "The anti-corruption industry: From movement to institution." In *Fighting Corruption in Eastern Europe: A Multilevel Perspective*, edited by Diana Schmidt-Pfister, and Holger Moroff, 193–210. Abingdon: Routledge.

Sartori, Giovanni. 1993. "Nem Presidêncialismo, Nem Parlamentarismo." *Novos Estudos CEBRAP* 35: 3–14.

Schelling, Thomas C. 1960. *The Strategy of Conflict*. Cambridge: Harvard University Press.

Schmitt, Carl. 2015. *Dialogues on Power and Space*. Cambridge: Polity.

Schulze, Günther G., and Nikita Zakharov. 2018. "Corruption in Russia." In *Handbook on the Geographies of Corruption*, edited by Barney Warf, 195–212. Cheltenham: Edward Elgar.

Schwarcz, Lilia M., and Heloisa M. Starling. *2018. Brazil: A Biography*. New York: Farrar, Straus and Giroux.

Schwartz, Christine R., and Robert D. Mare. 2005. "Trends in educational assortative marriage from 1940 to 2003." *Demography* 42 (4): 621–646.

Schwarz, Norbert. 1998. "Accessible content and accessibility experiences: The interplay of declarative and experiential information in judgment." *Personality and Social Psychology Review* 2 (2): 87–99.

Scott, James C. 1969. "The analysis of corruption in developing nations." *Comparative Studies in Society and History* 11 (3): 315–341.

Scott, James C. 1998. *Seeing Like a State: How Certain Schemes to Improve the Human Condition Have Failed*. New Haven: Yale University Press.

Senters, Kelly, and Matthew S. Winters. 2019. "Persistent malfeasance despite institutional innovations and public outcry: A survey of corruption in Brasil." In *Handbook on the Geographies of Corruption*, edited by Barney Warf, 154–168. Cheltenham: Edward Elgar.

Sergi, Anna, and Alberto Vannucci. 2023. *Mafia, Deviant Masons and Corruption: Shifty Brotherhoods in Italy*. Milton Park: Abingdon: Routledge.

Sharp, Alan. 2015. *Consequences of the Peace. The Versailles Settlement: Aftermath and Legacy 1919–2020*. London: Haus Publishing.

Shelley, Louise I. 2014. *Dirty Entanglements: Corruption, Crime, and Terrorism*. Cambridge: Cambridge University Press.

Shuster, Alvin. 1977. "Former Italian defense chiefs to stand trial in Lockheed Case." *The New York Times*, March 11, 1977. www.nytimes.com/1977/03/11/archives/2-former-italian-defense-chiefs-to-stand-trial-in-lockheed-case.html

SIPRI. 2020. "The financial value of national arms exports, 1994–2017." Accessed May 25, 2023. www.sipri.org/databases/financial-value-global-arms-trade

Sistema Garant. n.d. "система ГАРАНТ." Accessed June 11, 2023. http://ivo.garant.ru/

Skidmore, Thomas E. 1988. *The Politics of Military Rule in Brazil, 1964–85*. Oxford: Oxford University Press.

Skocpol, Theda. 1995. "The rise and resounding demise of the Clinton plan." *Health Affairs* 14 (1): 66–85.

Skocpol, Theda, and Caroline Tervo. 2020. "Conclusion: America at a crossroads." In *Upending American Politics*, edited by Theda Skocpol and Caroline Tervo, 317–330. Oxford: Oxford University Press.

Soldatov, Andrei, and Michael Rochlitz. 2018. "The siloviki in Russian politics." In *The New Autocracy: Information, Politics, and Policy in Putin's Russia*, edited by Daniel Treisman, 83–108. Washington, DC: Brookings Institution Press.

Solomon, Peter H. 2015a. "Post-Soviet criminal justice: The persistence of distorted neo-inquisitorialism." *Theoretical Criminology* 19 (2): 159–178

Solomon, Peter H. 2015b. "Understanding Russia's low rate of acquittal: Pretrial screening and the problem of accusatorial bias." *Review of Central and East European Law* 40: 1–30

Solow, Robert M. 1994. "Perspectives on growth theory." *Journal of Economic Perspectives* 8 (1): 45–54.

Stephenson, Matthew. 2018. "Some things are more important than corruption (Brazilian Elections Edition)." October 9, 2018. https://globalanticorruptionblog.com/2018/10/09/some-things-are-more-important-than-corruption-brazilian-elections-edition/

Stephenson, Matthew C. 2020. "Corruption as a self-reinforcing trap: Implications for reform strategy." *The World Bank Observer* 35: 192–226

Stickles, Brendan R., 2018. "How the US military became the exception to America's wage stagnation problem." *Brookings*. 29 November 2018. www.brookings.edu/blog/order-from-chaos/2018/11/29/how-the-u-s-military-became-the-exception-to-americas-wage-stagnation-problem/

Stimson, James A. 1999. *Public Opinion in America: Moods, Cycles, and Swings*. 2nd ed. Boulder: Westview Press.

Stimson, James, A. 2018. "The Dyad ratios algorithm for estimating latent public opinion." *Bulletin of Sociological Methodology* 137–138 (1): 201–18.

Stock, James H., and Mark W. Watson. 2015. *Introduction to Econometrics*. London: Pearson.

Stokes, Donald E. 1963. "Spatial models of party competition." *American Political Science Review* 57 (2): 368–377.

Stokes, Donald E. 1992. "Valence politics." In *Electoral Politics*, edited by Dennis Kavanagh, 141–164. Oxford: Clarendon University Press.

Swaine, John, and Dominic Rushe. 2018. "Payments to Michael Cohen show how 'shadow lobbying' eludes US law." *The Guardian*, May 10, 2018. www.theguardian.com/us-news/2018/may/10/payments-to-michael-cohen-show-how-shadow-lobbying-eludes-us-law

Taylor, Charles. 2004. *Modern Social Imaginaries*. Durham: Duke University Press.

Teachout, Zephyr. 2014. *Corruption in America: From Benjamin Franklin's Snuff Box to Citizens United*. Cambridge: Harvard University Press.

Teachout, Zephyr. 2018. "The problem of monopolies & corporate public corruption." *Daedalus* 147 (3): 111–126.

Teles, Steven M. 2008. *The Rise of the Conservative Legal Movement: The Battle for Control of the Law*. Princeton: Princeton University Press.

Telles, Edward E. 2014. *Race in Another America: The Significance of Skin Color in Brazil.* Princeton: Princeton University Press.

Tetlock, Philip, and Aaron Belkin. 1996. "Counterfactual thought experiments in world politics: Logical, methodological, and psychological perspectives." In *Counterfactual Thought Experiments in World Politics: Logical, Methodological, and Psychological Perspectives*, edited by Philip E. Tetlock and Aaron Belkin, 16–31. Princeton: Princeton University Press.

The Economist. 2014. "Why American elections cost so much." February 9, 2014. www.economist.com/the-economist-explains/2014/02/09/why-american-elections-cost-so-much

The Intercept Brazil. n.d. "As mensagens secretas da Lava Jato." www.intercept.com.br/series/mensagens-lava-jato/

The New York Times. 2012. "Editorial: The Power Broker." January 23, 2012. www.nytimes.com/2012/01/24/opinion/the-power-broker.html

Tian, Nan. 2021. "20 years of US military aid to Afghanistan." *SIPRI.* www.sipri.org/commentary/topical-backgrounder/2021/20-years-us-military-aid-afghanistan

Tomasi di Lampedusa, Giuseppe. 1958. *Il Gattopardo.* Milano: Feltrinelli.

Tooze, Adam. 2007. *The Wages of Destruction. The Making and Breaking of the Nazi Economy.* London: Penguin.

Torsello, Davide, and Bertrand Venard. 2016. "The anthropology of corruption." *Journal of Management Inquiry* 25 (1): 34–54.

Transparency International. 1995. "Press Release. New Zealand best, Indonesia worst in world poll of international corruption." July 15, 1995. Accessed June 30, 2023. www.transparency.org/files/content/tool/1995_CPI_EN.pdf

Transparency International. 2013. "Global corruption barometer." Accessed June 30, 2023. https://images.transparencycdn.org/images/2013_GlobalCorruptionBarometer_EN_200525_112757.pdf

Transparency International. 2018. "Corruption Perception Index 2017 shows high corruption burden in more than two-thirds of countries." February 21, 2018. www.transparency.org/news/pressrelease/corruption_perceptions_index_2017_shows_high_corruption_burden_in_more_than

Transparency International. 2019. "Corruption Perception Index 2018: Frequently asked questions." Accessed June 8, 2023. www.transparency.org/files/content/pages/2018_CPI_FAQs_EN.pdf

Transparency International. 2020. "Corruption Perception Index." Accessed June 30, 2020. https://web.archive.org/web/20200721083654/ www.transparency.org/en/cpi#

Transparency International. n.d.a. "TI Corruption Perception Index 1996." Accessed June 8, 2023. www.transparency.org/files/content/tool/1996_CPI_EN.pdf

Transparency International. n.d.b. "Bribe Payers Index 1999." Accessed May 23, 2023. https://web.archive.org/web/20120703025128/; www.transparency.org/research/bpi/bpi_1999

Transparency International. n.d.c. "Bribe Payers Index – Overview." Accessed May 23, 2023. https://web.archive.org/web/20120703025148/; www.transparency.org/research/bpi/overview

Treisman, Daniel. 2007. "What have we learned about the causes of corruption from ten years of cross-national empirical research?" *Annual Review of Political Science* 10 (1): 211–244.

Treisman, Daniel. 2018. "Introduction." In *The New Autocracy: Information, Politics, and Policy in Putin's Russia*, edited by Daniel Treisman, 1–28. Washington, DC: Brookings Institution Press.

Tribunal Superior Eleitoral. n.d. "Partidos políticos registrados no TSE". Accessed June 12, 2023. www.tse.jus.br/partidos/partidos-registrados-no-tse/registrados-no-tse

Tullock, Gordon. 1972. "The purchase of politicians." *Western Economic Journal* 10: 354–55.

Turno, Roberto. 2012. "La corruzione pesa per 60 miliardi." *Il Sole 24 Ore*, February 17, 2012. https://st.ilsole24ore.com/art/notizie/2012-02-17/corruzione-costa-miliardi-economia-063713.shtml?uuid=AaZLH7sE

Tversky, Amos, and Daniel Kahneman. 1973. "Availability: A heuristic for judging frequency and probability." *Cognitive Psychology* 5(2): 207–232.

UNCTAD. 1973. "Address delivered by Mr. Salvador Allende Gossens, President of Chile at the inaugural ceremony on April 13, 1972." *Proceedings of UNCTAD Third Session*. Vol. 1 Annex VIII.

United Nations. 2004. "United Nations Convention against Corruption." www.unodc.org/romena/en/uncac.html

United Nations. 2005. "Secretary-General's message to the Fourth Global Forum on Fighting Corruption and Safeguarding Integrity [delivered by Antonio Maria Costa, Executive Director, UN Office on Drugs and Crime]." June 7, 2005. www.un.org/sg/en/content/sg/statement/2005-06-07/secretary-generals-message-fourth-global-forum-fighting-corruption

UNODC. 2019. "Eighth session of the Conference of the States Parties to the United Nations Convention against Corruption. Resolutions and decisions." Accessed June 8, 2023. www.unodc.org/unodc/en/corruption/COSP/session8-resolutions.html

UNODC. n.d. "Conference of the States Parties to the United Nations Convention against Corruption. Accessed June 8, 2023. "www.unodc.org/unodc/en/corruption/COSP/conference-of-the-states-parties.html

United States Census Bureau. n.d. "Health insurance historical tables – HIA Series." Accessed June 14, 2023. www.census.gov/data/tables/time-series/demo/health-insurance/historical-series/hia.html

United States Department of the Treasury. 2014. "Treasury sanctions Russian officials, members of the Russian leadership's inner circle, and an entity for involvement in the situation in Ukraine." March 20, 2014. https://home.treasury.gov/news/press-releases/jl23331

United States Senate. n.d. "Supreme Court nominations (1789–present)." www.senate.gov/legislative/nominations/SupremeCourtNominations1789present.htm

Vajda, Zoltan. 2001. "John C. Calhoun's republicanism revisited." *Rhetoric & Public Affairs* 4 (3): 433–457.

Valarini, Elizangela, and Markus Pohlmann. 2019. "Organizational crime and corruption in Brazil a case study of the "Operation Carwash" court records." *International Journal of Law, Crime and Justice* 59: 100340.

Valente, Rubens. 2016. "Em diálogos gravados, Jucá fala em pacto para deter avanço da Lava Jato." *Folha De S.Paulo*, May 23, 2016. www1.folha.uol.com.br/poder/2016/05/1774018-em-dialogos-gravados-juca-fala-em-pacto-para-deter-avanco-da-lava-jato.shtml

Varese, Federico. 2001. *The Russian Mafia: Private Protection in a New Market Economy*. Oxford: Oxford University Press.

Vecchio, Giorgio. 2018. "Giovanni Leone." In *I Presidenti della Repubblica. Il Capo dello Stato e il Quirinale nella storia della democrazia italiana*, edited by Sabino Cassese, Giuseppe Galasso and Alberto Melloni, 259–294. Bologna: Il Mulino.

Veja. 2022. "Moro volta a flertar com Bolsonaro em propaganda eleitoral." September 1, 2022. https://veja.abril.com.br/coluna/maquiavel/moro-volta-a-flertar-com-bolsonaro-em-propaganda-eleitoral/

Villegas, Paulina. 2022. "Bolsonaro supporter fires on police, throws grenades as election looms." *The Washington Post*, October 24, 2022. www.washingtonpost.com/world/2022/10/24/roberto-jefferson-grenade-brazil/

Villoria, Manuel. 2015. "La corrupción en España: rasgos y causas esenciales." *Cahiers de civilisation espagnole contemporaine. De 1808 au temps présent* 15.

Villoria, Manuel, and Fernando Jiménez-Sánchez. 2012. "La corrupción en España (2004–2010): datos, percepción y efectos." *Revista Española de Investigaciones Sociológicas* 138 (1): 109–134.

Viroli, Maurizio. 1998. *Machiavelli*. Oxford: Oxford University Press.

Vlasov, Vladimir. 2019. "Триллионы на кону: почему миллиардер Аркадий Ротенберг передумал покидать большую стройку после Крымского моста." Interview by Julia Titova. *Forbes*, November 12, 2019. www.forbes.ru/milliardery/385425-trilliony-na-konu-pochemu-milliarder-arkadiy-rotenberg-peredumal-pokidat-bolshuyu

Vogel, Kenneth P. 2010. "GOP's big money men return." *Politico*, September 24, 2010. www.politico.com/story/2010/09/gops-big-money-men-return-042662

Volkov, Vadim. 2002. *Violent Entrepreneurs: The Use of Force in the Making of Russian Capitalism*. Ithaca: Cornell University Press.

Wahrman, Connor. 2020. "Competing to be corrupt: The multinational dynamics of public procurement public procurement bribery in Latin America." In *Corruption and the Lava Jato Scandal in Latin America*, edited by Paul Lagunes and Jan Svejnar, 35–48. Abingdon: Routledge.

Walker, Shaun. 2017. "Ex-minister's harsh jail sentence sends shockwaves through Russian elite." *The Guardian*, December 15, 2017. www.theguardian.com/world/2017/dec/15/russia-jails-former-economy-minister-alexei-ulyukayev-for-corruption

Wallis, John Joseph. 2006. "The concept of systematic corruption in American history." In *Corruption and Reform: Lessons from America's Economic History*, edited by Edward L. Glaeser, and Claudia Goldin, 23–62. Chicago: University of Chicago Press.

Wallis, John Joseph; Price V. Fishback, and Shawn Kantor. 2006. "Politics, relief, and reform Roosevelt's efforts to control corruption and political manipulation during the new deal." In *Corruption and Reform: Lessons from America's Economic History*, edited by Edward L. Glaeser, and Claudia Goldin, 343–372. Chicago: University of Chicago Press.

Wedel, Janine. 2014. *Unaccountable: How the Establishment Corrupted Our Finances, Freedom and Politics and Created an Outsider Class*. New York: Simon and Schuster.

Wedeman, Andrew H. 2012. *Double Paradox: Rapid Growth and Rising Corruption in China*. Ithaca: Cornell University Press.

Wedeman, Andrew. 2018. "The rise of kleptocracy: Does China fit the model?" *Journal of Democracy* 29 (1): 86–95.

Wedeman, Andrew. 2019. "The evolution of China's anti-corruption strategy." In *The Political Logics of Anti-corruption Efforts in Asia*, edited by Cheng Chen and Meredith L. Weiss, 201–228. Albany: SUNY Press.

Withlock, Craig. 2019. "At war with the truth." *The Washington Post*, December 9, 2019. www.washingtonpost.com/graphics/2019/investigations/afghanistan-papers/afghanistan-war-confidential-documents/

Whitlock, Craig. 2021. *The Afghanistan Papers: A Secret History of the War*. New York: Simon and Schuster.

Whitmire, Kyle. 2019. "Senate bill would fix Alabama's corruption problem – by making it legal" *AL.com*, April 5, 2019. www.al.com/news/2019/04/senate-bill-would-fix-alabamas-corruption-problem-by-making-it-legal.html

Williamson, John. 2009. "A short history of the Washington consensus." *Law & Business Review of the Americas* 15: 7–26.

Winters, Matthew S., and Rebecca Weitz-Shapiro. 2014. "Partisan protesters and nonpartisan protests in Brazil." *Journal of Politics in Latin America* 6 (1): 137–150.

Wolak, Jennifer, and David A. M. Peterson. 2020. "The dynamic American dream." *American Journal of Political Science* 64 (4): 968–981.

Wolfe, Joanna. 2010. "Rhetorical numbers: A case for quantitative writing in the composition classroom." *College Composition and Communication* 61 (3): 452–475.

Woolf, Steven H., and Heidi Schoomaker. 2019. "Life expectancy and mortality rates in the United States, 1959–2017." *Jama* 322 (20): 1996–2016.

World Inequality Database. n.d. "WID.WORLD." Accessed June 11, 2023. www.wid.world/wid-world

Wu, Tim. 2010. *The Master Switch: The Rise and Fall of Information Empires*. New York: Vintage.

Wylde, Christopher. 2012. "The economic policies of Lula's regime in Brazil." In *Latin America after Neoliberalism*, edited by Christopher Wylde, 131–160. London: Palgrave Macmillan.

Yaffa, Joshua. 2015. "The Double Sting, a power struggle between Russia's rival security agencies," *The New Yorker*, July 20, 2015. www.newyorker.com/magazine/2015/07/27/the-double-sting

Yuhas, Alan. "Trump names son-in-law Jared Kushner as senior adviser, testing anti-nepotism law." *The Guardian*, January 10, 2017. www.theguardian.com/us-news/2017/jan/09/jared-kushner-senior-adviser-donald-trump

Zaloznaya, Marina, and William M. Reisinger. 2020. "Mechanisms of decoupling from global regimes: The case of anti-corruption reforms in Russia and Ukraine." *Demokratizatsiya: The Journal of Post-Soviet Democratization* 28 (1): 77–111.

Zaum, Dominik, and Christine Cheng. 2011. "Selling the peace? Corruption and post-conflict peacebuilding." In *Corruption and Post-Conflict Peacebuilding: Selling the Peace?*, edited by Dominik Zaum and Christine Cheng, 19–44. Abingdon: Routledge.

Zingales, Luigi. 2017. "Towards a political theory of the firm." *Journal of Economic Perspectives* 31 (3): 113–130.

Zygar, Mikhail. 2016. *All the Kremlin's Men: Inside the Court of Vladimir Putin*. New York: Public Affairs.

Index